X-MEN
AND
PHILOSOPHY

X-MEN
AND
PHILOSOPHY

ASTONISHING INSIGHT AND
UNCANNY ARGUMENT IN THE
MUTANT X-VERSE

Edited by Rebecca Housel and
J. Jeremy Wisnewski

WILEY

John Wiley & Sons, Inc.

Library of Congress Cataloging-in-Publication Data:

    X-men and philosophy : astonishing insight and uncanny argument in the mutant
X-verse / edited by Rebecca Housel and J. Jeremy Wisnewski.
       p.   cm. — (The Blackwell philosophy and pop culture series)
    Includes index.
    ISBN 978-0-470-41340-1 (pbk:alk.paper)
       1. X-Men (Fictitious characters) I. Housel, Rebecca. II. Wisnewski, Jeremy.
PN6728.X2X24   2009
741.5'973—dc22

                                                    2008045526

Printed in the United States of America

10 9 8 7 6 5 4 3 2 1

To mutants everywhere

CONTENTS

ACKNOWLEDGMENTS

Superheroic Thanks to X-tra Special Humans
and Mutants Alike!

The editors wish to thank comic greats Stan Lee and the late Jack Kirby, the real X-perts!

We'd also like to thank series editor Bill Irwin for his X-vision and X-traordinary editorial instincts! Love ya, Bill! Special thanks go to our beloved contributors, whose lively intellects and creativity help make this volume a superpower-packed X-ploration into the vast space-time of the X-Verse. We also want to give our appreciation to Connie Santisteban, Eric Nelson, and the entire Wiley team for their publishing super-prowess.

As for the mutants: Beast, for being both a science geek and a badass; Wolverine, for being short; Mystique for bringing blue back into fashion; Phoenix Force, for being the ultimate sentient cosmic force of life and death (c'mon!); and every other mutant superhero, either in the pages of a Marvel comic or in the recesses of a human mind yet to begin a great hero's journey. . . .

Jeremy wishes to personally thank Meg Lonergan, now an old pro at making things happen; she did an X-cellent job helping with the copyediting and the index—keep it up, Sparky! Nico Meyering and Nick Forst read versions of the manuscript and offered some useful initial feedback. Nick gets an X-tra "thank you" for donating his illustrating abilities (and his imagination) to the book. (Nick is responsible for Jeremy's inner superhero at the end of chapter 17.) Jeremy is grateful to his wife, Dorothy, for putting up with his eccentricities (yet again), and his daughter, Audrey, for letting him play with her toys.

Rebecca would like to send special thanks to "Mighty" George Dunn, Bob Housel, Aaron Fields, Connie Santisteban, Stephanie "Shadowcat" Collins, and Marguerite Schwartz for lending super-vision to sections of the Marvel-ous manuscript. Bill Irwin gets a *Giant-Sized* shout out for reading countless e-mails over four years with eighties trivia and X-Men pleas. Tom Morris also gets a nod for accepting Rebecca's first article ever (!) on X-Men in his 2005 *Superheroes* volume. Rebecca's sincere appreciation goes to her husband, Bob, who lovingly made superhuman efforts in the domestic sphere while Rebecca typed away into the wee hours of the morning, and to her son, Gary, who has been her comic partner-in-crime for the better part of the last twenty years.

X-MEN
AND
PHILOSOPHY

INTRODUCTION

You Are About to Embark on an X-perience with "the Strangest Heroes of All"[1]

The X-Men franchise has made billions of dollars over the last forty-five years from major motion pictures, animated television shows, video games, and, of course, the best-selling comic series in American history.[2] The Marvel X-Verse is a large and diverse place full of complex storylines, timelines, seemingly endless characters (can you believe the first volume started with only seven?!), and—of course—*philosophy*.

The first X-Men comic featured Professor Xavier, Marvel Girl, Angel, Beast, Iceman, and Cyclops: five teenagers trying to learn how to control their mutant powers, or "extra" powers, at Xavier's School for Gifted Youngsters. Oh, and, of course, Magneto's villainous yet relatable character was also introduced as part of the original cast. And right there at the beginning, the big questions were being asked: What are our obligations to one another? What does it mean to be human?

1

What are the implications of evolution for the future of human (and mutant) civilization?

X-Men comics were one of the first Marvel series to feature female characters as the leads in multiple storylines. X-Women are shown as strong and powerful, equal to the men around them. X-Men comics also developed a diverse population of mutant superheroes that included African characters such as Storm, Native Americans like Dani Moonstar and Thunderbird, and Asian characters such as Jubilee and Lady Deathstrike. Originally, Stan Lee named the comic "The Mutants," a less gender-specific title, but his editor thought the audience would not understand what or who a mutant was, so Lee suggested X-Men because the main characters had "extra" powers and were led by a man named Professor X. That was also a rather new concept: having a handicapped leader in Professor X, who, despite being wheelchair-bound, is still one of the most powerful, influential heroes in the X-Men series. Here, too, we can see the underlying philosophical spirit of the X-Verse: All of our traditional hierarchies are scrutinized, questioned, and reimagined. The X-Verse is a deeply philosophical place where our world is dismantled, where our assumptions are turned against us, and where, strangely, we see ourselves in ways that only mutants (and philosophers) can show us. So if you're a human, this book is for you.

Your X-perience is about to begin. Enjoy the ride!

NOTES

1. This was the tagline used on the cover of the first X-Men comic in September 1963.

2. This is more money than philosophy has made since emerging on the cultural scene some 2,500 years ago.

THE X-FACTOR IN THE EXISTENTIAL

THE LURE OF THE NORMAL: WHO *WOULDN'T WANT* TO BE A MUTANT?

Patrick D. Hopkins

In the third X-Men movie, *The Last Stand*, a "cure" is discovered that suppresses the activity of the mutant gene, turning mutants into ordinary humans.[1] Storm, the weather-controller, reacts by asking, "Who would want this cure? I mean, what kind of coward would take it just to fit in?" Meanwhile, Rogue—whose touch can sap the life, energy, and abilities of other people—is preparing her trip to the pharmaceutical clinic.

Given the prejudice, fear, and persecution of mutants, some X-fans empathize with Rogue and can easily imagine wanting to be regular people. But other fans, especially those who have idealized or identified with the X-Men, roll their eyes and shake their heads about Rogue's decision, seeing in it the rejection of something glorious, unique, and desirable. Why would anyone choose the ordinary, the mundane, over the fantastic and the extraordinary? What kind of person wouldn't want to be a mutant?

Many of these issues revolve around the idea of the "normal." In philosophy, we make a distinction between the "descriptive" use of a word, which simply points to how a word is neutrally used to explain or characterize something, and the "prescriptive" use of a word, in which the term is used to indicate how something should be. The idea of "normal" can be used in both ways. As a description, it merely indicates that some condition is statistically average, as in, "Normally, humans have twenty-twenty vision," or, "Normally, people don't get angry about petty things." As a prescription, however, it indicates that something should be the case or should be done in a statistically average way, as in, "Her vision isn't normal, so she needs glasses," or, "It's not normal to get so angry over small stuff; there must be something wrong with him."

Whether the "normal" is a descriptive or a prescriptive idea, though, is a matter of debate. Is it true that just because something is normal, it should be our goal, our yardstick for how things should be? Does normality give us any guidelines? Or, is "normal" merely the way things statistically happen to be? And can we think of ways to make things much better?

What can the X-Men teach us about how the idea of "normality" works to shape and direct human lives? Is normality something to be valued or something to be transcended? Should a mutant's desire to be normal be congratulated or looked down on? What about our own desire to be normal or to be extraordinary?

The Paradoxes of Normality

For starters, there are only a limited number of ways to be normal: to fall within a small range around the average score for various traits, whether physical, mental, or social. But there are an unlimited number of ways to be abnormal. Not only can you be an extreme from average, but the way in which that extremity manifests can be wildly varied. Whereas you might be unusually talented, that talent could be specific to thousands of different areas—for example, an ability to play the many different types of musical instruments or sports or excel in the arts or the vocations. You might also be specifically deficient in one or more of thousands of areas. Whereas normality by definition requires the appearance of normality, your abnormalities might be visible or invisible, blatant or subtle, beneficial or detrimental.

Here the basic paradox of normality in the human species arises. On the one hand, we are social beings who feel a strong need to fit into a group (even "nonconformists" usually hang out with similar "nonconformists"—goths with goths, emos with emos, queers with queers), so there is a powerful desire to fit within an acceptable range. You don't want to stand out. On the other hand, we also want to attract attention to distinguish ourselves from others, so that we don't get ignored. These conflicting desires may both stem from a basic evolutionary pressure: the drive to be seen as reproductively attractive. We want to be normal enough to indicate to potential mates that there is nothing wrong with us—we don't have defective genes. But we also want to attract more attention than our competitors and indicate that we have some advantage over others—we have better genes or more social status.

It's a conundrum of the human condition: we want to fit in and we want to stand out. But there are lots of ways to stand out, some ways better than others. Some of these ways indicate to others that we are desirable; some indicate that we are undesirable.

The X-Men are mostly human, although they often refer to themselves as "mutants" and distinguish themselves from those whom they call "humans." For the most part, they have ordinary human brains and personalities housed in bodies that possess extraordinary abilities and qualities. Not surprisingly, then, they fall prey to all the vagaries of the ordinary human condition, including the desire to fit in and the desire to stand out. But the mutant gene has many effects, and these various effects in the mutant population demonstrate something about ordinary variation in human beings—namely, that being ordinary is largely a safe bet, whereas being extraordinary is very, very risky. When you pull a ticket for being different out of a hat, given the infinite ways you could be different, you run a risk.

How to Be Abnormal

When Storm asks why anyone would want to "cure" mutation, the blue-furred scientist Hank McCoy (aka Beast) responds, "Is it cowardice to save oneself from persecution? Not all of us can fit in so easily. You don't shed on the furniture." Clearly, there are distinctions to be made even among the mutants, even among the abnormal. Some mutants can pass as "normals" because of their appearance and capacity to control their abilities, such as psychic Jean Grey or sheathed-clawed Wolverine. Other mutants, however, are unable to pass as normal humans. And even these can be further distinguished. Some cannot pass because of their appearance, such as furry blue Beast or blue and devil-tailed Nightcrawler or winged Angel. Others cannot completely pass because of their incapacity to control their abilities, such as Rogue, who cannot touch anyone, or Cyclops, who can never show his eyes.

This concept of passing—successfully pretending to be normal—is an important and well-documented real-life experience among homosexuals and light-skinned African Americans. It gives the abnormal (the term here is understood to be simply descriptive) the ability to be treated as normal and thus can allow them to confront, or not confront, their own difference on their own schedules.

So within the range of the abnormal, we have a variety of possibilities of responding to the normal. Though exemplified in the extreme by mutants, these are familiar to many real humans as well. You could have an abnormality (the term here is used descriptively, simply to mean "statistically rare") that is beneficial (say, the ability to heal quickly, such as Wolverine). You could have an abnormality that is detrimental (say, a disability such as Professor Xavier's paraplegia). You could have an abnormality that is detectable (say by sight, touch, or smell) but is easy to keep hidden, for example, a third kidney, a photographic memory, or Shadowcat's phasing ability. You could also have an undetectable abnormality that causes distress when you attempt to hide it: say, a minority sexual orientation or social anxiety or Jean Grey's unruly telepathy. Maybe you have a detectable abnormality that causes distress, such as a missing limb, a deformity, or Nightcrawler's tail and three-fingered hands. There's also the detectable abnormality that causes no distress, such as Colossus's muscle-bound physique or Emma Frost's beauty.

To understand this more clearly, imagine the range of abnormality represented in a graph—not a two-dimensional graph, but a three-dimensional one, a cube, with the x-axis (width) representing the degree of utility, or how beneficial/detrimental the abnormality is; the y-axis (height) representing acceptability, or how the abnormality is received by society as desirable or undesirable; and the z-axis (depth) representing detectability, or how obvious/hidden the abnormality is. This doesn't in any way fully describe the psychological and social complexity of being abnormal (it doesn't even try to explain how your own personality might deal with being abnormal or specify in what way an ability might be detectable or used, for instance), but it is a start in helping you see what a range of experience you could have. Any trait outside the norm could fit anywhere within this space.

Now you can understand how falling in different places in the space can affect your attitude toward how good or bad it is to be normal. The philosopher Michel Foucault (1926–1984) described the history of the abnormal as beginning with the broad concept of the "monster" (a grand mix of the unnatural and the impossible) and moving on to the concept of the "individual to be corrected" (a more narrow medical and legal idea of humans who need to be fixed).² Much of Foucault's historical lesson is about how society handles the abnormal, but it can also be related to how any individual perceives his or her own abnormality. Are you a monster, someone needing to be fixed, or just different?

Storm despises as moral cowards people who would seek a cure for their mutations, but look at her experience and where she fits in that 3-D graph. Her mutation gives her the power to control the weather but is not in any way detectable unless she wants you to see it. The ability has great utility: it can be used for a wide variety of desirable goals. Weather control is mixed on the acceptability axis—some people may fear her power, but given the fact that she has control over it and it is not obvious, those who rate her ability low on acceptance don't ever need to know she is a mutant. As with many of the mutants, Storm is exceedingly beautiful, with a perfect physique and face. This abnormality is highly detectable but also highly acceptable and useful. In short, her particular location in the 3-D space means that Storm primarily benefits from her abnormalities and can always pass as someone normal when she chooses to.

Rogue, who is seeking a cure, is not so lucky. She is beautiful, healthy, and charming, but her mutation is complicated. She absorbs the energy, memories, and abilities of the people (abilities especially in the case of mutants) whom she touches, harming each person touched in the process. But she cannot control her power. Touch activates the transfer, regardless of her will. So, while in certain cases Rogue's ability may be useful, it is largely unacceptable and is largely detectable. Although Rogue can "pass" as an ordinary human for a while, she can do so only by avoiding all touch. This makes her seem quirky after a while and eventually downright strange. It also means that Rogue is unable to engage in certain activities that her otherwise very ordinary human brain and personality want to engage in. She wants, as anyone would, to be able to touch. She wants to kiss a boy, to have a mother stroke her face, to hug a friend. Her ability prevents her from having basic human experiences. No wonder Rogue wants to be normal! She is caught in a terrible situation: she has normal desires and needs but uncontrollable abilities that prevent her from satisfying those desires and needs.

Beast is another whose abnormality is not as beneficial as Storm's. He is blue and furry, so his mutation is highly detectable. Although his abilities (agility, strength, heightened senses) may be very useful, his appearance is perceived as scary, ugly, monstrous. Unlike Storm, Jean Grey, Wolverine, or Iceman, he cannot pass as normal.

Unfortunately, *The Last Stand* is not as informative as we would like it to be about why a mutant might want to be cured. For that information, let's turn to the comic book by Joss Whedon, which covers a version of the cure story.[3] Whereas in the film, the mutants who lined up for the cure look mostly normal, in the comic book there is a mix of those who could pass as normal and those who could not. Of course, in pictures, you can pick out only physical characteristics, but this is enough. The mutants who line up in the comic have scales, wings sticking out from beneath jackets, lobster claws for hands, and so on. One mutant actually has his face in his stomach, and in the testing lab, a girl has nightmares that come to life and kill those around her.

Perhaps no place in the X-Men universe is this problem of obvious abnormality explored better than in the story of the Morlocks, a group of mutants who mostly have very obvious and unsightly mutations.[4] They have chosen to live underground—a realm that befits their rejection by both normal society and mutants who can pass. In one story, the Morlocks have kidnapped the physically beautiful and winged Angel to be a husband and a consort for the leader of the Morlocks, Callisto. One of the Morlocks, Sunder, asks the others why they are fighting other mutants. He finds this strange since "they're mutants, like us." Another of the Morlocks, a mutant called Masque who is hideously deformed but possesses the ability to reshape others' bodies and faces into whatever form he wishes, says, "Not like us, Sunder. They pretty! Hate 'em. Want to hurt 'em!" Masque even thinks of Nightcrawler—the blue-skinned, three-fingered, three-toed, devil-tailed tele-porter—as "pretty" and wants to turn him inside out. Of course, this is ironic, considering that Nightcrawler is one of the mutants who cannot pass as normal. In the comic book, Callisto asks Nightcrawler to join the Morlocks since he is so obviously not human, and in the film *X2* Nightcrawler asks shape-shifter Mystique, herself usually blue and scaled, why she doesn't stay in a normal human shape all the time.

Some people may wish they had a Morlock's powers, but few, if any, wish to look like a Morlock. Why? Partly because we function with a cultural and evolutionary sense of what counts as attractive and thus find the abnormalities of the Morlocks "ugly." Also, because no matter what abilities they might have, people know if they looked like Morlocks, they would be despised by normal humans, perhaps even by normal-looking mutants. Angels and devils both have powers, but angels are prettier.

What most people seem to want, then, and this is part of the reason they might fantasize about being an X-Man, is to be different in a way that makes them stand out, but only in terms of being powerful, beautiful, and able to pass when desired. Some people might want to have abnormally good looks, abnormally high athletic ability, or an abnormally healthy immune system, but they would not want anything that inhibited them socially or physically. People want to stand out, and fit in, on conventional terms. How very normal, then, to want to be unusual only if it benefits us.

"Normal" Anxiety

Fantasy and science fiction provide an escape from the normal, allowing us to imagine the richness of a life that is enhanced by having special abilities and extraordinary experiences. We imagine the great and wonderful things we could do if only we weren't so limited, so ordinary. And it is no mere stereotype that the creators of works in speculative fiction and film have themselves often felt as if they didn't fit into society, thus turning to worlds in which characters who did not fit in were magnificent and enviable.

It is curious and telling, however, that so much of the fiction about the extraordinary belies an anxiety about normality and about abnormality. Characters routinely lament their special status and give long-winded monologues on how they just want to set aside the unique lives they experience and return to or become quintessential "average" people. We also find that the most evil or dangerous characters are most likely to cling to their differences, despising the normality of others as limiting them to banal experience, as with Magneto's insistence in *X-Men United* that mutants are "homo superior" and are as "gods among insects."[5] It's as if, at the same time that we envy the extraordinary or the uncanny, we also want to express our anxiety about being the outlier, about being special. There is excitement about being unusual, but there is also great comfort in being ordinary—which is often, and ironically, expressed by describing the normal person as having access to some experience that the extraordinary person cannot have (Rogue watching with envy as a mother caresses a child's skin, or Beast looking longingly at his ordinary unfurry hand when his mutation is temporarily suppressed). Somehow, we want to try to value the very ordinariness of life that science fiction and fantasy give us an escape from. Are we not perhaps trying to comfort ourselves, while at the very same time, *escaping* ourselves?

But not all of the anxiety about the uncanny and the extraordinary is science fiction. What about the real-world attempt to use technology to change into something extraordinary? Is such a desire understandable, even praiseworthy? Or is such a desire to be met with skepticism, horror, or even condemnation? We live on the edge of a world in which genetic engineering, pharmacological manipulation, and cybernetic implants open up the opportunity for a person to become something like a real mutant. Soon, perhaps, we may be able to alter ourselves to achieve what some fictional mutants possess: greater strength, intelligence, agility, immunity, longevity (though probably not weather control). Is this a bad thing? Is it wrong to push ourselves outside the limits of what is human? Transhumanists don't think so.

The transhumanist movement wants to use technology to enhance human beings, to push us beyond our biological limits until we become something grander and more transcendent.[6] Not surprisingly, transhumanists tend to adore the X-Men and most probably think Rogue is misguided to seek a cure for mutation.

Contrasting with transhumanists are "bioconservatives," who advocate conserving the normal biological status of human beings. One group of bioconservatives consists of natural law theorists. "Natural law" argues that morality comes from the given needs, abilities, and limitations we have as humans and says that trying to change human nature is the worst sort of pride and arrogance.[7]

So here we have two groups that already have real-world answers to the question of "Who wouldn't want to be a mutant?" Transhumanists don't want to be a certain kind of mutant—not the deformed or the weak or the kind of abnormal that interferes with living—but they love the idea of being extraordinary in all of the beautiful and powerful ways one could imagine. Bioconservatives don't want to be any sort of mutant at all. For them, the normal is a moral obligation.

But, of course, the "normal" is relative. If we all become extraordinary, then by comparison won't we end up simply being ordinary again? If everyone can fly, is flying special? This is where the tricky part of normality and abnormality comes into play. When we value something—an ability, a capacity, a trait—for what it can allow us to do, then possessing that ability may be reward enough. But sometimes, we value an ability or a trait only because others do not have it. Compare being healthy and being tall. Everyone could be healthy—no diseases, no injuries—and we would all benefit from being so. But everyone cannot be tall, because "tall" is a comparative idea. You are only "tall" in relation to someone who is shorter than you. Everyone could be 6 feet 5 inches high, but then 6'5" would be standard, not "tall." So we need to ask ourselves when we desire something whether we want it because it would benefit us no matter what or because it would benefit us only by comparison to someone who doesn't have it. The answer to that question partly determines whether we are acting on behalf of all humanity or acting only on behalf of ourselves. If you want to fly, even if everyone else could fly, too, then flying for you is valuable no matter what. But if you want to be able to become invisible only if others could not become invisible, then you are merely seeking a relative advantage. We could also ask a similar question about people's desire to be normal. Do they want to be normal because being abnormal (in the "greater ability" sense of the X-Men) would impose greater responsibilities on them and they don't want such responsibilities? Do they want to feel justified in not having to fight evil all the time? Funny. We might obviously be selfish in our desire to be extraordinary, but we might also be selfish in our desire to be normal. It makes you think . . .

So, there are your answers to the title question "Who wouldn't want to be a mutant?"—people who are limited by their abnormalities, people who are ostracized because of their abnormalities, and even people who don't want the responsibility that comes with having certain abnormalities. There can be great comfort in being normal, even if it is sometimes at the cost of never standing out.

The philosopher Friedrich Nietzsche (1844–1900) once wrote, "Man is something that should be overcome. What have you done to overcome him? All creatures hitherto have created something beyond themselves: and do you want to be the ebb of this great tide, and return to animals rather than overcoming man?"[8] Although in context, Nietzsche's character Zarathustra is preaching about humanity's religious experience, the general idea is well admired by transhumanists. They see humanity and its current normal range as something to be overcome, something that oppressively limits us. Our minds, curiously not as constrained as our bodies, can imagine what it would be like to be very different from what we are. Is this not obvious in the case of the fictional X-Men? We can imagine ourselves with abilities beyond what we can actually do. The question is, What is our motivation for wanting to overcome man? And equally important, What is our motivation for *not* wanting to?

NOTES

1. See director Brett Ratner's *X-Men: The Last Stand* (20th Century Fox, 2006), DVD.

2. Michel Foucault, *Abnormal: Lectures at the College de France 1974–1975* (New York: Picador, 2003).

3. Joss Whedon, *Astonishing X-Men, Vol. 1: Gifted* (New York: Marvel, 2004).

4. Chris Claremont, *The Uncanny X-Men* #169 (New York: Marvel, 1983).

5. See director Bryan Singer's *X2: X-Men United* (20th Century Fox, 2003), DVD.

6. See www.transhumanism.org/index.php/WTA/index/.

7. Patrick Hopkins, "Natural Law," *Encyclopedia of Philosophy*, 2nd ed. (Farmington Hills, MI: Macmillan Reference USA, 2006), chap. 6, pp. 505–517.

8. Friedrich Nietzsche, *Thus Spoke Zarathustra* (New York: Penguin Books USA, 1969), p. 41.

AMNESIA, PERSONAL IDENTITY, AND THE MANY LIVES OF WOLVERINE

Jason Southworth

In *Hulk* #180–182, Wolverine makes his first appearance as little more than a feral man in a colorful costume with no memories of his past or seemingly of anything (in fact, in *Giant-Size X-Men* #1, he has no memory of the Hulk appearance). The Weapon X stories in *Marvel Comics Presents* show us some of the things the character has done as an agent of the Canadian government, and *Origin* gives us a glimpse of the character prior to his time at Weapon X, when he was more at peace with the world.

Over the years, Professor Xavier and Wolverine had very little success in reversing the amnesia until *House of M*, when Wolverine finally recovered all of his memories. But rather than answer questions about his identity, the sudden emergence of these memories has raised more questions for Wolverine about who he really is.

What Is Personal Identity?

The issue of personal identity is actually a set of issues that are entangled and, at times, may be conflated. The questions philosophers try to answer when they discuss personal identity are: What constitutes personhood? Who am I? And what does it mean for a person to persist over time?

When establishing what constitutes personhood, philosophers are trying to figure out what makes a person *a person* (rather than, say, a comic book). What properties must that entity have to count as a person? Many nonphilosophers may not think this is an interesting or difficult question to answer, as our common use of the term *person* is synonymous with *human*. The case of the mutants in the X-books shows why this is an unsatisfactory answer, as they are not humans—they are Homo superiors, not Homo sapiens. If mutants are persons, then being a human is not a necessary condition (it is not required) for being a person. As you might imagine, philosophers do not spend a lot of time talking about Homo superiors, but we do spend quite a lot of time talking about other animals and artificial intelligence. You might consider whether Kitty Pryde's pet dragon, Lockheed, and the Scarlet Witch's robot husband, the Vision, are persons.

When we consider the question of "Who am I?" we are trying to establish the characteristics that make you the person that you are, as opposed to some other person. Again, this question appears deceptively easy to answer. You might think that you can just rattle off a description of your character traits, but the answer is going to have to be more complicated than that, because we can often be described in a variety of ways, some of which might be in tension. The question of *who* counts as a person and *why* is one of the recurring tropes of Wolverine's storyline. We see this when the Ol' Canucklehead goes on one of his tears, complaining that he is not the animal that some people think that he is.

Personhood and persistence over time also feature prominently in X-Men. Consider the classic story "Days of Future Past" (which appeared in *Uncanny X-Men* #141 and 142), in which we encounter characters who seem to be many of the X-Men we know (including Wolverine), but in the future. How do we know that they are the same characters? They *look* the same. This is the standard, unreflective first response people often give to the question of personal identity: people persist over time if they occupy the same bodies. Same claws and pointy hair? Well, it *must* be Wolverine. That's just common sense—which, as we'll see, isn't always as common or sensical as we might initially think.[1] Still, you might say, who cares?

Well, the main reason we should care about personal identity concerns moral culpability. All moral frameworks involve the attribution of blame and praise, and many call for punishment. In order to attribute praise and blame for an act, we have to be certain that the people to whom we are giving the praise and the blame are the ones who deserve it, based on their actions. If, for example, it turns out that the man called Logan is not the same person who committed atrocities for the Canadian government under the code name Weapon X, then he should not be punished for the behavior of that person. Likewise, if the current Wolverine is not the same person that he was in the past, Sabretooth and Lady Deathstrike would be wrong in their attempts to punish him.

Cassandra Nova, Charles Xavier, and John Locke

The philosopher John Locke (1632–1704) argued against the commonsense view that the body is the source of personal identity, using a modified example from the pop culture of his own time. Locke told a story that was essentially *The Prince and the Pauper*, except the individuals exchanged minds, rather than simply roles. If Locke were around today, he might instead have talked about Charles Xavier and Cassandra Nova. In Grant Morrison's run on *New X-Men* (if you haven't read it, you should be ashamed of yourself), we learn that Cassandra Nova placed her mind in Charles Xavier's body and placed Xavier's mind in her body. The Xavier body with Nova's mind forced Beak (if you don't know who Beak is, you should be doubly ashamed of yourself) to beat the Beast so badly, he had to be hospitalized, and started a war between the Shi'ar Empire and the X-Men.[2] When the body of Xavier manipulated Beak, it referred to itself as Cassandra. Likewise, later in the story, when Jean Grey communicates with the mind in Cassandra Nova's body, it reports to be Xavier. Prior to discovering the switch, the X-Men naturally believed the actions of Xavier's body to be those of Xavier. After finding out about this switch, however, they do not hold Xavier accountable for the actions taken by his body. Instead, they condemn Cassandra Nova for them and discuss how to defeat her. So, it seems personal identity is not a matter of body but of mind.

Having rejected the body theory in favor of something mental, Locke tries to determine the nature of the mental thing. What mental properties or characteristics could indicate persistence over time? Locke quickly rejects any type of character or personality traits because such traits are constantly in flux. We're always trying to become better people, and, as a result, our morality, tastes, and preferences tend to change often. Yet we remain in essence the same people.

By process of elimination, we come to memories as the source of personal identity. Locke does not mean that we need to have all and only the memories that a previous individual in time has had. You have "sameness of memories" even if you have additional memories that come after the memories that you have in common with yourself at an earlier time. So, we would say that Wolverine is still the same person he was the day he joined the New Avengers as he was the day after, since he has the same memories he had the day before.

Of course, we don't remember everything that happens to us—and some of us are more forgetful than others. Locke isn't forgetful on this account, though: he complicates things by introducing the concept of connected memories. One memory can be connected to another as follows: I remember a time when I had a memory I no longer have. As long as I can remember such a time, then those earlier memories still count as *mine*.[3] So, even if Wolverine no longer has memories of the first time he performed the Fast Ball Special with Colossus (in *Uncanny X-Men* #100. I didn't even have to look that up. I am a walking *OHotMU*), as long as he remembers a time when he *did* remember that day, then he is still the same person as he was *on* that day. Likewise, since on the day he joined the X-Men, Wolverine did not have memories of his encounter with the Hulk in *Hulk* #180–182, nor does he have memories of a time when he had memories of this, there are no connected memories, and he is, as a result, not the same person who encountered the Hulk on that day.

Bringing It All Back to Wolverine

If sameness of memory gives us sameness of person, then it seems several different people have inhabited the body we recognize as Wolverine's. Let's go through the history of Wolverine as it has been revealed to us so far and yell out, *"New Wolverine!"* every time we spot one.

The known history of Wolverine begins in *Origin* (2002). In this story, we learn that he was born in the nineteenth century on a plantation in Canada under the name James Howlett. Howlett left the plantation and adopted the name "Logan," the last name of the groundskeeper on the plantation. He had several adventures after leaving the plantation, first living with a pack of wolves, then with Blackfoot Indians (marrying one of them known as Silver Fox), joining the Canadian military, living in Japan under the name "Patch," and fighting in World

War II with Captain America.[4] After returning to Canada, Logan is recruited by Team X, and as a part of the program, Wolverine has his memory erased and replaced with memories of a life that no one ever lived.[5]

New Wolverine!

The man involved with Team X has no memory of the life prior to being a part of the team, so we are on the second life of Wolverine.

While a member of Team X, Logan was abducted by the people at the Weapon X program. As a part of the Weapon X program, he was given the name Mutate #9601 and once again had his mind erased.

New Wolverine!

And thus ended the short life of the second Wolverine.

Not all of the life of Mutate #9601 has been documented, but we have seen some of his nasty and brutish life in Barry Windsor-Smith's feature "Weapon X" that appeared in *Marvel Comics Presents* #72–84 (every comic fan should own a copy of this, as there is little better than Windsor-Smith art). Eventually, the Winter Soldier (a brainwashed Bucky) frees him, and the creature referred to as Weapon X goes feral in the woods of Canada and has his famous fight with the Hulk.[6] After some time, he is discovered by James and Heather Hudson (of Alpha Flight fame), with no memory of what he was doing in the woods, the fight with the Hulk, or the Weapon X project, and in time is civilized.[7]

New Wolverine!

At this point, the Wolverine we all know and love is born.

I will spare you a complete rundown of the rest of Wolverine's history (as I am sure you know it all), except to point to two other important events. When Apocalypse captures Wolverine to make him serve as his horseman Death, in *Wolverine Vol. 2* #145, he was once again brainwashed.

New Wolver—okay, that's probably enough of that.

With the conclusion of *House of M*, we discover that after Wolverine's body heals from the Scarlet Witch's messing with his mind, he finally has all of his memories restored, giving us one final new person, in Locke's view. Wolverine now has memories or connected memories to every person who inhabited that familiar body. At this point it seems that if Locke is right, the inhabitant of the Wolverine body will in one moment go from not being responsible for any of the things done by the other inhabitants of that body to being responsible for all of them.

Jamie Madrox and Derek Parfit

The contemporary philosopher Derek Parfit (b. 1942) has famously objected to the memory account of personal identity with a thought experiment about a brain being divided into two parts and placed in two separate bodies. Had Parfit been an X-Men fan, he could have used the example of Jamie Madrox, the Multipleman. For those who don't know, Madrox has the ability to create up to ninety-nine duplicates of himself at a time. To form a duplicate, a force must be applied to Madrox from outside himself, or he must apply the force to an outside object—in other words, he has to be hit by or hit something. At any time, two adjacent Madroxes can recombine by an act of mutual will.

When the Madroxes combine, all memories each of them had separately are joined into the new entity. Likewise, whenever a duplicate is formed, it has all of the memories of the Madrox from which it came. So, as we learn in the miniseries *Madrox* (2005), if one of the duplicates studies Russian or anatomy, then all other duplicates that are made after it has been reabsorbed will have this knowledge as well. From the moment it is created, each duplicate begins to have unique memories and experiences that no other Madrox has. So, Madrox is an even more complicated case than Parfit was concerned with, as there can be up to one hundred individuals that exist at the same time, with the same memories.

Parfit thinks that it would be wrong to say of the one hundred Madroxes that they are the same person. If they're the same, we get big problems: if one multiple were to go to the refrigerator and get a sandwich, but all of the other ones did not, it would follow that Madrox both did and did not get a sandwich. This certainly looks like a contradiction. Considering each of the Madroxes to be a different person who is unique until reabsorbed, at which time that particular Madrox is destroyed, seems like an obvious way to avoid this contradiction.

X-Factor #70–90, written by Peter David, features conflicts between the different duplicates. Some of the duplicates refuse to allow themselves to be reabsorbed, as they claim it would end their existence. In fact, one of the duplicates professes to hate the original Madrox. In addition, in the *Madrox* miniseries, it turns out that a duplicate ends up being the villain of the story, while the original Madrox and some other duplicates were the heroes fighting against him. Was Madrox getting into arguments with himself? Fighting himself? It doesn't seem like it. We thus have reason to conclude that sameness of memories is not a sufficient condition for sameness of identity.

This kind of thought experiment leads Parfit to conclude that there must be something physical involved in personal identity. Because the brain houses the mind, Parfit concludes that "sameness of brain" means sameness of identity over time. This is more complicated than it sounds, however, because the human brain changes over time. All cells in the human body, including neurons (a very special type of cell found only in the brain), break down and are replaced with new versions. It takes about seven years for all of the matter in the human brain to get completely broken down and changed. Due to this, Parfit concluded that personhood can persist for only, at most, seven years.[8]

Bringing It All Back to Wolverine (Again)

Wolverine's case is special. Wolvie is the head-trauma king. Every time he is severely injured in his brain, there is brain damage. And every time the old healing factor kicks in and repairs it, we are looking at a new Wolverine. In cases where there is only light brain damage (so the whole brain isn't affected), the healing factor still manages to reorganize his brain so quickly that the length of time to a new Wolverine is much shorter than seven years.

When you start thinking of all of your favorite instances of Wolverine brain damage, you realize there are so many that we will not be able to count all of the new selves in this short chapter. Just for fun, though, some of my favorites are: the Punisher running over Wolverine with a steamroller, leaving it parked on his head in *Punisher Vol. 3* #16; when the Wrecker hits him with his magic crowbar in *New Avengers* #7; and when Sabretooth thinks he has drowned him and walks away, only for the Ol' Canuklehead to get up again.

Be Slow to Judge

Now that you know Wolverine is in fact many individuals, you should see him in a new light. And if Parfit is right, it should make you think twice about how quickly you judge all of the characters in the X-Verse (and the real world). People who commit terrible acts of violence may need to be given the benefit of the doubt until it can be established that they are in fact the same person. In the X-Verse we should be less dubious of Emma Frost working with the X-Men; the less catlike Beast should question whether, even if the secondary mutation were reversed, he would be the character they miss; and the next time Jean Grey comes back from the dead, we should all stop complaining that she seems different from before.

NOTES

1. This is known as the bodily theory of personal identity.

2. *New X-Men* #118–121.

3. John Locke (1690), *An Essay Concerning Human Understanding* (Amherst, NY: Prometheus Books, 1994).

4. *Wolverine: Origins* #16.

5. *Wolverine Vol. 2* #68.

6. *Wolverine Vol. 3* #38.

7. *Alpha Flight* #33.

8. See Derek Parfit's "Personal Identity," *Philosophical Review* 80 (1971): 3–27.

IS SUICIDE ALWAYS IMMORAL? JEAN GREY, IMMANUEL KANT, AND *THE DARK PHOENIX SAGA*

Mark D. White

The Dark Phoenix Saga is the centerpiece of Chris Claremont and John Byrne's classic run on *X-Men* in the late 1970s–early 1980s.[1] Notable for many milestones in X-history, this storyline includes the introduction of Kitty Pryde and Emma Frost but is focused around the radical transformation and suicidal demise of one of the original X-Women, Jean Grey. Most of us would say that suicide is morally "bad," though for different reasons. But even if we agree that suicide is immoral, is it *always* wrong? What about cases of altruistic suicide, such as Jean's?[2] Are there cases in which ending your life may be moral—maybe even the only moral option?

"Oh, My God. You Teach Ethics?"[3]

In moral philosophy, there are three leading approaches to assessing whether an act is right or wrong: virtue ethics, consequentialism, and deontology. *Virtue ethics*, which dates from the days of the ancient Greeks, asks, What would the virtuous person do? Of course, it would help if we knew what made a person virtuous, and one typical answer is that a virtuous person leads a fulfilled and flourishing life. While that is still somewhat vague, it's enough to help us judge the morality of suicide, which by definition does not contribute to living *any* sort of life! But if, for some reason, a person can no longer live a fulfilling life—perhaps due to a severe brain injury or unthinkable emotional anguish—suicide may be justified.[4] So while there may be other convoluted arguments defending suicide based on virtue ethics, we can say that virtue ethics judges suicide, at least in most cases, to be wrong.

Next we have *consequentialism*, which judges the morality of acts based on their outcomes (or consequences). The best-known version of consequentialism is *utilitarianism*, in which acts are moral if they lead to the most happiness for the most people. Philosophers argue endlessly over what "happiness" means in this context—short-term or long-term, crude or sophisticated—but for our purposes we can take it to mean simply "well-being." We can already see that the morality of suicide is not as clear-cut under utilitarianism. Indeed, it's quite complicated, especially because of the concept of happiness or well-being. Consider this: if someone decides to end her life because she is miserable, then we may want to assume that she would be happier after her death. But if she's dead, then she can't experience happiness or well-being at all! So, has total happiness increased, because there is one less miserable person in the world, or has it decreased, because even a miserable person can enjoy at least a smidge of happiness (under all the gloom)?

But if we set that problem aside, we can see a valid contribution that utilitarianism makes to the debate. Even if the effects on the happiness of the suicidal person are questionable, perhaps the effects on other people's happiness aren't.

For the average person, these effects would probably be negative; she undoubtedly has family and friends who would miss her and mourn her death, perhaps even more so because of the particularly tragic nature of suicide. In addition, if she made a positive contribution to the world when alive, that effect would be lost upon her death. For most people, then, suicide would result in a loss of total happiness, even if we allowed that her "happiness" may rise (or her misery would fall).

But what about persons who have a net-negative effect on the world when alive? I'm not talking about your nasty boss, your mother-in-law, or the neighbor who plays his death metal CDs all night long.[5] I mean the serial murderer, the child molester, or the genocidal dictator—if any of these people (using the term generously) were to kill himself, the world would not likely mourn his passing. (True, even a monster can be loved, but not by many, and not much!) A utilitarian would say that such a suicide would be moral, since it increased total happiness more than it lowered it. More reasonably, if someone felt compelled to kill others, either because of mental illness or compulsion from another person, taking his own life would be justified because it would save one or more other lives.[6]

But the problem with utilitarianism, or consequentialism in general, is that these calculations of total happiness or well-being are very rough, vague, and—most important—contingent on the facts of the situation. As a result, suicide may always be moral, *if* the right conditions hold. We can rarely make unqualified statements about the morality of suicide, because that judgment always depends on the facts of the situation. Acknowledging particular circumstances is nice, don't get me wrong, but it would seem that with a topic like suicide, we might get something more definitive from our moral philosophers than *ifs* and *maybes*. But that's all that consequentialism gets us, and this stands us as a significant criticism of that ethical theory in general.

You Got Somethin' Better, Bub?

I think so, Logan (after all, I'm the best there is at what I do, too).[7] The third school of ethics is *deontology*, which judges acts according to their intrinsic moral quality, often based on a system of rules or duties. The most famous deontologist is Immanuel Kant (1724–1804), who developed his ethical system based on a belief in the intrinsic dignity of rational beings. His famous *categorical imperative* provides several guidelines that help determine the morality of a plan of action (or *maxim*) and generates *duties* that command us to do certain things and not to do others.

We can use two of these versions to show why cheating on your wife is immoral.[8] Let's suppose a man (call him Scott) has a "psychic affair" with a woman (call her Emma) other than his wife (call her Jean).[9] One version of the categorical imperative is commonly known as the *Formula of Universal Law*: "Act only according to that maxim whereby you can at the same time will that it should become a universal law."[10] According to this formula, cheating is immoral because if it were universalized, and everyone cheated on his wife (or her husband), the institution of marriage would lose all meaning. But since one has to have a wife to cheat on her, marital infidelity without marriage is a contradiction, and cheating fails this test. Therefore, there is a duty to be faithful to one's spouse.

Another version of the categorical imperative is the *Formula of the End in Itself*: "Act in such a way that you treat humanity, whether in your own person or in the person of another, always at the same time as an end and never simply as a means."[11] Rather than the cold, technical nature of the previous formula, this one focuses directly on the dignity of persons, who shouldn't be used solely to further one's own ends. In Scott's case, he is abusing Jean's trust in him in order to chill with Ms. Frost. Another way of putting it is that Scott is using his own good name (in Jean's opinion) to polish his pet diamond, which shows that you can use yourself wrongly, not only other people, as a means to an end. So this formula also generates the duty of marital fidelity but on somewhat different grounds. (I say "somewhat" because, ideally, all of the versions of the categorical imperative are identical.)

Luckily for us, Kant discussed suicide specifically in his *Grounding for the Metaphysics of Morals*. He first tested the maxim of suicide against the Formula of Universal Law and found that it failed: "One sees at once a contradiction in a system of nature whose law would destroy life by means of the very same feeling that acts so as to stimulate the furtherance of life."[12] He also explained how it failed the Formula of the End in Itself: "If [a suicidal man] destroys himself in order to escape from a difficult situation, then he is making use of his person merely as a means so as to maintain a tolerable condition till the end of his life."[13] Later, in *The Metaphysics of Morals*, he wrote, "Disposing of oneself as a mere means to some discretionary end is debasing humanity in one's person, to which man was nevertheless entrusted for preservation."[14] So, we can be fairly sure that in general, suicide is judged to be immoral in Kant's moral system.

Before we move on, I want to point out one benefit of Kant's deontology, especially compared to consequentialism: To Kant, the morality of specific acts did not depend on their consequences. Cheating on your spouse is wrong, even if total happiness is increased, or if the marriage comes out stronger in the end. Suicide is wrong, no matter how miserable one may be, because it uses one's capacity of reason to defeat itself. In other words, in Kant's ethics the rightness or wrongness of an act is not contingent upon circumstances but depends rather on the elements of the act itself.

Delving Deeper into the Mind of Professor K

Kant's ethical system generates a lot of "thou shalt nots," such as "do not kill" and "do not have 'psychic affairs' with wicked

blondes," but there is actually much more depth and sub-
tlety to Kant's ethics than he is given credit for. For instance,
although he said "do not lie," he was not saying that one had
to tell the truth at all times. It may be fine to keep quiet, dodge
the question, or change the subject—just as long as you don't
lie! Choices like that are left up to our judgment, for which
the duties given to us by the categorical imperative are simply
guidelines.

But "do not kill yourself" seems pretty clear, right? No two
ways about that one, right? Not so fast. In *The Metaphysics of
Morals*, Kant posed several questions suggesting that suicide
can be permitted. One of the cases he presented goes like this:
"A human being who had been bitten by a mad dog already
felt hydrophobia coming on. He explained, in a letter he left,
since as far as he knew the disease was incurable, he was taking
his life lest he harm others as well in his madness (the onset of
which he already felt). Did he do wrong?"[15] Gee—instead
of "human being," say "mutant," and instead of "bitten by a mad
dog," say "possessed by the Phoenix Force." Sound familiar?

There are several reasons why Kant may have been willing
to make a concession in such a case. The most obvious is that
if the hydrophobia or the Phoenix Force were going to take
you over, you would be likely to cause harm to others, which
would violate a duty not to—you know—harm others. While
you would technically not be responsible for this harm once it
happened, you do have the chance to prevent it, albeit by ending your own life.

For Kantians, this is an apparent case of conflicting duties or
obligations, in which a person finds herself between the proverbial rock and the hard place (think Colossus and Juggernaut).
On the one hand, you have a duty not to commit suicide,
but on the other hand, you also have a duty not to harm others.
Lenin's ghost—what do you do? It's not a matter of harming
others versus harming yourself; Kant makes no such distinctions, which are so popular in "everyday" ethics. It seems noble

to us that a person would sacrifice herself to save others—that's our definition of a hero, after all—but we don't assume that the hero's life is less worthy (far from it). To Kant, all human beings have an incalculable and incomparable worth, and he would never compare the value of one life against another (or even others, plural). That would be a consequentialist justification, and that's not the way Kant rolls.[16] He actually didn't leave much guidance for such situations, saying "simply" to observe the duty with the "stronger ground of obligation."[17] Thanks, Professor K. This open question has kept philosophers busy for the last two hundred years but doesn't help the X-Men very much.

Another reason Kant might have allowed such a suicide focuses less on the benefit to other people and more on the suicidal person herself. In the case of either the bite from a rabid dog or possession by the Phoenix Force, the affected person is not truly herself. Her rationality, her humanity, and her self are lost to the "madness" created by these circumstances. As we saw before, this may relieve her of responsibility for her actions, but we are more concerned here with how she feels about the effects on her self. In Kant's terms, she loses her *autonomy*, the ability to choose her own actions based on her rationality and morality. Indeed, autonomy is one of the most important concepts in Kantian ethics, representing the source of the dignity and the incomparable worth of human beings.

In his essay "Self-Regarding Suicide," Thomas E. Hill Jr., a contemporary Kantian philosopher, sorted through various motivations behind suicide, ruling out heroic, altruistic self-sacrifice to focus on those centering on the suicidal person herself.[18] Among these motivations is the desire to live according to moral principles or the desire not to live, if the only way to continue living is to abandon or renounce those principles.[19] For instance, some people would rather die than be enslaved, engage in prostitution, or fight in war. In those cases, suicide may be understandable, and Hill argued that it would be moral in a Kantian sense: "To be sure, one cuts short the time one could live as a rational, autonomous agent; but doing so can be a manifestation of autonomy, an ultimate decision of the author of a life story to conclude it with a powerful expression of ideals he autonomously chose to live by."[20]

Of course, we may hope that someone in such dire circumstances would be able to find another way, but at the same time we can recognize that there may be cases in which she can't. As Hill wrote, imagining a person to be the author of her life story, "if you value being an author and have just one story to write, you should not hurry to conclude it. But sometimes, to give it the meaning you intend, you must end it before you spoil it."[21] So if possession by the Phoenix Force would lead you (or the being that used to be you) to perform immoral acts against your will, such as mass murder, then suicide may be the moral alternative, tragic as it may be.

Let's Hear from Our Guests, Scott and Jean! (Applause)

I don't know whether Chris Claremont studied philosophy, but the dialogue he wrote for Scott Summers and Jean Grey in the final pages of *The Dark Phoenix Saga* closely resembles what we've been discussing. In particular, Jean's assessment of her situation reveals an awareness of the consequences of her possession, for others as well as for herself:[22]

> Jean: So long as I live, the Phoenix will manifest itself through me. And so long as that happens, I'll eventually, inevitably, become Dark Phoenix.
>
> Scott: You have an intellect, Jean, a will, a soul—use them! Fight this dark side of yourself!
>
> Jean: I can feel the Phoenix with me, taking over. . . . You want me to fight? I have. I am—with all my strength. But I can't forget that I killed an entire world—five

billion people—as casually, as unthinkingly, as you would crumple a piece of paper. I want no more deaths on my conscience. Your way, I'd have to stay completely in control of myself every second of every day for the rest of my immortal life. Maybe I could do it. But if I slipped, even for an instant, if I . . . failed . . . if even one more person died at my hands . . . It's better this way.

We can read Scott as trying to remind Jean of her human, rational, autonomous nature, that she has a will and she can use it to fight the influence of the Phoenix. But Jean realizes that while this is possible, she cannot guarantee that she will always be able to restrain the Phoenix within her—someday it will win, it will take her over, and it will kill again. After her death, Scott knows this, too: "I should have realized . . . that you could not become Dark Phoenix and remain true to your self, the Jean Grey I knew, and fell in love with."

Jean would rather die than live as the Phoenix, and it was her "ultimate decision," and the final expression of her autonomy, to make that choice. Perhaps the Watcher sums it up best on the final page: "When faced with a choice between keeping her god-like power—knowing she would then wreak death and destruction across the stars—and dying herself, she chose the latter. . . . Jean Grey could have lived to become a god. But it was much more important to her that she die . . . a human."

"Jean Grey Is Dead." "Yeah, *That'll* Last."[23]

Alas, Jean Grey has since returned to life and died several times over in the comics.[24] But that does not diminish the sacrifice she made to save countless lives—and herself—at the end of *The Dark Phoenix Saga*. Altruistic suicide may seem like the easiest type to defend in ethical terms, but it matters how we defend it. While virtue ethics would not approve of suicide in general, it would probably make an exception for altruistic suicide, because it is what we imagine the virtuous person doing, at least when there are no alternatives available. Utilitarians defend it—or, rather, demand it—based on its positive effects of total happiness, but this is a cold, calculating treatment of a human life.

Kant's deontological ethics ultimately provides the most satisfying defense of altruistic suicide such as Jean Grey's. She did not end her life solely to save the countless lives that Dark Phoenix would have taken but, more important, to make sure she didn't become someone she didn't want to be (and who would take countless innocent lives!). If, as Kant held, suicide is wrong because it sacrifices one's rationality and autonomy, then Jean's suicide can be seen as a way for her to save those faculties from being abused or sacrificed in a different way to the Phoenix Force. And that's not how she—or Chris Claremont and John Byrne—wanted her story to end.[25]

NOTES

1. *The Dark Phoenix Saga* originally ran in *X-Men* #129–137 (1980) and is available in its own trade paperback (2006, in color) and in *Essential X-Men Vol. 2* (2002, in black and white). Claremont and Byrne are credited as co-plotters on the tale, while Claremont wrote the script and Byrne provided the pencils (inked by the incomparable Terry Austin).

2. In an alternate universe, I would have written this essay around Colossus's self-sacrifice in *Uncanny X-Men* #390 (Feb. 2001), reprinted in *X-Men: Dream's End* (2004). (In that universe, I would also be thinner, and Emma Frost would love *me*.)

3. Kitty Pryde to Emma Frost, *Astonishing X-Men* #3 (Sept. 2004).

4. The Stoics were particularly clear on this point; see Michael Cholbi (2004), "Suicide," in the *Stanford Encyclopedia of Philosophy* (http://plato.stanford.edu/entries/suicide/, accessed November 7, 2008), section 2.1.

5. I said I'm sorry! Let it go, man . . .

6. This assumes that all lives are valued equally or contribute the same amount to total happiness, which we can doubt. This also leads directly to the morality of killing the murderer before he kills, which opens a completely different can of worms; on this, see my "Why Doesn't Batman Kill the Joker?" in *Batman and Philosophy: The Dark Knight of the Soul*, edited by Mark D. White and Robert Arp (Hoboken, NJ: John Wiley & Sons, 2008), pp. 5–16.

7. Not really, but I wanted to use that line *so* bad.

8. A third formula, the *Formula of the Kingdom of Ends*, is often understood to be a combination of the first two (though with a unique focus) and isn't commonly used to judge maxims.

9. *New X-Men Vol. 4: Riot at Xavier's* (2003).

10. Immanuel Kant, 1785, *Grounding for the Metaphysics of Morals*, translated by James W. Ellington (Indianapolis: Hackett, 1993), p. 421. (In my citations from Kant, I have provided the "Akademie" page numbers, which are given in any reputable edition.)

11. Ibid., p. 429.

12. Ibid., p. 442. Technically, this is a failure according to the *Formula of the Law of Nature*, a variation on the Formula of Universal Law: "Act as if the maxim of your action were to become through your will a universal law of nature" (ibid., p. 421). For our purposes, there is little difference between the two formulae, although they do generate slightly different tests of consistency.

13. Ibid., p. 429.

14. Immanuel Kant, 1787, *The Metaphysics of Morals*, edited by Mary Gregor (Cambridge: Cambridge University Press, 1996), p. 423.

15. Ibid., pp. 423–424.

16. A utilitarian, of course, would describe such a suicide as morally obligatory because it increases total happiness (one reason utilitarianism is often seen as too demanding an ethical system). But at least one scholar writing in a Kantian tradition has described such suicides as morally obligatory; see D. R. Cooley, "Crimina Carmis and Morally Obligatory Suicide," *Ethical Theory and Moral Practice* 9 (2006): 327–356.

17. Kant, *Metaphysics of Morals*, p. 224.

18. Thomas E. Hill Jr., "Self-Regarding Suicide: A Modified Kantian View," in his *Autonomy and Self-Respect* (Cambridge: Cambridge University Press, 1991), pp. 85–103.

19. Ibid., p. 91.

20. Ibid., p. 101.

21. Ibid. This recalls our virtue ethics discussion; the Stoic philosopher Seneca (1 BCE–CE 65) wrote that "the wise man will live as long as he ought, not as long as he can" (*Ad Lucilium Epistulae Morales*, translated by Richard M. Gummere, London: Williams Heineman, 1918), Epistle 70. It may not surprise you that Kant was greatly influenced by Seneca (and the Stoics in general).

22. All of the quotes in this section are from the final three pages of *X-Men* #137 (and the trade paperback).

23. S.W.O.R.D. Special Agent Abigail Brand replying to Emma Frost, *Astonishing X-Men* #6 (Nov. 2004).

24. "They'd have Jeannie spinning in her grave. That is, if she stayed in it for more'n five minutes" (Wolverine, commenting on several of Cyclops's orders, in *Wolverine* #46 [Nov. 2006]).

25. I thank Ariel Brennan for insightful and X-cellent comments on this chapter.

X-ISTENTIAL X-MEN: JEWS, SUPERMEN, AND THE LITERATURE OF STRUGGLE

Jesse Kavadlo

Although creator Stan Lee once claimed that the "X" in the X-Men's title stood for their "extra" power, the letter might as well have stood for "existential." The doubt, struggle, fear, and absurdity at the heart of existentialism are also the reasons why we respond so viscerally to the X-Men. But like the X-Men, existentialism isn't purely negative. Quite the contrary, existentialism can be a way to make sense of, and assign responsibility in, a world where God seems to be gone. But even more, to understand the X-Men it may be helpful to think of existentialism as a body of literature, a way of reading and writing, perhaps the most influential and important intellectual movement of the last century.

The X-Men's stories, then, may be best understood as literary examples of existential crisis. The mutant experience is anguished and absurd, a never-ending struggle not only to defeat bad guys—those staples of superheroism—but for safety and tolerance from the very people mutants protect. As each crisis passes, with another villain imprisoned, Magneto defeated (or dead or cloned or brainwashed or transported in space-time), yet another crisis inevitably begins, as the cycle has continued now for a half-century. Is the X-Men's eternal labor merely the nature of the serial narrative, the franchise in need of the next installment? Or has it come to represent the boundless, meaningless pursuit that is life? Even after the continuing deaths and resurrections, the alternate timelines and parallel universes, rewritten pasts and retroactively revised continuities—or, perhaps, as we will see, *because of them*—there is a moral, even redemptive, quality to the existential struggles and conflicts that characterize the X-Men.

The Jewish Question as Mutant Question

Even if it's easy to say that the mutant plight raises existential questions, as a movement, existentialism encompasses more than philosophy and more than literature. It is also bound up with the politics of its time. Although Martin Heidegger (1889–1976) was a Nazi sympathizer, Jean-Paul Sartre (1905–1980) published *Anti-Semite and Jew*, in response to persistent anti-Semitism in France, after the Holocaust saw six million Jews murdered.[1] The ideas that God was dead, the universe was cruel, and technology and modernity together stripped people of their subjectivity, suddenly, horrifyingly, seemed all too real.

One definition of existentialism suggests that man "is alienated from his authentic self and . . . thus an easy, indeed willing, victim of a vast and efficient collective modeled after mass-production processes and often, as in the case of Nazi Germany, a brutalized weapon in the arsenal of such a collective in its effort to achieve universality."[2] The Jewish philosopher Hannah Arendt (1906–1975) described existentialism's urgency in

Eichmann in Jerusalem, her chronicle of the Nuremberg Trials (the arraignment of Nazi war criminals). "Justice," she wrote, "demands that the accused be prosecuted, defended, and judged, and that all the other questions of seemingly greater import— of 'how could it happen?' and 'Why did it happen?' . . . be left in abeyance."[3] Since the trials and justice itself would not ask these questions, the moral imperative must fall on each of us.

The idea of the superhero, then, evokes the language of existentialism. That man himself may become a "brutalized weapon" sounds rather like Wolverine, except in the comic he is the hero and not the villain, a reversal we will return to. More important, though, the X-Men series continually asks its readers to consider the ways in which people treat others who are different from them. Yes, Spider-Man also exhibits existential angst and the Thing also experiences what it is like to be physically different. But unlike most of Marvel's greatest heroes, who gain their powers as the result of scientific accidents later in life, the X-Men's powers are, for lack of a better term, natural. At first glance, the use of mutation looks like lazy writing. After cosmic rays, gamma bombs, and even radioactive spider bites, deciding, "Ah, they were just born that way," may seem like a cop-out. But its simplicity is its brilliance: there can be no looking back, no self-recriminating "if only"—"If only we hadn't gone into space/saved Rick Jones/ been bitten on that day."

The X-Men, like most of us, were born into circumstances beyond their control, thrown into a world they did not choose. And their struggle, not simply to make sense of such a world, but to thrive in it, mirrors each of our own searches for authenticity and self-hood. That Professor X, the world's most powerful telepath, would continually put his team—his surrogate children—in danger, in essence *to protect his oppressors*, shows a morality and a selflessness that are themselves almost superhuman. No doubt, Charles Xavier could simply change people's minds to make them accept mutants. But to do so would be a science-fictionalized version of Sartre's "bad faith," or, "a lie to oneself within the unity of a single consciousness."[4]

Bad faith, for Sartre, is the cornerstone of anti-Semitism, the framework of which undergirds the entire nature of the X-Men stories. "The anti-Semite," Sartre wrote, "has chosen hate because hate is a faith; at the outset he has chosen to devaluate words and reasons."[5] In their consistent use of physical violence, so do the X-Men's adversaries.

Considering their creations' existential struggle, it is not surprising that most of the great comic book creators were Jewish: Superman's Jerry Siegel and Joe Schuster, Batman's Bob Kane and Bill Finger, the Spirit's Will Eisner, Green Lantern's Irwin Hasen, and many others. And fellow Jews Stan Lee and Jack Kirby, together and with other collaborators, created all of Marvel's major figures, including, of course, the X-Men. During the 1930s and the 1940s, many other professions restricted or discriminated against Jews, while comic books, seen as vulgar, provided an opportunity.[6] The Jewish influence shows from Superman (the first indisputable superhero) onward. Superman may have been an alien on the inside, but he disguised himself by hiding in plain sight: a clumsy, cowardly newspaper hack in glasses and an ill-fitting suit.[7] Any resemblance to his creators, then, was likely unconscious but surely there.

During the Golden Age of comics (for most readers, the late 1930s to the mid-1950s), writers often drew directly from the unique character of the American Jewish immigrant experience to create a powerful "assimilationist fantasy," as comic great Jules Feiffer put it, that "underneath the schmucky façade live men of steel."[8] Superman is a kind of super-immigrant himself, one who, like the immigrants of his day, assimilates flawlessly, speaks the language, and knows the natives better than they know themselves. As one character in Michael Chabon's recent novel *The Amazing Adventures of Kavalier and Clay*, puts it, "They're all Jewish, superheroes. Superman, you don't think he's Jewish? Coming over from the old country, changing his name like that. Clark Kent, only a Jew would pick a name like that for himself."[9]

The fantasy proved even more apt as superheroes went to war in the pages of comic books even before America itself had been attacked at Pearl Harbor. The most dramatic illustration (literally) of this phenomenon comes from the cover of 1941's *Captain America* #1 (another hero co-created by Kirby, who, like Jerry Siegel and Will Eisner, enlisted to fight in World War II). The comic featured the red, white, and blue supersoldier punching out Adolf Hitler himself. As historian Bradford Wright explained, "Like many patriotic superheroes of World War II, Captain America declared war on the Axis months before the rest of the nation did."[10]

But more than Superman and Captain America, the X-Men turned this Jewish subtext into the text itself, with depth and purpose that belie the comic-book label. In the aftermath of the Holocaust, Golden Age simplicities seemed hollow and naïve; not surprisingly, Superman retreated further into science fiction and fantasy, while Captain America disappeared for decades.[11] Meanwhile, the appearance of the X-Men in the 1960s (and particularly its 1970s revision in *Giant-Size X-Men* #1 that brought in Wolverine and saw the birth of Storm, Colossus, Nightcrawler, and others) by Len Wein and, later, Chris Claremont (both also Jewish), along with the emergence of the X-Men's popularity during the 1980s and the 1990s and film adaptations in the 2000s, radically complicate the largely positive immigration imagery of its comic forebears. First, like Superman, the X-Men are, metaphorically at least, Jewish. Not just Jewish like Kitty Pryde—Sprite, Ariel, Shadowcat—who wears a Star of David and refers to her faith semiregularly. And not just Jewish like Magneto. When we first met him way back in *X-Men* #1, he was a standard-issue megalomaniac in a bad helmet. But by the time of the first X-Men film, he had evolved into a Jewish Holocaust survivor.

The film's harrowing and not very comic-book opening, depicting a young Magneto torn from his parents in a Nazi concentration camp, together with the X-Men's own precarious relationship to human culture, wind up revising and maybe reversing Superman's Semitic semiotics. Clark Kent is a nerd and a nebbish on the outside but is really an Aryan ideal inside, yet crucially *in the service of truth, justice, and the American way.*[12] Superman is a perfect prewar fantasy: an American who uses Fascist-style power but in the service of freedom; a man like everyone else in all the ways that count, and his teensy-weensy difference—godlike powers—does not affect how he treats humans or *how humans treat him.* ("Thanks, Superman!") As Feiffer and, later, a similar monologue in the film *Kill Bill: Vol. 2* have suggested, Superman is the true, not secret, identity; Clark Kent is the disguise. In the aftermath of the Holocaust and the mainstream fear and acknowledgment of anti-Semitism as alive and well, the X-Men exist in a world where popular culture and fantasy are poised to tackle more disturbing truths than those of the earlier metaphorically Jewish superheroes. Unlike Clark Kent, Cyclops can never remove his glasses. Wolverine's healing factor makes him virtually invincible, but he, unlike Superman, is pierced by, and feels the pain of, each bullet. And Colossus may be a Man of Steel, but he has, in a sense, no secret identity; both flesh and organic metal are his true form.

If Superman represents a wish fulfillment, that the Jewish, immigrant, and assimilation experiences make people who they are (different, powerful) rather than what they look like (mild-mannered, bland), then the X-Men reverse the equation. Despite how they frequently look different, the experience of being a minority assimilating into a majority culture makes them the *same*, not different: entitled to equal and fair treatment and tolerance. Yet the experience does more than that. The only human in *Superman* who feels threatened by the presence of an omnipotent alien hiding among them is the arch-villain

Lex Luthor. Stan Lee, writing decades after Siegel and Schuster, knew better. Luthor's reaction isn't that of a psychopath but the way humans have always responded to those who are different from themselves.

The black-and-white Manichaeism of Superman's day, of good guys saving the world from the bad guys, would be replaced. There were humans who would help mutants and those who feared them, and vice versa. Magneto, the X-Men's Luthor, is not evil as much as chastened. He understands that the endgame of intolerance is death, and that it is better to kill than be killed. Indeed, in the recent comics, his separatist mutant island Genosha, which he had liberated from being a mutant forced-labor concentration camp, ended in mutant genocide at militant human hands. And in light of the series' Jewish roots, it should come as no surprise that other X-Men villains have had names like Apocalypse and Holocaust. Each storyline becomes a new attempt to rewrite human history through the lens of superhero science fiction, where the world can be saved—or, if not, time can be reversed or reality altered. And if not that, then the next threat to the world immediately segues from the last, without painful self-reflection or commentary. Indeed, if you chronicle the plight of even one X-Man over the years—Cyclops, Jean Grey, Beast, Angel, Wolverine, take your pick—it is a series of one severe trauma after another: torture, amnesia, disfigurement, displacement, transformation, disappearance, the death of loved ones, even one's own seeming death. Yet they move on, often, seemingly, unscathed, as if their psyches all have their own version of mutant healing powers. They can cope. But can we? If Superman is a wish, then the X-Men represent what Sigmund Freud (1856–1939) understood to be every wish's flipside: fear. Much of the superhero's appeal is the reader's desire to be a superhero, too. The X-Men embody that wish: Flight! Telekinesis! Claws! But unlike Superman, they also represent the terrifying possibility of what could really happen if the wish came true.

The X-Verse and Camus' *Myth of Sisyphus*—or, Why Can't the World Stay Saved?

Unlike other commentaries on the X-Men, this one didn't begin with the usual conundrum: which X-Men? In its long run, the team has accrued a vast assortment of lineups, permutations, spin-offs, and media representations, including the 1960s original lineup, the 1970s revision, *Alpha Flight*, *X-Force*, *X-Factor*, *New Mutants*, *X-Men 2099*, *Exiles*, the *Age of Apocalypse*, the *Days of Future Past*, *House of M*, *Ultimate X-Men*, the *X-Men: Evolution* cartoon, the three movies (and counting), and more. Undoubtedly, the decades to come will bring more reboots and newer television and movie incarnations. These multiple versions, variable timelines, and alternate universes have proliferated throughout comics in general, but they seem particularly prevalent in X-Men stories. Together, they demonstrate the ways in which these, too, are part of the existential crisis and fear, yet also fantasy, inherent to the storylines and the characters. For better or worse, the battle never ends.

These never-ending conflicts recall literary critic M. H. Abrams's textbook definition of existentialism,

> which is, in part, to view a human being as an isolated existent who is cast into an alien universe, to conceive the universe as possessing no inherent truth, value, or meaning, and to represent human life—in its fruitless search for purpose and meaning, as it moves from the nothingness whence it came toward the nothingness where it must end—as an experience that is both anguished and absurd.[13]

Taken as a checklist, Abrams's definition lets us see how the X-Men stack up existentially: "Isolated existent." Check. Aside from more X-puns, the whole notion of the X-Men as a team originated in Professor X's realization that each mutant has a lonely, isolated, and dangerous existence. Yet even then, to be a mutant is to be alone, even when surrounded by other mutants. Although certain powers, like, say, super-strength, abound, and while X-Men's colorists must love blue, each mutant is unique and not in the New Age feel-good way; that is, each mutant must learn to accept and control his or her particular powers and body, and the responsibility—sometimes even danger—that these inevitably bring. Even with Professor X and team-mates, each X-Man—"existent"—must ultimately cope alone.

"Alien universe." Check. Abrams didn't mean the worlds of the Shi'ar, Brood, or Phalanx, either, although these, plus the "alien worlds" of alternate timelines and dimensions, under-score the main point: how can we respond to the vast strange-ness and unknowability that surround us? If anything, these races, galaxies, and universes are no stranger than the oppres-sive forces the X-Men routinely face on Earth or even the notion of a race of superpowered mutants themselves.

I'll skip to the end of Abrams's description for a moment: "anguished and absurd." Although these words typically have negative connotations, they accurately describe the plight of many X-Men. However difficult life seems, at least your bones don't grow outside your skin into detachable weapons, as Marrow's do; at least the manifestation of your telekinetic ability didn't destroy the bottom of your face, as happened with Chamber. But even ignoring these obscure and grotesque mutants, what about Angel? Wings? Bird wings, sprouting out of your back? And you thought *your* puberty was awkward. As I said, anguished and absurd. Check.

It's the middle section of the definition that's debatable: "the universe as possessing no inherent truth, value, or mean-ing" and the "fruitless search for purpose and meaning" that "moves from the nothingness whence it came toward the nothingness where it must end." That's a bit dark, even for the X-Men. Or worse, consider the opening of Camus' *Myth of*

Sisyphus, one basis for Abrams's formulation: "There is but one truly serious philosophical problem, and that is suicide."[14] Not Jean Grey suicide-leading-to-resurrection-or-that-she-was-really-a-clone suicide either—the real deal. In the end, because of the never-ending battles in never-ending timelines in never-ending universes, do the X-Men, and by extension, do we, struggle for nothing? Or, as Mr. Incredible said, reasonably enough, in the movie *The Incredibles,* "No matter how many times you save the world, it always manages to get back in jeopardy again. Sometimes I just want it to *stay saved,* you know?"

His predicament, shared and magnified by the X-Men, is Sisyphus's problem as well. Condemned by the gods to Hades for punishment, Sisyphus must roll a boulder up a hill, only to have it tumble back down to the bottom before he can complete his task. Forever. Yet the suicide question and the question of whether existence is pointless belie Camus' optimism near the end:

> You have already grasped that Sisyphus is the absurd hero. He *is,* as much through his passions as through his torture. His scorn of the gods, his hatred of death, and his passion for life won him that unspeakable penalty in which the whole being is exerted toward accomplishing nothing. This is the price that must be paid for the passions of this earth. Nothing is told us about Sisyphus in the underworld. Myths are made for the imagination to breathe life into them.[15]

The X-Men, like Sisyphus, then, do not labor or suffer for nothing. Superheroes, as other critics have suggested, are a kind of modern mythology, and through their pursuits and struggles, their deaths and rebirths, their anguish and absurdity, we, as a readership and a viewership, get to exercise our imaginations and that deeply human power, our empathy. In light of the X-Men's, and comics', Jewish origins, the notion of alternate universes seems especially compelling, rather than especially hopeless. Who, in the aftermath of the Holocaust, doesn't wish that somewhere, somehow, the world could be different? That time travel—a kind of existential do-over—couldn't somehow make things right again? Although the seemingly futile struggle, the notion that the world cannot ever stay saved, seems like Sisyphus rolling the rock up the hill, only to watch it come crashing down, Camus understood that his plight is not torment but the most basic incarnation of *narrative* and *life* themselves. The rock, up, then down, is precisely how story itself works, as evidenced by the infamous parabolas from every high school English class that studies drama. The rock starts at the bottom, then rises, and rises, as the action rises, conflicts ensue, and characters develop, before it rolls back to the bottom in resolution—or, for serial narratives like the X-Men, resets the counter for the next adventure.

Fittingly, then, Camus ends *The Myth of Sisyphus* this way:

> I leave Sisyphus at the foot of the mountain! One always finds one's burden again. But Sisyphus teaches the higher fidelity that negates the gods and raises rocks. He too concludes that all is well. This universe henceforth without a master seems to him neither sterile nor futile. Each atom of that stone, each mineral flake of that night-filled mountain, in itself forms a world. The struggle itself toward the heights is enough to fill a man's heart. One must imagine Sisyphus happy.[16]

So let's imagine that the X-Men are happy as well. Perhaps satisfaction—for the reader, really, since the X-Men themselves are ink on paper—lies in the never-ending struggle, not in its completion. Like Sisyphus, and in a world forever transformed by the horrors of the Holocaust, we are happy to begin each adventure anew, even if we already know how it must, inevitably, end. For mutants, philosophers, or everyday folk, that ambiguity—existing, while lamenting the end—defines both stories and life itself.

NOTES

1. Six million Jews were only half of the twelve million murdered in Nazi concentration camps during the Holocaust; the victims included anyone who was considered "different," such as the ill, the aging, the handicapped, homosexual individuals, anyone of African or Gypsy ancestry, and so on. World War II resulted in the deaths of more than fifty million people.

2. William V. Spanos, *A Casebook on Existentialism* (New York: Crowell, 1966), p. 3.

3. Hannah Arendt, *Eichmann in Jerusalem: A Report on the Banality of Evil* (New York: Viking, 1966), p. 3.

4. Jean-Paul Sartre, *Being and Nothingness*, translated by Hazel E. Barnes (New York: Citadel, 1958), p. 547. The quotation here comes from the translator's Key to Special Terminology at the end of the book. Barnes added that the definitions given "will perhaps be confusing to the person who has read none of" the book. You can judge for yourself.

5. Jean-Paul Sartre, *Anti-Semite and Jew*, translated by George J. Becker (New York: Schocken, 1946), p. 16.

6. *ZAP! POW! BAM! The Superhero: The Golden Age of Comic Books, 1938–1950* (Atlanta: Breman, 2004), p. 14. This catalogue was a companion to the exhibit of the same name that appeared in New York City's Jewish Museum in 2004. The exhibition, I believe, cements the link between Jewish American culture and superheroes, as if more cement were needed. For much more on the Jewish roots of the comic book and Siegel and Shuster in particular, see Gerard Jones, *Men of Tomorrow: Geeks, Gangsters, and the Birth of the Comic Book* (New York: Basic, 2004).

7. Superman's Kryptonian name, Kal-El, means "vessel of God" in Hebrew.

8. Jules Feiffer, "The Minsk Theory of Krypton," 1996. Reprinted in *ZAP! POW! BAM! The Superhero*, p. 29.

9. Michael Chabon, The *Amazing Adventures of Kavalier and Clay* (New York: Random House, 2000), p. 585. Anyone reading this essay who has not already read Chabon's novel should run, not walk, to the nearest bookstore to get it. You won't be sorry.

10. Bradford W. Wright, *Comic Book Nation: The Transformation of Youth Culture in America* (Baltimore: Johns Hopkins University Press, 2001), p. 33. Wright is a particularly astute cultural historian.

11. A half-century later, Superman would be reinvented for TV's *Smallville* essentially as an existential, X-Men-style hero—that is, a teenager practically and existentially coping with his emerging powers, while concealing and celebrating his differences. It represents a powerful tribute to the X-Men's influence.

12. "Nebbish" is a Yiddish term for a poor, unfortunate, often timid and luckless individual. Yiddish is a Jewish language that combines German, Hebrew, and Slavic words. The word *Yiddish* itself means Jewish.

13. M. H. Abrams, *Glossary of Literary Terms*, 7th ed. (Fort Worth, TX: Harcourt, 1999), p. 1.

14. Albert Camus, *The Myth of Sisyphus*, translated by Justin O'Brien (New York: Vintage, 1942), p. 3.

15. Ibid., p. 89.

16. Ibid., p. 91.

CONSCIOUSNESS, CONSCIENCE, AND CURE

MAD GENETICS: THE SINISTER SIDE OF BIOLOGICAL MASTERY

Andrew Burnett

Nathaniel Essex is a serious scientist born into a comic-book world. Toiling obsessively to prove his theories, shunned by the scientific establishment for his unorthodox experiments, he stands on the brink of enlightenment or, perhaps, corruption. A fateful encounter with Apocalypse provides both. When offered genetic knowledge from outside his own timeline, Essex accepts transformation at Apocalypse's hands, refashioning his body and mind to eliminate mortal weakness—and with it, his essential humanity. Casting off his identity as Essex, he becomes the diabolical figure known as Mister Sinister. In decades to come, he will emerge as a geneticist of unparalleled brilliance and daring, a witness to great discoveries and travesties of medical history, and one of the most dangerous opponents the X-Men will ever face.

The mad geneticist is a mad scientist but with a difference. Mastery of the genetic code not only unlocks the powers of nature, it confers a certain seductive ability to redraw the boundaries of human and mutant existence. Heroic scientists such as Henry McCoy, Moira MacTaggert, and Charles Xavier, although sometimes tormented by the moral weight of their choices, are mostly able to resist temptations to misuse their knowledge and power. But many others succumb out of weakness, naiveté, or flawed motives, forsaking ethical restraint and leaving behind a trail of scarred, even dead, victims. Those with ordinary talent or luck often perish when their experiments get out of control. But Mister Sinister survives, driven by purposes that mystify others but burn with "the fierce light of clarity" in his scientific mind.[1]

Mister Sinister and other villainous geneticists illustrate a very real set of concerns about the moral interpretation and use of genetic knowledge, in our world as well as theirs. Even in ostensibly advanced societies, the progress of biomedicine has been shadowed by events that echo Mister Sinister's dark obsessions of genetic mastery. If biotechnological progress is not accompanied by ethical maturity, we may yet see more of these stories play out, exacting an awesome price in individual and global suffering.

The Burden of Dangerous Knowledge

Like the X-Men, bioethics is a child of the atom that came of age in the 1960s, outside of the cultural mainstream. Postwar revelations of Axis atrocities carried out by scientists and physicians had shaken the world. But the ongoing practice of ethically unsupervised research on vulnerable populations— under democratic as well as totalitarian regimes—came only slowly to public attention. Bioethics also went against current philosophical fashion, which emphasized analysis of ethical statements (metaethics) over making actual ethical judgments (normative ethics). Despite these difficulties, bioethics began to attract a wider public and professional audience. Few could deny the expanding influence of biomedical technology or the inadequacy of existing ethical guidance and regulations.

From its beginnings, bioethics incorporated a basic insight that is amply displayed in the X-Verse: knowledge is power, and power always has a dangerous edge. Power to heal includes power to kill. Power to preserve life includes power to prolong suffering. Power to identify differences includes power to isolate and oppress those who are different. Power to read genetic information includes power to take away individuals' freedom and responsibility. And power to reengineer humans, animals, or plants includes power to invite disaster, through hostile intent or simple miscalculation.

Ultimately, bioethics is about more than the balance of power or regulating biomedical activities relative to a given set of moral standards. Bioethics also involves wrestling with new moral questions posed by biomedical discoveries, realizing that our ethical standards appear differently as biology fills in our picture of humanity and its place in the world. This means there is a vital, if not always acknowledged, relationship between bioethics and the philosophy of biology, a difficult dialogue between the way things *ought* to be and the way things *empirically appear* to be. What is the meaning of justice and compassion in the larger life story of which humanity is only one part? On what basis would, or should, the strong feel solidarity with the vulnerable, evolutionary winners with those who are expected to lose? Should science model itself after the moral neutrality of the natural processes it studies? What happens when it does?

Nature, Red in Tooth and Claw

The rift between biology and ethics broke the surface in Victorian England, a society shaken by biological, industrial, and social revolutions. Even before Darwin's work was published, older conceptions of the natural order of things were coming under critical pressure. Evidence for a long history of life on Earth challenged literal readings of Genesis. But the real problem was not simply chronological. Nature was revealing multiple features that were hard to reconcile with divine design, such as natural cataclysms and the extinctions of multiple species, the apparent wastefulness of many biological processes, and the cruel adaptations of "torturing parasites, which outnumber in their kinds all other creatures."[2]

A generation earlier, the arguments of William Paley's *Natural Theology* impressed educated Britons (including the young Charles Darwin) with abundant natural evidence for a benevolent Creator. But if one could reason from Nature to God, how then should one interpret the widespread suffering due to natural causes, especially diseases that afflicted children and cut short so many lives? What kind of God would that reveal? Tennyson's "In Memoriam" expresses the dismay many Victorians felt:

> Are God and Nature then at strife,
> That Nature lends such evil dreams?
> So careful of the type she seems,
> So careless of the single life;
> . . . .
> I falter where I firmly trod,
> And falling with my weight of cares
> Upon the great world's altar-stairs
> That slope thro' darkness up to God,
> I stretch lame hands of faith, and grope . . .[3]

Reaching toward a loving God but confronted by Nature's indifference to individual suffering, it is no wonder that some Victorians began to wonder about the basis for their moral sensibilities or the possibility of using science as a weapon to rebel against the natural order, rather than meekly accepting it. These are just the questions that fire the imagination of Nathaniel Essex. The scene is London 1859, ground zero for Darwin's *Origin of Species*. Like Darwin himself, Essex has been emotionally devastated by losing a child to disease (implied to be a genetic condition). Energized by Darwin's theory, Essex gets into a heated debate with him about the potential to take control of future human evolution. Darwin counsels compassion and restraint and eventually expresses concern for Essex's mental stability. Stung by Darwin's rejection and devastated by his wife's death in premature labor, Essex rages in frustration at his own moral limitations and opens himself to the dreadful bargain offered by Apocalypse.

After his transformation, Mister Sinister exults at having "undergone what amounts to an industrial revolution of the mind," shedding Essex's moral restraint, which "prevented me from reaching the highest summit of knowledge."[4] Quickly rebelling against servitude to Apocalypse, he is freed to pursue his scientific agenda without interference from society or his own conscience. Like Nature, he, too, will be attentive to the type—whether Homo sapiens or Homo superior—and more careless when it comes to a single life.

Evolutionary Justice?

Is Mister Sinister's reading of evolutionary ethics correct? Is it really true that the only moral lesson of natural selection—if any—is victory in the struggle for existence, at any cost? Does evolution show that loving thy neighbor is not just an illusion, but actually an obstacle to real progress in economics, politics, and especially science? Such a view is hardly a necessary component of Darwin's theory, although it resonates with folk philosophies of biology such as "dog eat dog" and the "law of the jungle" that portray the natural world as an amoral world. But, in fact, it's not only possible but actually quite plausible to see a more harmonious relationship between biology and morality.

Herbert Spencer (1820–1903) was not merely an intellectual cheerleader for Darwin's theory, although it was he, not Darwin, who introduced the popular formula "survival of the fittest."

He was also an ambitious moral and political thinker with a huge influence on his contemporaries. Rethinking history in evolutionary terms, he pressed a claim Darwin had only hinted at, about the need for humans to evolve morally as well as physically:

> Here we shall assume it to be an inevitable inference from the doctrine of organic evolution, that the highest type of living being, no less than all lower types, must go on molding itself to those requirements which circumstances impose. And we shall, by implication, assume that moral changes are among the changes thus wrought out.[5]

Spencer saw a natural logic driving the development of human ethical behavior, just as it did the "quasi-ethical" behavior traits observed among higher animals. But the behavior patterns Spencer studied, at least among social animals, were based on the needs of the group, rather than of the individual organism. "Dog eat dog" turns out to be a losing strategy for dogkind, and even the law of the jungle includes the need to support young offspring who cannot care for themselves. Thus, instead of playing up the contrasts between biological facts and human moral feelings, Spencer encouraged the view that ethics had been, and would continue to be, shaped by a natural balance between cooperation and competition, between aggressiveness and restraint. Too little sympathy for one's fellow creatures could prove just as detrimental as too much.

If Spencer is right, then those who cite evolution to justify aggression and conquest are telling only part of the story. Egoists such as Mister Sinister, Apocalypse, Magneto, the Brotherhood, the Phalanx, and others may hail themselves as the next stage of evolution, agents of Nature's will, in eradicating those who stand in their way. And a collection of totalitarian villains has attempted similar rationalizations in our world. Yet a stronger case can be made—even on a strictly evolutionary basis—in support of altruists like Moira MacTaggert, Colossus, Cyclops, Cable, and Charles Xavier, whose "fitness" is reflected in sacrificing themselves so that others may survive. Evolution may have a cruel side, yet those who justify cruelty with genetic necessity are perhaps only making excuses.

The Eugenic Agenda

Another aspect of Mister Sinister's agenda poses a more subtle ethical challenge. What if, instead of plotting to dominate one's fellow humans or mutants, the goal is to improve their lot by improving their genetic constitution and increasing the number of "superior" individuals? Does the prospect of controlling evolution in a *beneficial* way confer moral legitimacy on the project? Do benefits to future genetically enhanced generations justify breaking a few eggs? Sir Francis Galton (1822–1911) believed they did. Galton coined and popularized the term *eugenics* to describe his project of taking control of human evolution. Rather than abandoning humanity to the randomness and misery entailed in the natural evolutionary process, eugenics would take a rational and (relatively) gentle approach to ensuring biological progress:

> Now that this new animal, man, finds himself somehow in existence, endowed with a little power and intelligence, he ought, I submit, to awake a fuller knowledge of his relatively great position, and begin to assume a deliberate part in furthering the great work of evolution. He may infer the course it is bound to pursue, from his observation of that which it has already followed, and he might devote his modicum of power, intelligence, and kindly feeling to render its future progress less slow and painful.[6]

Galton was a pioneer in the field of biometrics, devising ways to measure and quantify all manner of natural phenomena, with a special interest in human intelligence. Galton and his colleagues believed it possible to identify families and racial strains with clearly measurable variations in genetic giftedness. Working before the discovery of genetic engineering or testing—or even a basic theory of how genes work or what they are made of—the only "technology" available to Galton and the early eugenicists was selective breeding: maximizing reproduction among "fit" specimens, while discouraging or preventing the "unfit" from passing on their "inferior" genes.

It is easy to picture Mister Sinister, who would have been a contemporary of Galton, listening with approval to Galton's lectures. Although Mister Sinister is equipped with comprehensive knowledge of molecular genetics and yet-undreamed biotechnology, his methods often have an old-fashioned eugenic flavor. The offspring of exceptional individuals will be exceptional as well. Rather than working "from scratch" to produce a mutant powerful enough to defeat Apocalypse, he identifies a gifted bloodline—the Summers family—to be manipulated over multiple generations, culminating in the offspring of Scott Summers and Jean Grey. Mister Sinister also shows a preference for found materials in creating Madelyne Pryor as Jean's clone and implanting her with Jean's memories, only to be confounded when Madelyne nevertheless fails to manifest powers like Jean's. Apparently, even in the X-Verse, greatness is more than the sum of a person's DNA. Yet Mister Sinister is not deterred by this interruption in his plans; he continues without noticing the suffering inflicted on his genetic favorites (hence the name *Sinister*).

Is eugenics intrinsically indifferent to human suffering, at least when it is viewed as necessary to progress? This is the accusation that stung eugenics the most, based on its appeal as a progressive social movement propelled by seemingly benign motivations. Eventually, the track record of eugenics carried out by fascist regimes discredited the cause completely. But from the beginning, Galton had recognized and defended the ironies of carrying out genetic or racial hygiene for the benefit of humanity:

> There exists a sentiment, for the most part quite unrea-
> sonable, against the gradual extinction of an inferior
> race . . . [I]t may be somewhat brutally argued that
> whenever two individuals struggle for a single place,
> one must yield, and that there will be no more unhap-
> piness on the whole, if the inferior yield to the superior
> than conversely, whereas the world will be permanently
> enriched by the success of the superior.[7]

If the world must have winners and losers, who can object if the "superior" win? In fairness to Galton, he intended eugenics to proceed gradually and as humanely as possible, by persua-sion and policies to guide public opinion, rather than by force. Nevertheless, Galton's defense of the rights of the superior and his casual identification of inferior and superior races (which just happened to coincide with the prejudices of his audience) is chilling to those who know where ideals of racial hygiene would lead later in the twentieth century. Eugenic aims and government power would forge a dangerous alliance, not only in totalitarian regimes, but in democratic societies as well. Only later would bioethics develop an awareness of the spe-cific hazards of making governments the custodians of genetic health.

The Real "Menace" to Humanity

In a break with the conventions of Golden Age comics, where superheroes and the authorities usually get along swimmingly, the Silver Age writers of X-Men stories developed a new and much more fertile perspective on the inevitable conflicts between mutants and a government suspicious of difference and threatened by social change.

Not long after the advent of the X-Men, the comic story-line brought in eugenic elements with the U.S. government's approval of the Sentinel project engineered by Bolivar Trask. Introduced as an "eminent anthropologist," Trask is animated by a passion for the genetic future of humanity that Galton would find familiar.[8] But unlike Galton, Trask is not rooting for the winners. Trask sees mutants as a "menace," not only on an individual or a social basis, but as an evolutionary rival that will displace Homo sapiens if allowed to survive and repro-duce. Trask believes he can and must halt this evolutionary detour. To this end, he creates and programs the Sentinels, an army of adaptive robots theoretically capable of destroying even the most powerful mutant. The mutant menace will be brought under control.

Unfortunately for Trask, his scientific genius does not extend to predicting what his own robotic creations will do. The Sentinels, too, have been evolving, and soon Master Mold adopts a more aggressive approach to protecting humanity by completely taking over society. Trask's obsession with control has come full circle, with disastrous results. Learning only when it is almost too late who the true friends and enemies of humanity are, Trask sacrifices himself in the hopes of destroy-ing the true "menace" to humanity he has unleashed.

Deeper irony emerges as the story of the Sentinels con-tinues with Dr. Trask's son, Larry. Larry, who shares both his father's technical aptitude and his obsession with mutants, reactivates the Sentinels and their mission. What Larry does not know is that he himself is a mutant, and that the medal-lion he wears is actually a device engineered by his father to suppress his powers and conceal his mutant status from the Sentinels.

This storyline illustrates two key ironies that follow almost every definition of genetic health. One is the ease with which we forget that most of the "normal" among us also carry a load of genetic abnormalities, including a handful of lethal (but recessive) mutations. The other is the fact that like any form of discrimination, eugenic agendas feel most comfortable when directed against those we do not see as *people like us*. To view people as individuals and not as test subjects is to start making exceptions to rules about genetic fitness.

As it develops and reappears in multiple versions throughout the X-Men comics, the Sentinel project also raises disturbing questions about the will and ability of a democratic government to back projects that treat its own citizens as less than human. Can the same be said for our real-life environment of biomedical science?

Behind the Glass

Through the twentieth century and beyond, Mister Sinister turns up in the background of all manner of biomedical research projects, especially the darkest. To the children of Auschwitz, he is "Nosferatu," offering candy in exchange for blood samples. To the mutants who fall into the custody of the Weapon X program, he is Dr. Robert Windsor. On the Black Womb eugenics project, scientists such as Brian Xavier and Kurt Marko (Charles Xavier's father and stepfather) know him as their senior colleague, Dr. Nathan Milbury. David Moreau, the lead geneticist supporting the subjection of mutants into Mutates on the island of Genosha, draws on Mister Sinister's technology, if not his active assistance. Indeed, the full range of Mister Sinister's involvement in biomedical history can only be guessed at.

Of all of Mister Sinister's schemes, his collaboration with other scientists on large projects sounds the most morally pessimistic note about the nature of science in the X-Verse. Whether strictly in pursuit of his own agenda or contributing his expertise to others' research, Sinister mingles easily among scientific circles, sometimes barely in disguise. Perhaps Sinister takes pains to conceal his character and behavior from his scientific colleagues. Or, maybe no one raises objections to a brilliant, handsome figure who may be ethically questionable but obviously very talented?

Mr. Sinister's semi-anonymity in the corridors of Big Science illustrates a key insight about the possible ethical hazards of research in government—or corporate—sponsored contexts, where individual investigators may feel a diminished sense of moral responsibility. Unlike the archetypal mad scientist alone in his lab (a role Sinister is also happy to play), the scientists working on Weapon X or Black Womb feel their individual efforts swallowed up by a much larger whole. None sees the big picture or feels responsible for morally evaluating the project as a whole.

Thus, even sympathetic, albeit flawed, project staff members find themselves involved in unsavory research, knowing that if they don't participate, someone else will. Behind the glass wall, each is merely a faceless investigator doing research on nameless subjects. "They," superiors or sponsors, are in charge and have already decided what the protocol is.

Something like this moral alienation among real researchers emerges as an important factor in a wide variety of unethical research projects that were known to have been conducted in the postwar United States. Probably the most infamous is the Tuskegee syphilis study, where antibiotic treatment was withheld from African American men as their disease process was "followed" over a number of years. Other incidents involved injecting highly radioactive isotopes into terminal cancer patients without their knowledge or dusting public places, including schools, with a radio-tracing compound that was used to model the spread of a biowarfare agent. And these are only the declassified examples! Behind continuing walls of secrecy, the hazards of treating science and ethics as separate worlds are probably greater.

No one is currently in a position to assess whether, or how far, the end results of all biomedical research may justify the means. Since the 1970s, significant steps have been taken to require most biomedical research on humans or animals to be ethically reviewed at the local level, with careful documentation of informed consent in the case of human subjects. Still, with very limited resources for enforcement, the system relies almost completely on the willingness of individual investigators and staff to follow protocols and self-report problems.

A Sinister Purpose?

Mister Sinister is hardly a fair representative of geneticists, even within the X-Verse. Any character retaining a shred of genuine humanity would have more potential for redemption than he. By placing himself in Apocalypse's hands, Essex chose to deliberately dehumanize himself, hoping to irrevocably excise the moral sympathies that were, if Spencer is right, a part of his evolutionary heritage no less essential than his capacity for rational thought is. Yet through a centuries-long conflict with Apocalypse, Mister Sinister ultimately functions as a preserver of the human future, saving the world on more than one occasion. And ultimately, whatever his own twisted motives may be, all of his actions combine with the efforts of the X-Men to defeat Apocalypse—almost as if by divine design.

With Apocalypse defeated, Mister Sinister presumably continues his scientific work, his current purposes and goals unknown. His successes have been dearly bought, but Sinister is not consumed by his work. He is defined by it.

NOTES

1. *Further Adventures of Cyclops and Phoenix* #4 (September 1996).

2. Herbert Spencer, *Principles of Ethics*, vol. 2 (New York: D. Appleton, 1898), p. 248.

3. Alfred Lord Tennyson, "In Memoriam A. H. H.," stanza 55.

4. *Further Adventures of Cyclops and Phoenix* #4.

5. Spencer, *Principles of Ethics*, p. 261.

6. Francis Galton, *Inquiries into Human Faculty and Its Development* (London: Dent & Dutton [Everyman], 1907), p. 198.

7. Ibid., p. 201.

8. *X-Men Vol. 1* #14 (November 1965).

LAYLA MILLER KNOWS STUFF: HOW A BUTTERFLY CAN SHOULDER THE WORLD

George A. Dunn

If you happen to bump into a saucy mutant girl larking down the street, snapping a mouthful of bubble gum and twirling her Hello Kitty umbrella, don't be surprised if she introduces herself by saying, "Hi. I'm Layla Miller. I know stuff." And don't be misled by the ragamuffin apparel and the raffish bearing. This girl is a formidable mutant, playing a pivotal role in the two biggest X-Men stories of recent years, *House of M* and *Messiah CompleX*.

"Nostradamus Reborn as Wednesday Addams"

Layla Miller "knows stuff," meaning she can anticipate the future, but her ability doesn't seem to depend on mystical premonitions, prophetic auguries, or any of the other forms of precognition that are usually encountered in the sci-fi and comic-book worlds. Rather, her power takes the form of an eminently practical, albeit uncanny, grasp of the minute details of the causal pathways that determine the shape of things to come. This insight gives her the power, the practical know-how, to intervene effectively in the causal nexus, performing seemingly trivial actions at one end of a causal series in order to produce, often by way of some improbably tangled chain of events, the outcome she desires on the other side.

Removing a couple of screws from the faucet handles in an upstairs bathroom, she foils an assassin who is electrocuted when, after a soaking-wet ceiling collapses on top of him, he's struck by a flying electric cable. Placing some food orders over the telephone, she arranges for four pizza delivery trucks to collide at an intersection, obstructing the getaway of a pair of kidnappers. Pint-sized Layla (she's only 4'10" and 90 pounds, according to the Official Marvel Wiki) does small things that, in league with the celebrated Butterfly Effect, cause big things to happen.[1]

The *Butterfly Effect* is a term coined by the pioneering mathematician and meteorologist Edward Lorenz (1917–2008) to express the idea that the flapping of a butterfly's wings can cause an ever-so-slight change in the atmosphere and thereby set off a chain reaction that can snowball into a tornado. As Layla explains, flapping her wings and whipping up storms is "kind of what I do. I have a sense of what's to come from a distance away. Of how things might turn out . . . and should turn out. And if it's not going the way it should, I . . . "

"Flap your wings?" asks another mutant.

"Right," says Layla, "I do one little thing on one end that makes things turn out the way they should at the other end."[2]

Layla's debut in *House of M* #4 was heralded by a publisher's solicitation that gushed about how "The fate of the entire world rests on the shoulders of one young girl," this "newest of new mutants" who was "about to become the most important person in the Marvel Universe."[3] Layla's shoulders have toted around a lot of weight since then, placing her in the elite company of a handful of heroines who have at one or time or another borne responsibility for the fate of the world, such as world-class ass-kickers Buffy Summers, Ellen Ripley, and Kara "Starbuck" Thrace. But Layla is unique even within this rare group for, unlike the others, her power resides not in physical strength and agility but entirely in the "stuff" she knows.

For those who may not be up-to-date on some of the more recent developments in the Marvel X-Verse, let's quickly review the extraordinary series of events that have thrust Layla to prominence. It all begins when Magneto's daughter Wanda Maximoff, also known as the Scarlet Witch, suffers a mental breakdown and uses her powers to remake reality, granting herself, the members of her family, the X-Men, and the Avengers (the superhero team of which she had been a member) their fondest wishes, while leaving (almost) no one with any memory of how the world used to be. One consequence is that Magneto now rules over a mutant-dominated world as patriarch of the House of M. Another consequence is that Wolverine, who had always anguished over the memories stolen from him by repeated mind-wipes, wakes up with total recall of every moment of his life—including every detail of how the world had been before it was altered by Wanda.

Enter Layla Miller. She seemed at the time to be little more than a deus ex machina, a somewhat contrived plot device to facilitate the discovery by the other X-Men and Avengers that their world had been created through the reality-warping powers of the Scarlet Witch. Not only does Layla retain memories of how the world once was, but she also manages, with the help of telepathic mutant Emma Frost, to resurrect the buried memories of the other heroes, who are then assembled for an assault on the House of M to put the world back as it should be. The battle concludes with the Scarlet Witch, in a fit of rage at her father's insolent ambition for mutants to rule the world, once again altering reality with devastating consequences for mutantkind. With three fateful words—"No more mutants"—the Scarlet Witch slashes the world's mutant population from millions to less than three hundred. Decimation Day, as this cataclysm will be called, looks like the beginning of the end for Homo superior.

Layla's work, in any event—along with her entire raison d'être within the Marvel Universe—appears to be done. But *House of M* hints that she may harbor other untapped powers and more than a few surprises. Telepathically examining Layla, a bemused Emma Frost remarks, "These psychic powers of yours . . . They're psychic but they're *not* psychic. Not like mine. Not like anything I've ever seen."

Layla: What does *that* mean?

Emma: It means you're a conundrum.

Layla: Is that good?

Emma: Rarely. But you never know.[4]

Conundrum is an apt description of Layla, as is the concise profile supplied by Theresa Cassidy, the mutant detective also known as Siryn: "If Nostradamus was reborn as Wednesday Addams, that'd be her."[5] Layla has annoyed and unnerved Siryn since that first night when this preternaturally well-informed waif sauntered out of the shadows that Decimation Day had cast over Mutant Town and into the headquarters of X-Factor Investigations, the mutant detective agency headed by Jamie Madrox, the Multiple Man.[6] Her association with the team begins with her merry announcement that she's there to help: "I'm joining your group. It'll be fun."[7] And it has been fun, great fun, thanks entirely to Peter David, who, as the author of the X-Factor series, has reimagined a more or less throwaway character from *House of M* as a winsome avatar of the old philosophical adage "Knowledge is power." For Layla now lays claim to a new power that will prove to be of inestimable value to her adopted teammates, an uncanny ability to—as she never tires of repeating—"know stuff."

But what kind of power is *that*?

"The Greatest Power of All"

Magneto's son Pietro Maximoff (Quicksilver) is under siege by members of X-Factor. Pietro is currently allied with X-Cell, a terrorist band of former mutants who mistakenly hold the U.S. government responsible for Decimation Day. He has just restored some of their powers using the Terrigen Crystals he stole from the Inhumans and has dispatched a strike force of these repowered mutants to defend his headquarters against the assault. Surveying the battle from a window, he's startled from behind by Layla Miller. The superpowered fracas down in the street, she explains, is really just a distraction staged to allow her to walk through the back door unnoticed. He scoffs when she denounces him as an evil person who "thinks that all that matters is power" and parries with a menacing jeer.

"And you, Layla," he replies, "for all your talk, remain—in person—a mere girl. Helpless. *Powerless*."

Arms akimbo, a defiant glint in her eye, she corrects him. "Actually, I have the greatest power of all. Knowledge."[8]

Layla may be right about this—and, let's face it, when is she ever wrong?—but we can't award her any points for originality. She's simply paraphrasing one of the greatest philosophers of the sixteenth and seventeenth centuries, Sir Francis Bacon (1561–1626), who coined the phrase that could serve as Layla's motto, "Knowledge is power."[9] (Her *motto*, mind you, not her *catchphrase*. Her catchphrase is, "I'm Layla Miller. I know stuff.") This precept may have become a bit shopworn and clichéd over the centuries, the fate of many revolutionary ideas that have degenerated over time into tired platitudes. But when Bacon first identified knowledge with power, these were fighting words, as defiant on his lips as they are on Layla's. For they announced a bold assault on what his most esteemed predecessors, including the philosophers Aristotle (384–322 BCE) and Thomas Aquinas (1225–1274), had lauded as the noblest and most beneficial employment of our cognitive faculties.

Francis Bacon is best known today as a tireless champion of the experimental method of uncovering the secrets of nature, whose writings helped to inaugurate a new era of scientific progress in the seventeenth century. He's one of those proverbial giants on whose shoulders have stood a long train of later scientific geniuses, including a few X-Men, such as geneticist Charles Xavier (Professor X) and biochemist Hank McCoy (the Beast). Bacon died a martyr to his method when, as a result of an experiment to determine whether packing a gutted chicken with snow would help to preserve the meat, he caught a chill that developed into fatal pneumonia. (Happily, the chicken was preserved, so Bacon didn't die in vain.) But his chief contribution to modern civilization wasn't the invention of frozen dinners or even the particular strategies for scientific research that he advocated, some of which are judged by contemporary philosophers of science to be flawed. No, his most important legacy was the introduction of a new paradigm of knowing that both redefined what could count as genuine knowledge and proposed a drastic reappraisal of what made knowledge worthwhile.

It's this revolutionary new paradigm of knowledge, rather than a specific method of acquiring it, that links Bacon to Layla Miller. After all, while we may not be privy to how Layla knows stuff—she tells Jamie she would be struck dead were she to disclose that information, but she's such an adroit manipulator that anything she says is suspect—it's a safe bet that it's not through any of the methods pioneered by Bacon.[10] Nonetheless, she's thoroughly Baconian in her assessment of the value of knowledge and the uses to which she puts it, matters that may be every bit as fundamental to modern science as the experimental method.

Bacon was more than simply a dry theorist of the methods of modern science. Above all, he was a philosopher of hope, urging his contemporaries to stake their future on the prospect that scientific investigation, conducted in the right way, could uncover the hidden forces at work in nature and put them to work for us. His *New Atlantis*, one of the first works of science fiction and a powerful advertisement for his groundbreaking aspirations, imagined a society wholly dedicated to the pursuit of science and as a result able to produce such technological wonders as flying machines, submarines, robots, and, needless to say, some mighty formidable weapons. Research is conducted at the House of Solomon, a state-sponsored institute whose stated goal is "the knowledge of Causes, and secret motions of things; and the enlarging of the bounds of Human Empire, to the effecting of all things possible."[11] In Bacon's vision of science, knowledge of nature is inseparable from power over nature.

Baconian science is able to put nature *to work* because it studies nature *at work*, which is why Bacon put such a premium on careful and controlled experiments. If science is to yield practical results, its methods must themselves be practical, that is, experimental, designed to uncover the hidden mechanisms through which natural phenomena are generated. Armed with knowledge of how nature works its wonders, we should be able to produce similar wonders of our own, just as skilled mechanics apply their understanding of dynamics and material properties to construct devices that lift enormous weights, hurl huge projectiles, and perform other feats that employ the powers of nature in ways that seem to defy its ordinary course. In fact, for Bacon the mechanical arts served as the prototype of the form of knowledge that he believed experimental science would be able to extend without limit. But they also offer an illuminating analogue to the kind of power that Layla is able to exercise by knowing stuff, as we see in the following scenario.

X-Factor is looking for X-Cell, the band of ex-mutants who, as they later learn, have allied with Pietro Maximoff. Layla initially refuses to help, insisting, "These guys will self-destruct all on their own without our help. Trust me. I'm Layla Miller. I know stuff." But when they refuse to trust her assurance that matters will take care of themselves, she hands out assignments. Jamie and Rictor are dispatched to an address that, to their considerable surprise and chagrin, turns out to be a deli where a sandwich for Layla is awaiting pickup. She stations Theresa and Monet St. Croix (M) on a street corner where they're simply to stand and wait, their exasperation mounting as they ward off lewd propositions from passing motorists who mistake them for streetwalkers. (Monet squints menacingly and bends a lamppost when some jerk asks, "How much for both of you together?") Rahne Sinclair (Wolfsbane) and Guido Carosella (Strong Guy) are even more unlucky. Assigned the supremely distasteful chore of lifting the manhole cover at a certain intersection and crawling into the sewer, they abandon their assignment, along with the open manhole, when they find the stench of the sewer intolerable. It all seems like a pointless snark hunt, until Jamie and Rictor are attacked on their way back to the office by a member of X-Cell, the depowered but still very hungry Blob, who demands their sandwich. In the ensuing fight, Blob is joined by Fatale, also depowered, and the two of them manage to make their getaway in a car that whizzes by Theresa and Monet, still stationed at their corner a few blocks away. They give pursuit but might have lost their quarry had the car not lost a tire and flipped over as a result of hitting the manhole left open by Rahne and Guido. And these are just the first of many gears set in motion by Layla's peculiar assignments.[12]

These gears turn and mesh in way that resembles a Rube Goldberg machine. For the benefit of the uninitiated, a Rube Goldberg machine is an elaborate apparatus built to accomplish some simple task in a needlessly—and often comically—complicated manner. Think of those convoluted contraptions that drop a tea bag in your cup or put toothpaste on your brush through some ridiculously complex process involving inclined planes, cranes, catapults, and just about anything else that might help accomplish the task in the most roundabout way possible. (As it happens, Layla's assignations in the scene we're considering are especially Goldbergian in their complete abandonment of the principle of parsimony, since, as she had forecasted, matters were already on track to take care of themselves.) The delight we experience in watching Layla at work is akin to the joy and surprise we feel when we witness the improbable feats of those wacky products of bold human ingenuity. But this helps us to notice something significant about Layla. It's as though she knows the world in a way that allows her operate it like a vast machine, whose levers, pulleys, gears, and cranks are ordinary objects and events. And this is precisely how Bacon and his followers have invited us to conceive the world and our role in it.

"Small in Bulk but Surpassing Everything in Power"

To fully appreciate the magnitude of Bacon's revolution, we need to take a look at the paradigm of knowledge that he helped to overthrow. In the sixteenth century into which Bacon was born, the highest ideal of knowledge was personified by the ancient Greek philosopher Aristotle, whose writings had been reintroduced into Europe only a few centuries earlier but had in that short span of time come to dominate the university curriculum. Students of anatomy studied Aristotle's *De animalibus* (On the Parts of Animals) and astronomers pored over his *De caelo* (On the Heavens). In *The Inferno*, the poet Dante Alighieri (1265–1321) christened him "the master of those who know" and imagined lesser lights such as Plato (428/427–348/347 BCE) and Socrates (469–399 BCE) as members of the entourage that waited on him in the underworld.[13] Thomas

Aquinas, his greatest medieval disciple, referred to him simply as "*The* Philosopher," the definite article signifying his preeminence, compared to his (presumably) second-rate forerunners and followers. But as erudite as Aristotle may have been—or maybe just *because* he was so erudite—he didn't see very much value in knowing the sort of "stuff" that is of interest to Layla Miller and Francis Bacon. And to Bacon, that signified a serious defect in Aristotle's conception of knowledge.

Like most ancient philosophers, Aristotle was preoccupied with the question of what set of activities constituted the best possible life—or, as we commonly say nowadays, the best *lifestyle*—for a human being. The finest activities, he believed, were not only intrinsically pleasurable but also put into play our highest and most distinctively human capacities, specifically our aptitude for intellectual contemplation and rational deliberation. While honoring the lifestyle of the virtuous statesmen as praiseworthy because it brought practical reason to bear on how best to organize the life of a political community, Aristotle reserved his highest accolades for the life devoted to the pursuit of knowledge solely *for its own sake*, not for the uses to which it could be put. Knowledge per se, apart from its practical applications, is inherently rewarding. More significantly, the activity of knowing lifts up and ennobles the soul, offering us a fleeting taste of the blessedness enjoyed without interruption only by the gods. This applies, however, only on condition that the light of the intellect has been directed toward the right sort of beings.

For Aristotle, knowledge is genuinely edifying only when it concerns the most perfect objects, the unchanging *essences* of things that we attempt to capture in definitions. Consider Julio Esteban Richter, better known as Rictor, one of Layla's X-Factor teammates. Rictor is a human being, a member of the class Homo sapiens, at least since he was depowered on Decimation Day. Aristotle would say the essential thing about Rictor is that he is human, for that defines the *kind* of being he is. Other particulars about his life—such as the fact, somehow known to Layla Miller, that if he goes to a certain gas station one evening, he will have the opportunity to save a young woman, an ex-mutant like himself, from her homicidal boyfriend—are considered "accidents" of negligible importance to our knowledge of Rictor, since they can vary without in any way disturbing his essence.[14] And even if Rictor hadn't survived that nasty altercation, his essence would remain unaffected. After all, his essential human nature is hardly unique to him but is shared with Nick Fury, Tony Stark, Val Cooper, and about seven billion others at last count. Each of them is what Aristotle calls a "substance," a particular individual bearing some essential characteristic that defines it as a member of a class, in this case, the human race. Accidents and substances come and go, but essences endure, making them both the highest and the most edifying objects of knowledge.

The human intellect, through which we are able to understand and contemplate these unchanging essences, is what lifts us above the other animals, making it our most distinctively human attribute. It's also the most powerful part of us, "for even if it is small in bulk, much more does it in power and worth surpass everything."[15] This may sound like a description of Layla Miller, but the power Aristotle imagined the intellect to possess was very different from what she wields. He believed it made us semi-divine, since the knowledge of eternal things, which we mortals can enjoy in only a fleeting and imperfect fashion, most properly belongs to God or the gods. "[T]he activity of God, which surpasses all others in blessedness, must be contemplative," he wrote, adding that "of human activities, therefore, that which is most akin to this must be most of the nature of happiness."[16] Aristotle's God is reminiscent of the Watchers, cosmic entities who inhabit the Marvel Universe and whose sole occupation is compiling knowledge on every facet of that Universe, all the while maintaining a firm commitment never to interfere in its affairs.[17] This lofty disdain for the travails of lesser beings makes them kin to Aristotle's God, although the Watchers monitor, among other things, the course of cosmic and human history, something the Aristotelian divinity would certainly dismiss as merely a senseless tumult of substances and their accidents that remains blessedly off their radar.

This doesn't mean that Aristotle had no interest in investigating things that undergo change. He was in fact one of the founders—some would say *the* founder—of the science of biology, a study that takes as its subject matter things that start out small, get bigger, grow old, and then die. But if we experience delight in studying these mutable natural beings, it's because we discern in them traces of something eternal when we contemplate the beauty and artistry of design that appears to be present in the orderly arrangement of their parts and their purposive movements and activities. In the arresting language of Aristotle's great teacher Plato, in the processes of particular beings undergoing change we may glimpse the "moving likeness of eternity."[18]

But the contemplative study of nature, undertaken for its own sake, was something Aristotle sharply distinguished from the practical know-how that puts us in a position to manipulate and control the world. As Thomas Aquinas wrote, clarifying Aristotle's distinction:

> Of the sciences some are practical, some are speculative; the difference being that the former are for the sake of some work to be done, while the latter are for their own sake. The speculative sciences are therefore honorable as well as good, but the practical ones are only valuable.[19]

"Only valuable" means, in this context, second-rate. Consequently, philosophers who followed in the footsteps of Aristotle often sneered at the rough-and-ready know-how of the mechanical arts for being preoccupied with impermanent things and the process of change. The mechanical arts are not windows through which we spy faint glimmers of eternity but are mere instruments to be commandeered and pressed into service for improving the material conditions of human life.

Bacon's epochal innovation was to reverse that appraisal, as he argued that any knowledge worth having must be practical. Real knowledge should resemble the expertise of our skilled mechanics, prying open the hidden causal mechanisms of nature and putting them to work for us. Not lofty knowledge of essences, but lowly knowledge of "stuff"—that's knowledge as power, Layla's power.

"I've Got Bigger Things on My Mind Than God"

Layla Miller's heart weighs heavy as she sits on the stoop outside the offices of X-Factor. Inside, her teammate Theresa Cassidy lies in bed, the battered and bruised victim of an ambush that occurred the night before in a nearby alley and that Rictor suspects (rightly, it turns out) Layla could have prevented. His accusations still ringing in her ears ("Did you know Terry was going to be jumped, Layla? And if so, why didn't you do whatever you do to stop it?"), she's greeted by another colleague, the devout Rahne, arriving home from Sunday morning church service. Rahne takes the opportunity to ask Layla about her religion.

Layla: I'm *between* religions right now.

Rahne: What does that mean?

Layla: It means my parents died, I was orphaned, and I've got bigger things on my mind than God right now.[20]

Words like that would have scandalized Aristotle and Aquinas, for whom nothing could be greater or more worthy of contemplation than God and the eternal essences contained in the divine intellect. Bacon, however, believed that philosophy and science would never make any headway as long as they remained bogged down in fruitless religious speculation, which, in any case, only distracts us from the pressing business of improving the conditions of human existence right here and now. We should pursue knowledge of mundane "stuff" instead, not as an end in itself but only in order to contribute to human welfare. Bacon admonishes us:

> to reflect on the true ends of knowledge; not to seek it for amusement or for dispute, or to look down on others, or for profit or for fame or for power or any such inferior ends, but for the uses and benefits of life, and to improve and conduct it in charity.[21]

To use knowledge charitably means to place it in the service of others. When Layla says she has bigger things than God on her mind, it's likely that her thoughts are occupied with how best to make use of the stuff she knows in ways that benefit others, rather than causing harm. For, as she will soon be reminding Quicksilver, "Helping is good. Harming is evil. Sometimes it's hard to tell them apart."[22]

Does *X-Factor* #8 supply a clue to Layla's moral perspective? In this book, she spends all of her scenes clutching Ayn Rand's (1905–1982) philosophical novel *Atlas Shrugged* and even quotes passages from it to Quicksilver ("Evil is impotent and has no power other than what we let it extort from us").[23] But it seems unlikely that Layla would be a full-fledged adherent of Rand's moral philosophy. For Rand is famous—or notorious, depending on who you ask—for praising *selfishness*, the single-minded pursuit of one's own personal happiness, as the highest value and for denouncing *self-sacrifice* as inherently irrational and immoral. "Accept the fact that the achievement of your happiness is the only *moral* purpose of your life," proclaims John Galt, the grandiloquent hero of her novel, and he means just that—*your* happiness, not the happiness of others, ought to be your sole priority.[24]

The figure of Atlas, a Titan who in Greek mythology bore the world on his shoulders, becomes in Rand's work emblematic of the highest achievers who were, in her opinion, unjustly compelled by society to support their less productive brethren.[25] Layla also identifies herself with Atlas, telling one of Jamie's duplicates, who's just teased her for looking "so *serious*, like you have the weight of the world on your shoulders," that she really *does*.[26] But her attitude toward this lonely burden is almost diametrically opposed to that of Rand's hero, John Galt, who resents having to shoulder any responsibility for the fate of others. He's a far cry from Layla, who embraces her responsibilities as defining who and what she is as a unique individual.

This attitude is conspicuous in her therapy session with Doc Samson, the superhero psychiatrist whom Jamie insists everyone in X-Factor must see in order to work through their recent traumas. When asked which chess piece best represents her, she lifts up a pawn and says, "This one." When asked why she would choose the most *powerless* piece, she explains, "Because I'm part of a different game than everybody else. And only I can see the players. I know the endgame. And I know . . . I'm expendable."[27] She announces this with her usual sunny nonchalance, but her words strike a somber note. They leave us wondering in what way an awareness of her own expendability might be a corollary of the other stuff she knows. Presumably, the extraordinarily wide purview of her knowledge frees her from the egocentric illusion that tempts most of us to imagine that the Powers That Be have arranged everything for our benefit or, as it all too often seems, just to spite us. But at the same time that her knowledge deflates the pretension of her ego, it grows her sense of responsibility to Atlaslike proportions.

Layla calls herself a pawn not because she's the helpless victim of some higher power that shoves her around like a stubby piece of wood. If we take the chess board as a metaphor for the causal matrix that Baconian science helps us understand and manipulate, Layla is the chess master extraordinaire, with an unparalleled knowledge of the "players" and the "end-game" that puts her in complete control of the board. At the same time, however, she recognizes herself as just another piece, one more intersection of causal forces, and not herself the point of the game. As she explains on another occasion, "I'm a chess piece. So's everybody *else*, really. Except I see the hands of the players, and *because* of that I don't have the right to make my own moves." To this description of her plight, she adds, in a rare moment of grumbling, "You might say I've been rooked."[28] It's not that she hasn't the *power* to use her knowledge to maximize her own self-interest at the expense of others—far from it!—but she realizes she has no *right* to do so, given the stakes of the game. She's the noble soul philosopher Friedrich Nietzsche (1844–1900) celebrated when he wrote, "I love him whose soul is overfull, so that he forgets himself, and all things are in him: thus all things become his going-under."[29] Because of her knowledge, *all things are*—in a manner of speaking—*in* Layla. For their sake, she's willing to sacrifice herself or, as Nietzsche puts it, *go under*.

Layla demonstrates her willingness to go under in *Messiah CompleX*, the other big Marvel Comics event in which she plays a pivotal role, just as she had in *House of M*.[30] For the greater good of mutantkind, she makes an unscheduled and possibly one-way leap into the time machine designed by the mutant inventor Forge, disembarking eighty years later in a dystopian future where mutants are detained in concentration camps. Because of what she learns there and relays back to the present, the X-Men are able to protect the first and only child born with the mutant gene since Decimation Day threatened to turn Homo superior into an evolutionary cul de sac. But the price she pays for this good deed is horrific: trapped in a nightmarish future, she's interned in a Mutant Containment Center, her head shaved and her face marked with a grotesque tattoo declaring her dehumanized status. As she tells Scott Summers (Cyclops) in a heartbreaking speech:

> I knew what they were going to do to me before I stepped foot in Forge's time machine, Cyclops! I'd wake up screaming, shaking in my bed, knowing what was to come! But I did it anyway, because I had to! *I had to!*[31]

It's hard to imagine the purely contemplative knowledge of Aristotle's philosopher-gods and Marvel's Watchers ever occasioning such anguish, since these rarefied knowers are neither pawns nor players in the game they observe from their "blessedly" elevated heights. But enviable as their existence may be, isn't it nobler to be lowly Layla Miller, willing to "go under" because she has "bigger things on [her] mind than God," such as the weal and woe of countless mortal beings like herself, whose fates depend on her choices?

As this volume goes to press, our diminutive heroine remains trapped in that horrible future where mutants are shaved and inked and herded into pens, but also where, according to a recent Marvel Comics press release, "the liberation of mutants rests on the shoulders of"—care to guess?—"Layla Miller!"[32] Ah, those shoulders again! One little butterfly flapping her wings, one saucy mutant girl shouldering the world.

NOTES

1. See www.marvel.com/universe/Miller,_Layla.

2. *X-Factor* #6 (April 2006). Collected in the graphic novel *X-Factor Vol. 1: The Longest Night*, written by Peter David and illustrated by Ryan Sook and David Calero (New York: Marvel Comics, 2006). Good explanations of the Butterfly Effect can be found in James Gleick, *Chaos: The Making of a New Science* (New York: Penguin, 1988), pp. 9–31; and, at a more technical level, in Stephen H. Kellert, *In the Wake of Chaos: Unpredictable Order in Dynamical Systems* (Chicago: University of Chicago Press, 1993), pp. 10ff. According to Layla, Jeff Goldblum also explained it really well in *Jurassic Park*.

3. *House of M* #4 (July 2005). The eight-part *House of M* series has been collected in graphic novel format as *House of M*, written by Brian Michael Bendis and illustrated by Olivier Coipel (New York: Marvel Comics, 2006). The original solicitation can be read at www .comixfan.com/xfan/forums/shoethread.php?t=33259, accessed November 10, 2008. Brian Bendis and Tom Brevroot, *House of M* writer and editor respectively, discuss Layla in general and this solicitation in particular in an interview that is available at http:// forum.newsarama.com/showthread.php?s=&threadid=32619, accessed November 10, 2008.

4. *House of M* #5 (August 2005).

5. *X-Factor* #7 (May 2006), collected in *X-Factor Vol. 2: Life & Death Matters*.

6. Fans of the movie franchise will remember Jamie Madrox, the Multiple Man, from *X-Men: The Last Stand*. In the movie he's a bank robber recruited into Magneto's Brotherhood of Mutants, but the Jamie Madrox who inhabits the standard Marvel Universe is one of the good guys (or at least tries real hard to be).

7. *X-Factor* #1 (November 2005). Collected in the graphic novel *X-Factor Vol. 1: The Longest Night*, written by Peter David and illustrated by Ryan Sook and David Calero (New York: Marvel Comics, 2006).

8. *X-Factor* #20 (June 2007). Collected in the graphic novel *X-Factor Vol. 4: Heart of Ice*, written by Peter David and illustrated by Pablo Raimondi and Khoi Pham (New York: Marvel Comics, 2008).

9. The source most often given for this line is Bacon's *Meditationes sacræ: De hæresibus* (Religious Meditations: On Heresies), where he declares *ipsa scientia potestas est* (knowledge itself is power). See *Meditations Sacrae and Human Philosophy* (Whitefish, MT: Kessinger Publishing, 2005), p. 71. But this passage is almost always quoted out of context, since Bacon's not speaking about human knowledge and power but is making a theological argument against those who claim that while God's power is unlimited, his knowledge isn't. To the contrary, Bacon reminds his readers, God's knowledge is one of his powers. *The New Organon*, Bacon's major work on the methods of science, is a much better source for his identification of knowledge as a form of power. "Human knowledge and human power come to the same thing," he avers, "for ignorance of effect frustrates effort" (New York: Cambridge University Press, 2000), p. 33.

10. *X-Factor* #6.

11. *"New Atlantis" and "The Great Instauration,"* edited by James Weinstein (Arlington Heights, IL: Harlan Davidson, 1989), p. 70.

12. All of this occurs in *X-Factor* #18 (April 2008), collected in *X-Factor Vol. 4: Heart of Ice*.

13. *The Inferno*, Canto IV, line 130, in *The Divine Comedy*, translated by John Ciardi (New York: NAL, 2003), p. 43.

14. See *X-Factor* #2, collected in *X-Factor Vol. 1: The Longest Night*.

15. *Complete Works of Aristotle*, Vol. 2, edited by Jonathan Barnes (Princeton, NJ: Princeton University Press, 1984), p. 1861 (1178a1).

16. *Complete Works of Aristotle*, Vol. 2, p. 1863 (1178b20).

17. The Watchers were first introduced in *Fantastic Four #13* (April 1963).

18. *Plato's Timaeus*, translated by Peter Kalkavage (Newburyport, Mass.: Focus/R. Pullins, 2001), p. 67 (37d).

19. *Aristotle's de Anima: In the Version of William of Moerbeke and the Commentary of St. Thomas Aquinas*, translated by Kenelm Foster and Silvester Humphries (Eugene, OR: Wipf & Stock, 2007), p. 45.

20. *X-Factor #6*.

21. *The New Organon*, translated by Michael Silverthorne (New York: Cambridge University Press), p. 13.

22. *X-Factor* #8, collected in *X-Factor Vol. 2: Life & Death Matters*.

23. Ayn Rand, *Atlas Shrugged*, 35th Anniversary Edition (New York: Signet, 1992), p. 942.

24. Ibid., p. 974.

25. Ibid., p. 424.

26. *X-Factor* #8.

27. *X-Factor* #13 (November 2006). Collected in the graphic novel *X-Factor Vol. 3: Many Lives of Madrox*, written by Peter David and illustrated by Pablo Raimondi (New York: Marvel Comics, 2007).

28. *X-Factor: Layla Miller* #1 (August 2008).

29. *Thus Spoke Zarathustra: A Book for Everyone and Nobody*, translated by Graham Parkes (New York: Oxford University Press, 2005).

30. The comics in this cross-over series are all collected in *X-Men: Messiah Complex*, written by Mike Carey, Ed Brubaker, Christopher Yost, and Peter David and illustrated by Marc Silvestri, Billy Tan, Chris Bachalo, Humbert Ramos, and Scot Eaton (New York: Marvel Comics, 2008).

31. *X-Factor: Layla Miller* #1.

32. The press release, issued on July 15, 2008, can be read at www.marvel.com/news/comicstories.4227.X-Factor apos s_Layla_Miller_is_Back?utm_source=rss_new_news_feed, accessed November 10, 2008. A clue to this "endgame" was perhaps hinted at by the numbers emblazoned on Layla's tank top the day she leaped into the future: 46664, Nelson Mandela's prisoner number during his twenty-seven-year incarceration by the South African apartheid regime. See *X-Factor* #25 (November 2007), collected in *X-Men: Messiah CompleX*. Interestingly enough, Layla also wears a tank top adorned with Mandela's prisoner number in *House of M* #4–6 (July and August 2005).

X-WOMEN AND
X-ISTENCE

Rebecca Housel

To the ocean of being, the spirit of life leads the
stream of actions.

—from the Isa Upanishad[1]

Why X-Women? Because X-Men comics were one of the first
Marvel comics to consistently sustain female superheroes as
leads, and a diverse population of female superheroes, too!
Think of it as an homage to the great Stan Lee, who first
conceived of "The Mutants" in the early 1960s, bravely going
where only one other man had gone before, under a different
comic publisher with Wonder Woman. Lee and Kirby co-created
an unprecedented world of gender equality, beginning in 1963
in the midst of the civil rights movement and women's liberation. As a little girl in the 1970s, I had female superheroes to
read about and relate to because of Stan Lee's X-Men, not just
glamazons in thigh-high boots and breastplates. X-Women
are "real" heroes from diverse backgrounds with intriguing
storylines and equally intriguing interior lives. There are so

many X-Women to choose from in the Marvel X-Verse that it would be impossible to cover them all in this short chapter. So my modest goal here is to give a brief existential history of some of the main X-Women from the major comic storylines over the last four and a half decades.

Genesis-X

In the beginning, Stan Lee and Jack Kirby created Marvel Girl, Professor Xavier's first female student at his School for Gifted Youngsters in *X-Men* #1 (September 1963). Jean Grey was one of the original seven mutants introduced in *X-Men* #1 as a young girl with tremendous mental abilities. From her debut, Jean has had to fight for her life. Whether being taken over by a sentient cosmic entity or duped by the mutant Mastermind or killed by Xorn (who was posing as Magneto) or cheated on by her one true love, Scott Summers (aka Cyclops, with Emma Frost), Jean's been through hell and back. Jean Grey has had more resurrections than any other X-Men character, which means she's also died more than any other mutant in the series. Who better to have an existential crisis?

Jean-Paul Sartre (1905–1975), the twentieth century's best-known existentialist, summed up the basic tenet of existentialism in the phrase "existence precedes essence."[2] This means that your *essence*, the meaning and purpose of your life, is undefined until you freely choose what your life will be, as opposed to the definition of your life being imposed by forces beyond your control, such as illness or genetics. According to Sartre, this is what makes human existence different from a manufactured object that exists only because of an idea its maker had formed about the purpose of its existence. The *essence* of this object precedes its *existence* because its maker first settled on its purpose and only *then* brought it into being. We're different, declared Sartre, because we exist *first* and then assign meaning to our lives. Recognizing this fact can induce feelings of anguish or existential angst, for our freedom to choose means that we can't escape responsibility for what we finally become. Sartre is convinced that many of us would gladly hand this responsibility over to others (our families, our peers, religious authorities), conforming to outside expectations. But this is "bad faith" (more on this later), a self-deluded and ultimately futile attempt to flee our existential freedom.

Let's consider Jean Grey in terms of her existence and her essence. As a fictional character in the Marvel X-Verse, conceived in someone else's imagination and beginning her life as an etching on paper, her essence isn't hers to choose. She *can't* be responsible for the meaning of her existence because she is, after all, just a comic book character, in the same boat as the object that has its meaning imposed by a creator. On the other hand, Jean Grey is brought to life on the silver screen by actress Famke Janssen, whose performance makes us believe that Jean is real. And *that* Jean, the one sustained in existence by our suspension of disbelief, *is* responsible for giving meaning to her life. If that's not enough of a paradox for you, stay tuned.

From the day of her inception, Jean Grey has been fighting and sacrificing, fighting and sacrificing, and doing so ad infinitum in countless futures, dimensions, and timelines. In a future timeline, she and Scott have a daughter, Rachel; in another timeline, Jean's genetic clone, Madelyne Pryor, marries Scott and has a son, who is still Jean's son genetically, Nate Summers. Jean Grey merges with the Phoenix Force while in a continuation of that reality and later is duped into believing she lived a life in the eighteenth century, leading her to adopt the persona of the Black Queen, which triggers Jean's evolution as the Dark Phoenix. Jean must also face her genetic clone and kill her in battle—essentially, kill herself.[3] Jean dies again in a conflict with the first Xorn but rises once more as the "the White Phoenix of the Crown."[4] Her existence is seemingly infinite because her mutant powers allowed her to call to, and merge with, the sentient cosmic force of life and death. In that single act and in that singular timeline, Jean Grey effectively influenced every other X-Men storyline to come. And there we have it, paradox lovers. We—the writers, the artists, and the fans whose imaginations conspire together to bring Jean to life—are the ones who assign meaning to her fictional existence. Yet that fictional existence belongs to someone who perennially re-creates herself out of the ashes of her past, someone who might be thought to embody the existentialist ideal to an unparalleled degree, since through her choices she repeatedly redefines the meaning of her existence and reshapes the X-Verse she inhabits.

Let's keep it all in the family and move on to Rachel Summers or Phoenix II or Marvel Girl II or Mother Askani. Talk about existential angst!

Evolutions

Rachel Summers, the daughter of Scott and Jean from the *Days of Future Past* alternate timeline, becomes Phoenix II, Marvel Girl II, and Mother Askani all in one fiery package. Rachel has multiple identities and crosses multiple storylines and timelines, first appearing in *The Uncanny X-Men* #141 (January 1981). She transcends Jean Grey's paradox, in that she was the creation of a horrible future, which is reversed through Rachel's actions as Mother Askani, sending Kate Pryde into thirteen-year-old Kitty to stop an assassination that leads to the *Days of Future Past* storyline, where Rachel Summers originates. Kate then returns to the alternate future and sends Rachel to the mainstream X-Men timeline, where Rachel bonds with the Phoenix Force and adopts the code name "Phoenix." Both Kate and Rachel are founding members of Excalibur, the British version of X-Men.

In another storyline, featured in *New Mutants Vol. 1* #18 and *Excalibur Vol. 1* #52, Rachel is a mutant "hound" as a captive of Ahab aka Dr. Roderick Campbell, who made his first appearance in 1990 in *Fantastic Four Annual* #23. During her hound-days with Ahab, Rachel was forcibly given facial tattoos to signify her status. Rachel is able to hide the tattoos with her powers, but the images of the tattoos show up when Rachel is in battle; she is both physically and psychologically marked by her past, present, and future. How does someone like Rachel find meaning in such an existence?

José Ortega y Gasset (1883–1955) was an existentialist writer-philosopher, who used literature to convey philosophical ideas. His *Historia como sistema* (History as a System, 1941) speaks to Rachel Summers's existentialist predicament: "The stone is given its existence; it need not fight for being what it is—it is a stone in the field. Man has to be himself in spite of unfavorable circumstances; that means he has to make his own existence at every single moment."[5] The stone in this quote stands for all of those natural beings that never need to trouble themselves over the nature of their existence because they simply are what they are, without any prospect of becoming something else through their own efforts. Compare that "stone in the field" to a human being. We can't adequately describe a human being's way of existing without taking into account what Ortega calls her "project," by which he means her aspirations or what she's striving to become. Unlike the stone, the human being helps to shape her own existence every time she exerts herself to become who she will be.

With Rachel Summers, the audience sees again and again, as we follow her through alternate futures and multiple story-lines, despite her "unfavorable circumstances" (among which is the destruction of her original timeline and therefore potentially herself), that Rachel makes her own existence "at every single moment." Whether rebelling against Ahab, sending Kate to the mainstream timeline to save the future, bringing Nate to the future to save her people, or claiming her connection to the Phoenix Force and her mother, Jean Grey, and becoming the second-generation Phoenix and Marvel Girl, Rachel seizes what Ortega called the "abstract possibility of existing" that can be made a concrete reality only through our own efforts, earning her existence, her meaning, at every turn.[6] No matter how or where or when the Marvel writers and illustrators place or portray her, Rachel Summers rises like the Phoenix she is.

Origins

Wanda Maximoff (aka the Scarlet Witch) first appeared in *X-Men* #4 in March 1964. Wanda is Magneto's long-lost daughter from his estranged wife, Magda, and the twin sister of Pietro Maximoff (aka Quicksilver). The siblings were adopted and raised by gypsies and never knew their father. Almost killed by fellow villagers when their powers began to manifest, Wanda and Pietro were saved by Magneto and reluctantly joined Magneto's Brotherhood of Evil Mutants out of gratitude to their rescuer. Not until years later did the twins learn that Magneto was their father. Let's note, however, that the Scarlet Witch, although a daughter of Magneto, has never herself had the same ambitions. She's a hero in her own right, recruited into the Avengers along with her brother after their short stint in the Brotherhood. In time, Wanda found momentary happiness with the Vision, another member of the Avengers, and the two were married.[7] Wanda gave birth to two children, believing them to be products of her loving marriage to the Vision. The revelation that they were not her children at all, only shards of the soul of the demon Mephisto (who then reabsorbed them), signaled the beginning of Wanda's descent into insanity.

Her mutant powers originally consisted only of the ability to cast "hex-spheres" that changed probabilities, but the Scarlet Witch augmented her powers over the years until she became capable of altering reality as a whole, which made her quite possibly the most powerful mutant of all time. Existentialism urges us to assume responsibility as the authors of our own existence, but Wanda's powers allow her to take this to an extreme no existentialist philosopher had ever envisioned. At their highest point, Wanda's powers enable her not only to create herself in the face of "unfavorable conditions" but to alter those very conditions by decree. Tragically, the boundless scope of her power ultimately causes her downfall. Coupled with the mental strain of suppressing her memories of the two children she lost, her powers lead to mental instability, breaking open what we might call a "philosophical fracture." As Jean Baudrillard (1929–2007) observed, "[T]here is, as it were, a line beyond which, for every expanding system—every system which, by dint of exponential growth, passes beyond its own end—a catastrophe looms." This line is the point of fracture, at which "the system cracks up from excess."[8]

Wanda's "crack-up" results in her attacking the Avengers and killing many of her former friends and colleagues, a conflict that is recounted in the *Avengers Disassembled* storyline. Not long afterward, she uses her powers to restructure reality, restoring her lost children and creating the alternative reality of *House of M*, in which mutants dominate the world. But when, with the help of Layla Miller, the Avengers and the X-Men discover what Wanda has done and launch an attack on her residence, she alters reality one last time and depowers most of the world's mutant population, herself included.[9] The lesson of Wanda's downfall is one we might have learned from Baudrillard: there are limits to how far we can remake the world into a "virtual landscape" that simply reflects back the meaning we put there—and the price paid for ignoring those limits.

But don't the existentialists tell us that we're the ones who must give meaning to our lives? It may seem that Wanda is just being faithful to the existentialist creed when she refuses to acknowledge her limits and shapes her own existence, but in fact she isn't. According to Ortega, we aren't free to fashion ourselves any old way we choose, for there is one constraint to which everyone is bound and no one may ignore, "one fixed, pre-established, and given line by which he may chart his course, only one limit: the past. The experiments already made with life narrow man's future."[10] Human existence is defined only in part by the "project" that focuses our aspirations for the future. In addition, said Ortega, "Man is what has happened to him, what he has done."[11] From an existentialist perspective, when Wanda wipes out her real past and replaces it with a pipe dream, even going so far as to create fraudulent memories for herself, she's guilty of "bad faith" or self-deception. Her denial of her past is tantamount to rejecting the fundamental aspects of who she is.

Astonishing '70s

The X-Women of the 1970s, such as Storm and Mystique, reflected the social change of the era. Unlike Jean Grey, who was brought in as the fifth of five students (the other four male), at Xavier's School for Gifted Youngsters, the X-Women who were developed in the 1970s were independent thinkers, strong-willed, and tough as nails. Let's begin with Storm (aka Ororo Munroe), who made her first appearance in *Giant-Size X-Men* #1 in 1975.

Storm is a born leader, smart and sensitive, with a dedication to duty that produces unparalleled loyalty. In true existential fashion, Storm embraces freedom and responsibility. Despite being orphaned at a young age, trapped with her dead mother under rubble, abandoned and alone on the streets of Cairo, Storm manages to always make the right choices. The reason: She experiences no angst, no temptation to flee from responsibility. Life is beyond absurd in the existential sense for this X-Woman who faced tragedy and death at an early age and, later, suffered forced vampiricism on an alternate Earth. It would be easy for someone like Storm to be angry all the time, to hate, to do evil. But even as the vampire-mutant Bloodstorm, she does not feed on anyone but Forge, and only with Forge's consent. Despite all the many difficulties that have befallen her, Storm always makes free and responsible choices.

But is an angstless existence really possible? Many existentialist philosophers have doubted that it is, simply because the responsibility our freedom confers on us is so great and often feels so cumbersome. "There are many, indeed, who show no such anxiety," admitted Sartre. "But we affirm that they are merely disguising their anxiety or are in flight from it."[12] This fact may explain why it is that however much we may admire Storm, we find it so much easier to relate to the more deeply flawed, but by the same token much more human, Mystique.

Mystique (aka Raven Darkholme, aka Mallory Brickman, aka Ronnie Lake) is a shapeshifter who made her first appearance in *Ms. Marvel* #16 in April 1978. Like the other ladies of the seventies, Mystique is not the "perfect" image of womanhood and goodness and is certainly no victim. Mystique is cunning, as her scaly exterior implies, and can always slither out of bad situations, living to fight another day. But Mystique has gotten a bad rep as being "evil."[13] In fact, Mystique is probably the most human of all the X-Women in her behaviors, in her flaws and foibles, in her loves, in her losses, and in her life. As confident and straightforward as Storm is, Mystique, in her humanity, is the opposite.

Mystique makes what existentialists call "bad faith" decisions *all* the time, just like the rest of us. What Sartre called "bad faith" is really a matter of self-deception, lying to yourself. Because lying to yourself implies that you really know the truth, Sartre called this a "cynical consciousness," a label that perfectly describes Mystique—as well as most of the human population on planet Earth. She is in a perpetual existential conundrum, much like her sixties predecessors Scarlet Witch and Polaris, with reality pulling her one way and self-deception pulling her another.[14] No matter what befalls Mystique, she always manages to get up, dust herself off, and walk tall. Perhaps one of the greatest achievements of Stan Lee's X-Men comic series is the relatable, almost lovable nature of X-Villains like Mystique and Magneto.

Generation NeXt

Rogue and Kitty Pryde are part of the next generation of X-Women, following greats like Jean Grey, Scarlet Witch, Ms. Marvel, Storm, Psylocke, and Mystique.[15] There are many, many other new X-Women who deserve to be included as well, such as Nightcrawler's daughter, Nocturne, and the only nonpsychic psychic, Layla Miller.[16] But because I am not a mutant superhero, just an ordinary human, I'll limit my focus to Rogue and Kitty Pryde.

Rogue (aka Anne Marie) first appeared on the X-scene in *Avengers Annual* #10 in 1981. Traumatized by a first kiss that drained her boyfriend, Cody Robbins, of all his energy and left him in a coma, Rogue left home. She has the uncontrollable ability to absorb the energy from humans and mutants, and when this occurs with mutants, she can also take on that mutant's powers. This is often a temporary side-effect of direct contact, as seen in the *X-Men* films when Rogue touches Wolverine and Iceman.[17] Though the foster daughter of Mystique and a member of the Brotherhood, Rogue went to the X-Men out of a desperate need to control her newly acquired powers.

Imagine a life without touch. A life where you can see the people around you, talk to them, but never, ever *touch* them. We humans are tactile creatures, constantly watching how others move their bodies, constantly touching one another, whether through a handshake, a hug, or a pat on the back. Because of Rogue's limitations, she is isolated and lonely and desperately wants to feel someone's touch. The absurd nature of Rogue's condition brings to mind the great existentialist philosopher and writer Albert Camus (1930–1960).

In his famous essay *The Myth of Sisyphus*, Camus uses an ancient myth to illustrate the human condition. In Greek mythology, Sisyphus was a man who, due to his offenses against the gods, was compelled to roll a boulder up a hill every day for all eternity, only to have it roll back down as soon as he reached the top. Camus described Sisyphus as the tragic hero, not only because he had to relentlessly repeat the same pointless task each day, but because he *knew* what would happen each time he rolled the burdensome boulder back up the hill. Had Sisyphus been ignorant of the futility of his daily chore, he could have awakened each morning refreshed and hopeful. But the fact that he knew what he was doing, while doing it over and over, added to the overall torture and tragedy. Sisyphus symbolizes the human condition; he stands for all of us, perhaps especially Rogue.

Because Rogue at one time knew touch, her fate is all the more tragic. Even if Rogue were to engage in the self-deception of Sartrean bad faith, the very nature of her self-lie would indicate that she already knows the truth. Rogue was not born unable to touch; cruelly, that "power" came on in her teen years, the time when we are most vulnerable, the time when we long for reassuring touch. This is truly absurd in Camus' sense; the world is indifferent to our hopes and dreams. Kitty Pryde must also face absurdities, but she does so with a different existential perspective.

Kitty Pryde (aka Kate Pryde aka Shadowcat) made her first appearance in *The Uncanny X-Men* #129 in October 1994. Shadowcat was a protégée of Wolverine, who taught her how to fight like a samurai in the comics. Kitty becomes a major force in mainstream X-Men when her older self, Kate Pryde, is sent into Kitty's thirteen-year-old body to correct the incident that set the *Days of Future Past* timeline in motion. When she is successful, Kate returns to the alternate timeline, sending Rachel Summers into the mainstream, where the two work together again through Excalibur.[18]

As Ortega might say, Kitty is a "substantial emigrant on a pilgrimage of being," a phrase that signifies an existence that is never static but always changing.[19] Ortega believed that human beings had no fixed nature prescribed from birth, but rather came to be who they are over the course of their personal histories through the choices they made along the way. "Man lives in view of the past," he wrote, meaning that what we are at this moment is the sum of everything we have done and undergone.[20] Kitty—with her alternate timelines and altered perceptions of history—is a prime example of Ortega's "substantial emigrant," moving from place to place, from one alternate reality to another, acting from what he calls "the relentless trajectory of experiences," everything we carry with us from our past.[21] In fact, Kitty's first experience with the X-Men was the reason she joined the mutant superheroes to begin with: Emma Frost, then associated with the Hellfire Club, and Charles Xavier for X-Men, were both attempting to recruit thirteen-year-old Kitty to their respective "private schools."[22] Not long after Emma paid a visit to her home, Kitty witnesses Frost's abduction of three X-Men. Kitty helps Cyclops in the rescue and immediately signs on. Shades of this were seen in X3, where Kitty and a handful of other mutant students were led into the ultimate battle by Storm, Wolverine, and Beast. It remains to be seen what Kitty will face in upcoming comic and film storylines. One thing is certain, though: Shadowcat will emerge as a formidable X-Woman, regardless of adaptation.

The Ultimate Conclusion

Though it is my heart's desire to talk on about other X-Women such as Jubilee, Polaris, Psylocke, Moonstar, Meltdown, Husk, Ms. Marvel, and so many, many others, for the purposes of this particular chapter in this particular book, we have come to our end.[23] We, like Rachel, like Kitty, are also immigrants on our own pilgrimages of being. We may not be mutant superheroes in skin tight costumes with voluminous hair, but we are *all* human. Like Mystique, we, too, often live in deliberate self-deception, making mistakes over and over again. Like Phoenix or the Scarlet Witch, we are all in the midst of an existential predicament, struggling to heal philosophical fractures. This is what makes the X-Men, and particularly the X-Women, so relatable, so intriguing, and, ultimately, so entertaining.

In the style of the great Stan Lee: *Excelsior!*[24]

NOTES

1. *The Upanishads*, translated by Juan Mascar (New York: Penguin Books, 1965), p. 49.

2. In Walter Kaufman, ed., *Existentialism from Dostoevsky to Sartre* (New York: Plume, 2004), p. 349.

3. For more on Jean Grey, suicide, and "The Dark Phoenix Saga," please see Mark White's essay "Is Suicide Always Immoral? Jean Grey, Kant, and *The Dark Phoenix Saga*," in chapter 3 of this book.

4. Xorn, a mutant, is part of the "New Mutant" series and was revealed to be one of the X-Men's archenemies; Xorn was first thought to be Magneto, but it was revealed later that Xorn was never Magneto. There are multiple incarnations of the Xorn character in different X-Men comic storylines.

5. From Ortega; see Kaufman, *Existentialism from Dostoevsky to Sartre*, p. 153.

6. Ibid., p. 153.

7. Vision was a synthozoid; Quicksilver, the Scarlet Witch's brother, did not approve of the relationship.

8. Baudrillard's idea of "Lines of Fracture" corresponds with his work on Integral Reality, Dual Form, and the Great Game, a social criticism and a corresponding philosophy of how twenty-first-century society is obsessed with creating false realities by overassigning meaning to everything. For more, please see Baudrillard's *The Intelligence of Evil or the Lucidity Pact*, translated by Chris Turner (New York: Berg, 2005), p. 191.

9. For more on Layla Miller, please see George Dunn's essay "Layla Miller Knows Stuff: How a Butterfly Can Shoulder the World," in chapter 6 of this volume.

10. Kaufman, *Existentialism from Dostoevsky to Sartre*, p. 157.

11. Ibid.

12. Ibid., p. 351.

13. In my 2005 essay "Myth, Morality and the Women of X-Men" in *Superheroes and Philosophy*, edited by Morris and Morris, an editing glitch rendered the final copy as reading Mystique as "evil." I don't believe people, or mutants, are strictly good or evil. It is not possible, in my humble opinion, in the past, present, or future. I finally get the chance to set the record straight. My deepest apologies, Mystique . . . keep on keepin' on!

14. Polaris aka Lorna Dane first appeared in *Uncanny X-Men* #49 (October 1968).

15. Ms. Marvel aka Carol Danvers was part of the Avengers, then became Warbird for a time before readopting her Ms. Marvel persona. She first appeared in *Marvel Super-Heroes Vol. 1* #13 (March 1968). Psylocke aka Elizabeth "Betsy" Braddock first appeared in *Captain Britain Vol. 1* #8 (December 1976).

16. Nocturne is the daughter of Nightcrawler and the Scarlet Witch in a parallel reality and was one of the first recruits to the interdimensional team of "time-fixers," Exiles, first appearing in *Exiles* #1 (August 2001).

17. However, Rogue's initial battle with Ms. Marvel left Rogue with the flying Ms. Marvel's powers permanently.

18. Kitty, with her ability to "phase" through solid matter, was also an agent with SHIELD.

19. See Ortega in Kaufman, *Existentialism from Dostoevsky to Sartre*, pp. 152–157.

20. Ibid., p. 157.

21. Ibid., p. 157.

22. First appearing in *X-Men* #132 (January 1980), Frost is known as the White Queen of the Hellfire Club, a secret organization, but in recent years has worked with the X-Men and Charles Xavier at the new School for Gifted Youngsters in Massachusetts as an instructor to mutants in *Generation X*.

23. Jubilee aka Jubilation Lee first appeared in *Uncanny X-Men* #244 (May 1989). Moonstar aka Danielle "Dani" Moonstar first appeared in *Marvel Graphic Novel #4: The New Mutants* (June 1982). Meltdown aka Tabitha Smith first appeared in *Secret Wars II* #5 (November 1985). Husk aka Paige Elisabeth Guthrie first appeared in *X-Force* #32 (March 1994).

24. My thanks to Bill Irwin, J. Jeremy Wisnewski, and especially Bob Housel and "Mighty" George Dunn (my personal editors), for help on this chapter . . . there really is no "I" in team!

MUTANT RIGHTS, TORTURE, AND X-PERIMENTATION

Cynthia McWilliams

Mutants Are Different

Magneto claims that mutants are a new stage in human evolution. "We are the future, Charles, not them," he tells Professor Xavier. "They no longer matter." When Xavier explains to his old friend and nemesis that humankind has evolved since the Nazis confined the young Magneto in a concentration camp and murdered his family, Magneto simply replies, "Yes, [they have evolved] into us."

While Xavier and Magneto continue their philosophical debate over how mutants should treat "normal" humans, we humans can argue about how we should treat mutants. Is it acceptable for humans to experiment on mutants like Wolverine, as long as we don't cause them long-term physical harm? Can we send out the Sentinels to capture, confine, and control the mutants? As we shall see, the central issue in answering these questions is whether mutants have "human" rights.

The X-Gene

Does the presence of the X-gene in a mutant place him or her outside of the realm of human moral consideration? For help in answering this question, let's consider another genetically unique group of individuals, people with Down syndrome (which in 95 percent of cases is caused by the presence of an extra copy of chromosome 21 at conception).[1] Historically, many people with Down syndrome have been sterilized and placed under the care of the state, either against their will or without their consent. Let's assume, for the sake of argument, that such treatment is morally permissible. Is it the presence of the extra chromosome that justifies treating people with Down syndrome differently? No, the justification is rooted in the supposition of a low level of functioning and competence. People with Down syndrome generally cannot function independently.

The average mutant, by contrast, functions perfectly well and is competent to make decisions for him- or herself. So, although the average mutant is in some ways different from the average human being in terms of "extra" abilities, both humans and mutants possess the same reasoning abilities. The concern of normal human beings regarding mutants is, therefore, not so much a question of mutant competence, as in the case of people with Down syndrome. Rather, concern arises because of the *potential* harm mutants can cause humans.

But They Can Look Just Like Everyone Else . . .

Mutant powers often manifest at puberty, although some are brought on by duress, and others are even present at birth. Many mutants are visually indistinguishable, even after power manifestation (except while using their powers). So whereas it would be difficult for the average human to hide a weapon that could kill hundreds of people, the average mutant can easily hide his or her tremendous power. How does this affect mutants' rights and responsibilities?

Of course, it is just this problem of mutants looking like everyone else, yet possessing incredible potential for harming others, that leads Senator Kelly, in the first X-Men movie, to argue in front of an eager crowd for legislation requiring the registration, and one can only assume the eventual confinement, of mutants: "There are mutants who can enter our minds and control our thoughts, taking away our God-given free will."

So does power-potential place mutants outside the protection of human rights?

The U.S. Declaration of Independence (1776) asserts that "all men [people] are created equal . . . with certain unalienable [inalienable] Rights, that among these are Life, Liberty, and the Pursuit of Happiness."[2] The United Nations' Universal Declaration of Human Rights (1948) states:

> All human beings are born free and equal in dignity and rights. They are endowed with reason and conscience and should act towards one another in a spirit of brotherhood. Everyone is entitled to all the rights and freedoms set forth in this Declaration, without distinction of any kind, such as race, colour, sex, language, religion, political or other opinion, national or social origin, property, birth or other status. Furthermore, no distinction shall be made on the basis of the political, jurisdictional or international status of the country or territory to which a person belongs, whether it be independent, trust, non-self-governing or under any other limitation of sovereignty. Everyone has the right to life, liberty and security of person. No one shall be held in slavery or servitude; slavery and the slave trade shall be prohibited in all their forms. No one shall be subjected to torture or to cruel, inhuman or degrading treatment or punishment.[3]

These declarations are intended as statements of how we ought to treat others. Everyone has the right to life, liberty, and security; slavery, torture, and "inhuman" treatment are wrong. Fair enough. But who counts in the category of "everyone" deserving these rights?

Morality and Impartiality: Aliens vs. Mutants

Are mutants included in "everyone"? Consider the following thought experiment. If a spaceship were to land tomorrow in Iowa (they always land somewhere desolate, after all!), and peaceful, non-carbon-based life forms that we could recognize as distinct entities emerged from it, would such beings deserve our moral consideration? Would they fall into the category of "everyone"? It seems that what matters in delineating "everyone" here would be the abilities of the individuals in question. If the aliens could demonstrate advanced reasoning ability (landing on Earth in a spaceship would count in this category) and some communication skills and sentience, then why wouldn't they count in the category of "everyone" deserving of moral consideration? Surely, it would be problematic to exclude a creature from moral consideration simply because it is not of our species.[4] The aliens' functioning and abilities would make the difference in moral consideration on this account. It would be wrong, for example, to imprison and torture and experiment on these peaceful aliens. And if strange-looking aliens deserve "human rights" and moral consideration, then why wouldn't mutants?

The U.S. Supreme Court has ruled that privacy and autonomy rights follow from the rights granted in the Constitution. And court cases involving patients' and subjects' rights to make decisions regarding health care and experimental participation have upheld such autonomy rights, the rights to be self-determining and to make our own decisions.

Rights and duties are usually thought to be correlated. That is, if an individual has a certain right, the right to autonomy, for example, then someone else has the corresponding duty not to interfere with that right. So if mutants have basic human rights, then other people, normal humans and mutants alike, have the corresponding duty and responsibility not to interfere with them.

The Duties of Mutants and Magneto on Mutant Superiority

Magneto claims in the first X-Men movie that mutants are the future of humanity. His statements suggest that mutants are a subspecies of humans, Homo superior, a recent step on the evolutionary ladder. Of course, it may be argued that mutants like Magneto and the rank and file of the Brotherhood of Evil Mutants are dangerous and threaten humanity and, as such, deserve to be treated in a less-than-humane manner. Sure, some mutants are dangerous, but so are some humans. Of course, the level of threat or the possibility of harm that a mutant can cause (especially omega-level mutants like Phoenix, for example) is significantly greater in most cases than the average human could ever cause. Separating themselves from human-kind, Magneto and the Brotherhood of Evil Mutants use the oppression of mutants at the hands of average humans as a rallying cry and a reason to harm, even kill, humans as they see fit. One of their implicit arguments is: if mutants do not deserve the same degree of moral consideration that we afford to average human beings, then mutants are justified in plac-ing humans outside of mutants' moral consideration. We have seen, however, that mutants should be included in the class of "everyone" deserving of basic human rights. But do mutants have any extra responsibilities?

Considering the power that many mutants wield, perhaps they should have greater moral constraints placed on their behavior and thus have greater moral duties than the average human being. Even though they deserve the same moral consideration and have the same basic moral rights as average human beings, they may have greater responsibilities to other sentient creatures. The average human being has the right not to be harmed unnecessarily, and so mutants who have a greater potential for harm have greater duties not to harm. Although these may not be different and distinct duties, they are at least duties that follow from mutants' potential.

But mutants' added moral responsibilities do not undermine the duties we owe to them. If it's wrong in general to torture or experiment on normal human beings, as most moral reasoning would lead us to believe, then it is wrong to torture or experiment on mutants. So let's look at the reasons for thinking that torture and experimentation on humans are wrong.

Experimentation without Consent and Torture

There are many good reasons why it is morally wrong to torture human beings or to use them in potentially harmful experiments without their consent. The most obvious is that competent human beings have the right to be self-determining and to make their own decisions—the right to autonomy. A consequence of the recognition of autonomy is the practice of informed consent. It is morally (and typically legally, as well) required that we attempt to obtain an informed consent from an individual before performing any medical procedure on the individual or before using him or her in any potentially harmful experiment. Using people in experiments, either without their consent or against their explicit wishes by coercion or force, is thus problematic as it infringes upon their right to autonomy—their right to make their own decisions regarding their own best interests.

It is uncontroversial that we have the rights not to be tortured or experimented upon without our consent. It is controversial, however, whether these rights can be overridden by the possibility of benefit to others.

Rights vs. Beneficial Consequences

Wolverine leaves Xavier's school at the end of the first X-Men movie to confront his lingering demons from the surgical implantation of adamantium onto his skeleton, a procedure that was seemingly done without his consent.[5] A similar theme of experimentation on mutants recurs in the two subsequent X-Men movies, as well as in numerous storylines from the X-Verse. In *X-Men: The Last Stand*, many mutants are incited by Magneto's quite plausible claim that the recently developed "cure" for mutants will be forcibly inflicted on them against their will. Now let's add a utilitarian twist: what if experimentation like this, performed on some mutants, yields results that greatly benefit both humankind and mutantkind?[6]

Even if mutants have the same basic human rights as normal human beings, these rights may be overridden, under certain circumstances. On this line of reasoning, causing harm to a few to save many may be justified. Even if we reject such consequentialist moral reasoning in general, almost everyone agrees that basic human rights can be overridden in some circumstances. We can imprison people against their will when they have been found guilty of a crime, for example, thus overriding their basic rights to liberty and autonomy. We reason that such punishment is warranted to protect others, to reform the criminal, or simply because the criminal deserves to be punished.

Consequentialist arguments are typically offered to support torture in certain circumstances.[7] For example, we see scenarios on television and in the movies involving the "necessary" torture of a supposed terrorist to extract information that could save hundreds or even thousands of lives. The implication is that the suspected terrorist, like the convicted criminal, and like the evil, overly powerful mutant, is not innocent and can therefore be sacrificed to save innocent lives.

We are then faced with a related but quite different problem: given that mutants have the same basic human rights as average human beings, when, if ever, is it morally permissible to override these rights for the good of the many?

And like any good story arc, this one ends on a cliffhanger.

NOTES

1. See www.nlm.nih.gov/medlineplus/ency/article/000997.htm, accessed November 10, 2008.

2. See http://usinfo.state.gov/products/pubs/hrintro/declare.htm, accessed November 10, 2008.

3. See www.un.org/Overview/rights.html, accessed November 10, 2008.

4. For a discussion of "speciesism," see Peter Singer's *Animal Liberation*, 2nd ed. (New York: Random House, 1990).

5. Although this lack of consent is questioned by Colonel William Stryker in the 2003 movie *X-Men 2: X-Men United*, when he claims that Wolverine volunteered for the program that led to his adamantium skeletal grafts.

6. Utilitarianism is a moral theory that contends that the rightness or wrongness of an action is determined solely by the consequences of the action. Although there are numerous versions of utilitarianism, they all share the same commitment to the consequentialist principle that actions lack inherent moral worth and are to be judged on the basis of consequences.

7. See, for example, Bob Brecher, *Torture and the Ticking Bomb* (Malden, MA: Blackwell, 2007; and Vittorio Bufacchi and Jean Maria Arrigo, "Torture, Terrorism and the State: A Refutation of the Ticking-Bomb Argument," *Journal of Applied Philosophy* (2006): 3–23, 355–373.

WHEN YOU KNOW YOU'RE *JUST* A COMIC BOOK CHARACTER: DEADPOOL

Joseph J. Darowski

You are reading an essay in a book. I was, at one point, writing the words on this page, but that was a long time ago and probably in a place far away. Now the words are just ink on a page, and I have nothing to do with them. Please do not get confused. I know that right now I'm speaking as though I was a voice in your head, in the present, but really I'm likely napping. Or playing video games. Or I could be working hard on another scholarly article (I need to say something like that in case this article is read when I'm going for tenure . . . which could be at this very moment if you are a member of a certain committee). The important thing that you need to know is that when I wrote and revised and revised this article, I was writing in a way that would make Deadpool proud: I was a consummate postmodern. Of course, Deadpool is a fictional character and therefore can't be proud, but you already know that. Or do you?

Deadpool is not one of the most iconic comic book characters ever created, so perhaps you've never heard of him. Comic
book superheroes have existed for decades, and although literally thousands of characters have been created, publishers still
seek to introduce new, unique characters. Superman, Batman,
and Wonder Woman introduced the superheroic archetypes
in the 1930s and 1940s, and more than seventy years after
Superman first appeared on the cover of *Action Comics* #1,
superheroes continue to evolve. As creators seek to find ways to
make their characters stand out from the spandexed crowd,
superhero character traits stray further from the archetype
embodied by the archetypes of the genre. Deadpool has a quirk
different from Superman's kryptonite, Batman's lack of powers,
or Wonder Woman's Amazon origins: Deadpool knows he is a
character in a comic book. Under the hands of skillful comic book
creators, this postmodern character trait has been used not only
for humor, but to explore and raise philosophical questions.

Definitions of Postmodernism and Ontology, and a Brief History of Deadpool

Let's go ahead and acknowledge that on some level, the term
postmodern seems oxymoronic. Many students sitting in college
classrooms, perhaps even you, have paused to ask, "*Post*-modern?
How can anything be happening after the current moment?" The
"modernism" in postmodernism, however, does not refer to the
present time but to a movement that immediately proceeded postmodernism. Postmodernism, then, is a movement that reacted to
modernism. As Edward Quinn (1920–1997) explained,

> Where modernist literature was characterized by its
> commitment to the value of a unified, coherent work of
> art employing symbol and myth, exhibiting alienation
> from ordinary life, postmodernism celebrates incoherence,

discontinuity, parody, popular culture, and the principle of metafiction.[1]

Postmodernism can be found in any art form, from architecture to painting, from film to comic books. Quinn further noted that postmodernism often has a "playful element" that is used to explore deeper issues. This playful element is on full display in the Deadpool comic books, as Deadpool's awareness that he is a comic book character is generally used to deliver the punch line of a gag.

Ontology has a decidedly longer history than postmodernism. Ontology is a branch of philosophy concerned with the nature of being. A basic definition is provided in *The Blackwell Dictionary of Western Philosophy*:

> Ontology deals with the essential characteristics of being itself (of Aristotle's being qua being), and asks questions such as "What is or what exists?" "What kind of thing exists primarily?" and "How are different kinds of being related to one another?"[2]

The word *ontology* is "derived from the Greek word for being, but a seventeenth-century coinage for the branch of metaphysics that concerns itself with what exists."[3] Many philosophers before the seventeenth century considered ontological issues. In Western philosophy, Plato's Allegory of the Cave is a famous experiment in ontology. Plato imagines prisoners who have never seen anything but shadows play across a cave wall. These shadows are the prisoners' "reality," because they experience nothing else. If these prisoners were freed to become enlightened to the true reality, full of colors and depth, would they accept this new reality or believe only the world of shadows? Plato implies in this allegory that there are levels of existence to be explored, and as people learn more, they can leave behind their old existence to explore a new understanding of the world around them.

Postmodernism and ontology are related in many ways. Postmodern texts make the reader aware of the factors involved in bringing the text and the narrative into existence, while ontology considers the nature of existence. Narratives inherently create a universe, often inviting the reader or the viewer to become immersed in the fictional world. As a narrative medium, comic books require the reader to actively participate in the creation of a narrative, to aid in bringing the story into existence. In the adventures of Deadpool, the writers and the artists use the comic book medium in a postmodern manner to explore ontological questions.

Deadpool was created by writer Fabian Nicieza and artist Rob Liefeld for Marvel Comics in 1991. His first appearance was in the *New Mutants*, a comic book featuring a junior team of X-Men characters, and the character has been closely associated with the X-Men franchise of the Marvel Comics universe ever since. Deadpool was initially a villainous mercenary who would perform any job if the money was right. Through the events of two miniseries, however, *Deadpool: The Circle Chase* (1993) and *Deadpool: Sins of the Past* (1994), as well as two monthly comic book series, *Deadpool* (1997–2002) and *Cable & Deadpool* (2004–2008), Deadpool has become a somewhat more noble character. At times, Deadpool has even gone on quests to become a respected hero, although he still lacks the clear moral and ethical motivations of most superheroes.

Initially, Deadpool did not demonstrate what has become one of his defining characteristics: the knowledge that he is a character in a comic book. When Deadpool was introduced in 1991, the most distinguishing aspect of the character was his wise cracking pop culture–referencing attitude. Yet as any comic book fan knows, gun-toting characters with strange muscular proportions who are unafraid to joke around while killing people were prevalent in comics at the time. Thus, there was not much to distinguish Deadpool, the so-called Merc-with-a-mouth, from these other early-1990s creations.

As Deadpool began to headline his own comic books, depth and layers were added to the character. When Joe Kelley began writing *Deadpool*, incidents of the metafiction started to occur. Most particularly, Deadpool began to reference the fact that he was a comic book character, with allusions to writers, panels, word balloons, and an audience. Later writers, such as Christopher Priest, Gail Simone, and Fabian Nicieza (Deadpool's co-creator, who returned to the character and wrote the entire *Cable & Deadpool* series), emphasized Deadpool's knowledge that he was a comic book character, and the Merc-with-a-mouth became the Merc-with-a-meta-awareness.

Metafiction draws attention to its own fictionality. This can be done when a character breaks the fourth wall in the theater, addresses the audience in a television show, or references writers and artists in a comic book. Imagine that Wolverine, in *X-Men Origins: Wolverine*, turns to the camera and advises that the young boy in the third row cover his eyes, because this fight scene is going to be inappropriately violent for a child of his unseasoned years—*this* is postmodernism at its peak.

Tactics like this can force the audience to consider the text more deeply than if they are focused on the narrative. Furthermore, this postmodern technique can highlight elements of a medium that are normally processed unconsciously and can thus bring to light intricate interactions that are often overlooked. Metafiction also raises ontological issues. Acknowledging the falseness of the narrative's reality encourages readers to ponder existence. Deadpool will insist to readers that nothing they read is really occurring, because it is all in a writer's imagination. This causes readers to step back from the false world they have been reading about in the comic book and acknowledge the reality that a writer did imagine everything that is on the page. Metafiction, when used successfully, can raise the same issues concerning levels of existence that Plato explored in his Allegory of the Cave. When the writers of the Deadpool comic books engage in postmodern exercises, readers are invited to step back and consider their understanding of comic books and the manner in which they combine texts and images into a cohesive narrative. Readers then become aware of their collaborative work in creating a comic-book universe inhabited by fictional characters.

Reading between Panels

As a series of still images juxtaposed to create a sense of story, comic books require the participation of the audience in order for a story to be understood. A viewer watching a film can largely be passive, perhaps drawing conclusions about location and the passage of time following scene changes but otherwise simply watching the action unfold. A comic book reader, however, must participate in the creation of the story by inserting action in the transition between panels. The space between comic book panels is called the gutter. When readers look at two panels and decide what action occurs in between them, the process is called closure. Scott McCloud, a noted comic book theorist, argued that comic books are "a medium of communication and expression which uses closure like no other. A medium where the audience is a willing and conscious collaborator and closure is the agent of change, time and motion."[4] Without the reader collaborating in the process of forming a narrative, the comic book would be a series of individual drawings that might look beautiful but would fail to signify anything, much less tell a complex story. A picture of Wolverine standing still placed next to a picture of Wolverine in the same pose with claws now appearing out of his fists does not signify any action occurring unless readers imagine the claws sliding out in the gutter between the panels.

Though McCloud calls the readers "conscious collaborator[s]" in the process of closure, in truth the process should become unconscious in a well-constructed comic book. Ideally, readers are unaware that they are participating in the narrative, because the art and the dialogue operate so seamlessly that the readers' act of closure is completely natural. If the comic book in question is deliberately postmodern, however, it may draw attention to this natural process.

One simple example of a writer recognizing the readers' completion of the action between panels occurs in *Deadpool* #2. In one panel, Deadpool is sitting at a kitchen table in a bathrobe and is about to take a bite of cereal, not knowing that he has been tricked by his blind roommate into pouring a large amount of salt onto his breakfast instead of sugar. The next panel shows Deadpool, now in costume, entering his friend Weasel's room, and it contains a text box in which Deadpool provides first-person narration, stating, "Five tooth brushings and a scene change later . . ."[5] A more standard caption may read, "In Weasel's room . . ." and allow the reader to surmise that time has passed, based on Deadpool's wardrobe change.

When Joe Kelley, the writer of the issue, included the line "a scene change later," he drew attention to the reader's traditional role of providing closure between the panels by having a character who should have been unaware of a scene change recognize the occurrence. In classic narrative form, the characters go on with their lives as normal in the periods the reader does not see. Deadpool would have gone to brush his teeth and put on his costume and walked to Weasel's room without ever being aware that a scene change occurred, and the reader would have imagined those actions taking place in the gutter between the panels. But in a postmodern comic book, which resists the traditional narrative style and instead emphasizes the fiction of the story and the conventions of the medium, the character references the scene change, rather than stepping into it. Deadpool recognizes his presence in a narrative that is being presented to an audience. Readers, in turn, recognize the story as being prepared for their consumption and should analyze the story not only for its narrative, but also as a product being produced for their benefit. Furthermore, readers are made conscious of the fact that they have unconsciously been completing the narrative action between the panels.

When First-Person Narrative Text Boxes Go Wrong

McCloud, in explaining the role of the reader in comic books, stated, "Every act committed to paper by the comics (plural?) artist is aided and abetted by a silent accomplice. An equal partner in crime, known as the reader."[6] The reader's role in understanding a comic book goes far beyond completing the action between the panels. Readers are also expected to understand the conventions of the comic book medium. Failure to understand the vocabulary of comic books will result in an incomprehensible narrative, and the writers of Deadpool again use postmodern techniques to emphasize this complex interaction between reader and text. Explaining the vocabulary of comic books in textual form seems a bit counterproductive, so let's see what other options we can explore.

Now that we all understand some comic book conventions, we can appreciate how the writers of Deadpool frequently toy with them. The first issue of *Deadpool*, written by Joe Kelley, begins with text boxes containing expository dialogue that a reader acquainted with comic book conventions would assume to be Deadpool's thoughts. The text boxes read, "The Bolivian jungle. Steamy rank. More humid than a church pew on Sunday. And quiet . . . so deathly quiet." At this point a soldier, using a word balloon, states, "Sir? I think I hear him. I—I think he's talking—?" The next text box reads, "Duh. It's called narration, you ignorant simp."[7] The gag here is dependent on the reader reading the text boxes as internal narration by Deadpool and then discovering that he has been speaking aloud. The text

boxes are simply words on the page. There is no reason text boxes should be read as a silent internal monologue, but that is how they are traditionally portrayed. By manipulating the conventions that comic books have developed, Kelley stresses the conventions' very existence.

Fabian Nicieza also manipulated the common role of text boxes in *Cable & Deadpool*. *Cable & Deadpool* #30 begins with Deadpool fighting the intentionally lame superhero team the Great Lakes Avengers. Deadpool provides exposition through text boxes; however, the Great Lakes Avengers continually respond to Deadpool's narration. This leads to the following exchange between Deadpool and Big Bertha, with Deadpool's dialogue presented in text boxes and Big Bertha's in traditional word balloons:

Deadpool: What's going on here?

Big Bertha: You're saying everything out loud!

Deadpool: I am?

Big Bertha: Yes!

Deadpool: *Oh. Weird. Coulda sworn I was in first person narrative form.*[8]

Later in the same issue, Deadpool is thinking through his problems in text boxes. In the final text box Deadpool congratulates himself, stating that "First person captions are working again." Then a woman walks by and says, "Y'talkin' t'you'self, dude."

These examples all prevent the reader from becoming immersed in the story. Not only that, they force awareness of the reader's role in creating this narrative world. The reader aids in the creation of Deadpool's world, and if the reader initially reads the text boxes as "audible" narration, the joke is lost. Referring back to Plato's Allegory of the Cave, Deadpool knows he is in a world of shadows and that his text boxes are one aspect of this reality, but with these postmodern touches readers discovers their involvement in creating that shadow reality.

Writers, Artists, and Editors, Oh My!

The creation of comic books is collaborative on many levels. Writers, artists, editors, inkers, and colorists are all involved in producing the comic book. Furthermore, you, the reader, are required to collaborate with the finished product in order to create a story. Postmodern texts resist the impulse for works to stand on their own. You should be made aware that the work has been produced for consumption, and in the case of comic books, many people have had a role in that production.

When Christopher Priest began to write *Deadpool*, he took a self-deprecating approach to informing readers of the change in writer for the title. The first issue of Priest's run on the title, which immediately followed Joe Kelley's run, begins with a sequence in which Deadpool is welcomed to a trailer park. He is carrying a bag with him, which in various panels is labeled "Every good idea Kelley ever had" and "Everything that made this book work," that Deadpool then throws into a river. Deadpool then meets the inhabitants of the trailer park, who are all characters that Priest previously wrote comic books for, but the comic books were canceled while Priest was writing them. Deadpool realizes that all those characters' comic books have been canceled and tries to leave, yelling, "I will not end up like those losers! That will never happen to me!" But he is told, "It's already happened to you. Why do you think they brought *him* in? Name me one healthy project he's ever been assigned to. The man has one purpose in life, and now he's been assigned to you."[9] This revelation causes Deadpool to jump into the river to seek the bag containing Kelley's good ideas. When Priest's run as writer comes to an end, *Deadpool* has not been canceled but is instead being passed on to another writer. Priest's final issue features Deadpool triumphantly returning to the trailer park, but this time carrying a bag with a body in it. He reveals to the characters living there that the body is of Christopher Priest, and that by killing the writer he managed to have his series continue.

Another way in which Priest reminded readers of the writer's presence and simultaneously employs ontological philosophy is with Deadpool's frequent references to the fact that "There is a man . . . sitting at a typewriter . . . this is all his imagination." Although other characters in the comic book believe Deadpool's assertions to be insane ramblings, the reader knows Deadpool is correct. In fact, these statements by

Deadpool can be compared to the ancient ontological thought experiment devised by Plato. Deadpool has left the world of shadows that the other characters still exist in and has seen the true reality—he is only a fictional character. Deadpool spouts so much nonsense, however, that the truth of his statements is dismissed by the other characters. These moments when Deadpool correctly identifies his reality emphasize to you, the reader, that you and the writer exist in the true reality, and you both collaboratively construct a false reality for Deadpool.

Fabian Nicieza also made fun of himself as the writer of *Cable & Deadpool*. In issue 8 of that series, Deadpool is giving an interview to a reporter, when the following exchange occurs:

> Irene Merryweather: And who is paying you to stop Cable?
>
> Deadpool: That would be telling. I am putting together pieces of a puzzle—missing parts of some future tech device that once was on Cable's ship.
>
> Apparently, that'll prove to be the plot device that stops him when his powers become too much to make work in the context of a monthly comic.
>
> Merryweather: Excuse me?
>
> Deadpool: Never mind. Fabian doesn't want me breaking the fourth wall in this book.
>
> Merryweather: Who is Fabian?
>
> Deadpool: He's the hack who co-created me. Personally, I like Kelley and Simone better, but I think they're both exclusive at DC now.
>
> Merryweather: What?
>
> Deadpool: I better shut up now or else I'll end up in a dress or something.[10]

Joe Kelley and Gail Simone were both writers who had previously worked on titles featuring Deadpool, and at the time this issue was published, both writers had contracts to work exclusively at DC Comics, Marvel Comics' chief rival. In the following issue, Deadpool did appear in a dress.

The collaborative nature of comic books suggests that a postmodern comic book should allude to more than simply the writer. In creating the comic-book world, the artist works closely with the writer to produce the story. Ontologically, recognizing the collaborators who create the narrative emphasizes the multiple voices that are required to create a narrative reality. The most blatant example of artist referencing comes in *Deadpool* #36. Deadpool is not in his costume for most of this issue, but when the reader turns to page 25, Deadpool is shown in full costume in a full-page image. The word balloon reads, "Oh hi, kids—Deadpool here. Hate to interrupt the story like this, but our fine artist had the overwhelming urge to draw me in this pin-up shot even though it's nowhere in the script."[11] The fact that this dialogue appears raises the question of whether this page was included in the initial script. Was the dialogue a reaction to a disobedient artist, or was it a planned joke that was included in the original script? These are precisely the types of questions that postmodern texts hope to raise.

Nicieza also brought the role of editors to the forefront in *Cable & Deadpool* #36. The first page of *Cable & Deadpool* was often a recap page, meant to remind readers of previous events. As such, the page was not part of the continuity of the story, and Deadpool's recap page almost always explicitly broke the fourth wall. In this recap page, Deadpool appears at Marvel's publishing offices while looking for a particular character, Taskmaster. Marvel was in the midst of a massive crossover involving most of its characters. Deadpool therefore went and threatened Marvel editors, who keep track of which writers are using specific characters, at gunpoint to discover the whereabouts of Taskmaster.[12] Though this page does not fit into the continuity of the issue, it still makes the reader aware of the editors' involvement in the book. It also raises the issues of large crossovers, narrative cohesiveness in the Marvel universe, and large-scale continuity, which all affect the creation of a Marvel comic book.

This Is the Last Section Heading You Will Have to Read

Postmodernism seeks to distance readers from the text and invites them to consider the process inherent to the production of the narrative. *Deadpool* is one example of a postmodern comic book that forces the reader to become aware of the his or her role in interpreting the story, the conventions of the comic book medium, and the role of multiple creators and editors in producing a single issue. Although there have been other postmodern comic books, such as Grant Morrison's *Animal Man* or John Byrne's *She-Hulk*, those titles are more often associated with the creator than with the character. When other writers pen the adventures of Animal Man, the postmodern elements are abandoned. Deadpool is unique in that the postmodern elements have become part of his personality and are now adopted by all writers who take on the character. When producing the adventures of a postmodern comic book character such as Deadpool, comic book creators can inspire readers to think about the medium that a story is delivered in as much as the story itself.

Yet the invitation to think more deeply does not stop with the medium Deadpool's adventures. Ontological questions are raised, as Deadpool is more enlightened about his true nature than are the characters he interacts with. In the Marvel universe, Deadpool is considered insane because he knows the truth about his fictional "reality." Complex issues can be considered by the reader, as layers of reality are dissected. The creators, the product, and the reader collaborate to forge a reality that we all know to be fiction. Deadpool, working in a medium often dismissed as juvenile, raises the same ontological issue that Plato raised in his Allegory of the Cave.

Are you ready for this essay to end? I sure am.

NOTES

1. Edward Quinn, *A Dictionary of Literary and Thematic Terms* (New York: Checkmark, 2000), p. 255.

2. Nicholas Bunnin and Jiyuan Yu, eds., *The Blackwell Dictionary of Western Philosophy* (Malden, Mass.: Blackwell Publishing, 2004). Blackwell Reference Online, www.blackwellreference.com/subscriber/tocnode?id=g9781405106795_chunk_g978140510679516_ss1-38, accessed June 18, 2008.

3. Simon Blackburn, *The Oxford Dictionary of Philosophy* (Oxford: Oxford University Press, 1996). Oxford Reference Online, Oxford University Press, Michigan State University Library, www.oxfordreference.com.proxy1.cl.msu.edu:2047/views/ENTRY.html?subview=Main&entry=t98.e1711, accessed June 18, 2008.

4. Scott McCloud, *Understanding Comics: The Invisible Art* (New York: HarperCollins, 1993), p. 65.

5. Joe Kelley, writer, and Ed McGuinness, illustrator, *Deadpool* #2 (1997), p. 7.

6. McCloud, *Understanding Comics: The Invisible Art*, p. 68.

7. Joe Kelley, writer, and Ed McGuinness, illustrator, "Hey, It's Deadpool!" in *Deadpool Classic*, edited by Mark D. Beazley (New York: Marvel Comics, 2008).

8. Fabian Nicieza, writer, and Staz Johnson, illustrator, "The Hero Hunter: A Marvel Civil War Tie-In," in *Cable & Deadpool: Paved with Good Intentions*, edited by Jennifer Grunwald (New York: Marvel Comics, 2007).

9. Christopher Priest, writer, and Paco Diaz, illustrator, "Sending in the Clowns," *Deadpool* #34 (1999), p. 6.

10. Fabian Nicieza, writer, and Patrick Zircher, illustrator, "The Burnt Offering Part Two: Lepers at the Table" in *Cable & Deadpool* Vol. 1 #8 (2004), p. 1.

11. Christopher Priest, writer, and Paco Diaz, illustrator, *Deadpool* #36 (2000), p. 25.

12. Fabian Nicieza, writer, and Reilly Brown, illustrator, "Unfinished Business: Part One," in *Cable & Deadpool Vol. 7: Separation Anxiety*, edited by Jennifer Grunwald (2007).

HUMAN ETHICS AND MUTANT MORALITY IN THE X-VERSE

MAGNETO, MUTATION, AND MORALITY

Richard Davis

The question is not whether evolution is
connected with ethics, but how.

—Michael Ruse, *Evolutionary Ethics: A Phoenix Arisen*

Charles Darwin's *The Origin of Species* (1859) may well be
the most influential and controversial book ever written. It
contains an idea so revolutionary that it has been compared
to Copernicus's discovery that the Earth revolves around the
Sun, and not (as previously thought) the other way around.
What *is* that idea? That individuals everywhere are engaged
in a "struggle for existence"—a struggle whose outcome is
determined not by God but by Nature herself. Those individuals possessing features that are conducive to survival and
reproduction (an opposable thumb, say, or perhaps webbed
feet) have an adaptive advantage; they are more likely to beat
out their competitors in the game of life. Nature looks on
them (or rather on their traits) favorably and passes them down

the family tree to the next generation of offspring. And thus organisms change and *evolve*—in our case, as the first *X-Men* reminds us, "from a single-celled organism into the dominant species on the planet."

It is difficult to overemphasize the importance of Darwin's thought. "If I were to give an award for the single best idea anyone has ever had," said philosopher Daniel Dennett (b. 1942), "I'd give it to Darwin, ahead of Newton and Einstein and everyone else."[1] Hefty praise indeed. The idea is also deemed "dangerous," in that it has expansionist tendencies; it tends to creep into other areas, sometimes stepping on the toes of disciplines outside the realm of biology. There are, for example, evolutionary explanations of art, love, mathematics, and even religion.[2] If Dennett is right, Darwin's dangerous idea "unifies the realm of life, meaning, and purpose with the realm of space and time, cause and effect, mechanism and physical law."[3] In other words, it explains the meaning and the purpose of our lives in a purely naturalistic way.

The story of the X-Men is the story of genetic mutation and the incredible powers and advantages it confers. With PhDs in genetics, biophysics, psychology, anthropology, and psychiatry, Charles Xavier, mutant mentor, is no intellectual slouch. One of the world's most powerful telepaths, he can project his thoughts into the minds of others. With Cerebro—a device that magnifies telepathic ability—at his disposal, it is within his power to annihilate the entire human race. Yet he doesn't. Indeed, in the face of compulsory mutant registration, Xavier is hopeful. He pleads with his friend Erik Lehnsherr (Magneto), "Don't give up on them, Erik." But Magneto merely replies, "I've heard these arguments before," referring, of course, to the forced registration of Jews in Nazi Germany, a seemingly innocuous request that ultimately led to the death camps (where in the first X-Men movie we are introduced to Magneto as a boy).

How can we be sure the nonmutants aren't proceeding down a similar slippery slope? Professor Xavier assures us, "That was a long time ago. Mankind has evolved since then." Magneto retorts, "Yes, into us." But that's not what Xavier has in mind. What he says suggests that human morality is evolving *along with* human biology: that evolution and ethics are intimately connected. This raises all sorts of fascinating philosophical questions. If mutation and morality are linked, then wouldn't morality simply be a biological adaptation: "a feature helping us in the struggle for existence and reproduction—no less than hands and eyes, teeth and feet"?[4] Evolutionary ethicists think so. But then wouldn't those *most capable* of surviving and reproducing in effect be the *most moral*? In a Darwinian world, if I can eliminate my rivals—say, by manipulating magnetic fields or creating hurricane-force winds—then what would be *wrong* with that, if that's what I wanted to do? You might reply that I should respect other human beings. Well, perhaps I should. As Professor Xavier points out to Wolverine, however, "There are mutants out there with incredible powers, Logan, and many who do not share my respect for mankind." What do you say to them? Magneto tells the young Pyro: you are "a god among insects." Well, from a mutant point of view, if that's what humans beings *are*—mere insects—then why isn't Magneto's attempt to kill off all of the nonmutants (by way of Cerebro) morally justifiable? After all, he is merely ensuring his survival by eliminating those he perceives as threats to his fitness. What could be more laudable than that?

"Nonsense on Stilts"

Most of us, I dare say, see little difference between Magneto's plan to exterminate all nonmutants and the Fuehrer's "Final Solution." In words that echo those of Hitler, Magneto declares, "We are the future, Charles, not them. They no longer matter." Perceived threat or not, what's in view is mass genocide of billions of innocent human beings. We can quibble about the morality of stem cell research or abortion if we like, but clearly a holocaust of this sort is morally unconscionable, an absolute wrong—no ifs, ands, or buts. Still, the question arises: Why are we inclined to think so? What accounts for that?

Darwin has a handy explanation. Human beings once lived in a very primitive state—a state famously described by Thomas Hobbes (1588–1679) as "solitary, poor, nasty, brutish, and short." Basically, we were at one another's throats. Survival was a beastly struggle. Somewhere along the way, however, bands of humans realized that by overcoming their differences, life lasted longer and everyone produced more offspring. Those individuals with altruistic impulses, who showed concern for others—today we call them "emotionally intelligent"—were subject to less aggression on the part of others, attracted better mates, and so on. Accordingly, "Those communities, which included the greatest number of the most sympathetic members, would flourish best and rear the greatest number of offspring."[5] What we consider moral behavior is therefore the result of genetic mutation and instincts hardwired into us by socio-biological evolution. The fact is, says Richard Dawkins,

> Natural selection favours genes that predispose individuals . . . to remember obligations, bear grudges, police exchange relationships and punish cheats who take, but don't give when their turn comes.[6]

You and I are therefore the happy recipients of certain moral impulses or urges; we possess a "moral sense," if you will. As a result, we tend to engage in what Dennett calls "rule worship"; we are strongly inclined to embrace, and at times enforce, such prescriptions as *You ought to respect human life* or *You shouldn't have more than one spouse at a time*. But why so? Because, Dennett says,

> "rule worship" of a certain kind is a good thing, at least for agents designed like us. It is good not because there is a certain rule, or set of rules, which is probably

the best, or which always yields the right answer, but because having rules works—somewhat—and not having rules doesn't work at all.[7]

In short, following "rules" produces social order and cohesion; it sets the stage for human flourishing. We kid ourselves, though, if we think there is a foundation for morality apart from human evolution.[8] These "moral rules," to borrow Jeremy Bentham's phrase, are "nonsense on stilts." And yet they're "good nonsense," Dennett tell us, precisely because they are on "stilts"; that is, they've got enough clout to rise above those who decide to impose their selfish agendas on the rest of us. They're "conversation-stoppers" that can be used to silence the opposition. And that's all they are—end of story.

Something like this view of "moral rules" seems to be lurking behind Magneto's ongoing battle of wills with Charles Xavier over the nonmutant problem. As we all know, Xavier meets his match in William Stryker, the former military man bent on wiping out every mutant on the face of the planet. After kidnapping Xavier, Stryker uses his telepathic son, Jason, to take over the professor's mind, hook him up to Cerebro, and then carry out a final solution of his own. Behind the scenes, of course, Magneto is redirecting events for his own purposes: to modify Cerebro and wipe out humankind.

With Stryker out of the picture, Magneto triumphantly strides to the end of the ramp where the professor is perched, still under the effects of brainwashing. Listen to what Magneto says to his old friend:

> How does it look from there, Charles? Still fighting the good fight? From here it doesn't look like they're playing by your rules. Maybe it's time to play by theirs.

Something has gone seriously wrong. How in the world did Xavier get into this mess? It's perfectly obvious. He bought into the wrong set of rules: *human* rules that guarantee *human* superiority. He is one of Darwin's "sympathetic" individuals, desperately trying to produce a new consensus, a new set of cooperative standards by which humans and mutants can live in harmony. Magneto's point, however, is pure Dennett. "Charles, it's not working." Xavier thinks the rules he follows are good (fighting the good fight by following good rules). But "good" here just means "what enhances fitness." If your "respect for humanity" rule were really working, Charles, why are you on the verge of telepathically annihilating every member of *your own* kind?[9] Your rule is an absolute dud.

Yes, I know. Professor Xavier is ultimately rescued, heads off the forced registration of mutants, and helps usher in a new era of cooperation with humanity. But things could easily have gone the other way. Indeed, if a "good" rule is one that confers an evolutionary advantage, then it's difficult to see why Magneto's rule "You ought to eliminate any group that poses a potential threat to your existence" isn't the better of the two rules as far as natural selection goes. After all, wouldn't a homogeneous community consisting only of mutants be far more cohesive, far more conducive to mutant survival and reproduction, than a mixed community of humans and mutants, with its radically unequal (and therefore divisive) distribution of powers and opportunities?

You Can't Get an *Ought* from an *Is*

The Harvard professor E. O. Wilson once announced that "the time has come for ethics to be removed temporarily from the hands of the philosophers and *biologicized*."[10] Admittedly, we all feel more confident about the claims of a discipline when we're told they have a scientific basis. If scientists can study it, we're on solid ground. But what do scientists study? Simply the way the world *is*. By way of the scientific method and using their five senses, they tell us *what is the case*: chemically, biologically, and so forth. Do they also study ethics? There is a very good reason to think not. For, as most of us recognize, "Ethics has to do with what is good or right—in other words, with what *ought to be* the case."[11] Do you see the difference between *what is* and what *ought to be*? The claim that we can ground ethics in evolutionary biology assumes that we can deduce how the world ought to be from the way it is in fact.

Unfortunately, this assumption commits what the distinguished Cambridge philosopher G. E. Moore (1873–1958) called "The Naturalistic Fallacy."[12] What precisely is that? It's a mistake in reasoning that occurs every time we try to identify what is good or right with some scientifically measurable, natural property. Let's suppose, for example, that "good" means "whatever contributes to your personal pleasure." Then consider one of Wolverine's many sexual advances toward Jean Grey, who is already in a committed relationship with Scott Summers (Cyclops). Does that activity increase his personal pleasure? You bet. Now ask yourself this question:

> Q1: Making sexual advances to Jean Grey has the property of increasing Wolverine's pleasure, but is it good?

That's an open question, isn't it? For even if Wolverine finds this sort of thing pleasurable, we can still ask whether it's right or good for him to do so. She's someone else's girl, for goodness sake! Now here's the kicker. If "good" simply means "whatever contributes to your personal pleasure," then Q1 asks the very same question as:

> Q2: Making sexual advances to Jean Grey has the property of increasing Wolverine's pleasure, but does it have the property of increasing Wolverine's pleasure?

But that's clearly ridiculous. Unlike Q1, Q2 isn't an open question at all. You don't have to ask whether something is pleasurable if you know that it's pleasurable. What you do have to ask is whether it's good, whether it ought to be so.

What this shows, in general, is that the attempt to equate right and wrong with purely natural properties is an abject failure. "Come back in a hundred years," Sam Harris said, "and if we haven't returned to living in caves and killing one another with clubs, we will have some scientifically astute things to say about ethics."[13] Don't hold your breath. What science might help with is explaining how our moral beliefs *arose*; it cannot hope to provide a natural *ground* or *basis* for them. This is actually a welcome conclusion, because the list of things that nature has selected for includes some of the most sickening behaviors any of us could ever imagine: rape, infanticide, siblingcide, and even sexual cannibalism (killing and eating one's mate after impregnation).[14] Even Harris, a diehard naturalist, concedes that these are things "we would have done well to leave behind us in the jungles of Africa."[15] And he's right. But then where does that leave Xavier, Magneto, and those who see a link between evolution and ethics?

Are Ethics an Illusion?

Frankly, it's a bit of a pickle. If, like Professor Xavier, you want to denounce Magneto's behavior, your judgments need some sort of moral bite (you would think). They have to prohibit and condemn certain actions as ones that *ought not* to have been done, morally speaking. Surely, we need something on which to hang our deepest moral convictions. If that something isn't natural, then what is it? Here, philosopher of biology Michael Ruse (b. 1940) bites the bullet:

> The evolutionist argues that, thanks to our science, we see that claims like "You *ought* to maximize personal liberty" are no more than subjective expressions, impressed upon our thinking because of their adaptive value. In other words, we see that morality has no philosophically objective foundation. It is just an illusion, fobbed off on us to promote biological "altruism."[16]

What's he saying? Evolution has basically tricked us into thinking that morality is objective and real when it isn't; evolution does this so that we obey the illusion, rather than ignore it. Things work better for all of us that way. The fact of the matter, however, is that "morality has no more (and no less) status than that of the terror we feel at the unknown—another *emotion*."[17] So what is morality? It's a sentiment or a feeling. A moral statement such as "It is wrong to force mutants to register with the authorities" doesn't make a factual claim at all. In her showdown with Senator Kelly, Jean Grey might just as well have blurted out, "Mutant registration!!" in disgust. That's all she's doing: announcing her feelings. Believe it or not, she's not saying anything true or false. It's a little bit like "booing" an athlete at a sports event.

Ruse and Magneto have a lot in common. Did you ever notice how Magneto never engages anyone in moral debate? He *listens* to Senator Kelly crush Jean Grey in debate and then tells his friend Charles, "I've *heard* these arguments before." Okay, then, why not join the discussion? Put a counterargument on the table. Feed the good Dr. Grey some better material. Get with it! All you'll ever see Magneto do is act on feeling and impulse. At one point, he actually kidnaps Senator Kelly. Then we get the following exchange:

Magneto: "I think what you are really afraid of is me—me and my kind, the brotherhood of mutants. . . . Mankind has always feared what it doesn't understand."

Senator Kelly: "What do you intend to do to me?"

Magneto: "Let's just say that God works too slowly."

You've got the senator alone; it's a perfect time to reason with him. And what does Magneto do? Instead of persuading Kelly to change his position, he jumps in his gyroscope machine and blasts the senator with waves of radiation, transforming him into jellyfish man. Like Ruse, Magneto knows that moral reasoning is impossible; there are no facts in the moral realm. Morality is all about feelings, desires, urges, and impulses. The senator is in the grip of fear, a very powerful emotion that drives his anti-mutant behavior. The point of changing him into a mutant is to replace fear with sympathy, a much more mutant-friendly emotion. Reason is not involved.

Now, it's certainly true that we find ourselves with powerful impulses to act. The thing to see, however, is that if Ruse and Magneto are right, these are not *moral* impulses. For morality is sheer illusion. This has a number of rather devastating implications. For one thing, it implies that there is no such thing as real moral disagreement.[18] If you're cheering on Michael Phelps to his eighth Olympic gold medal, and I'm viciously booing him, we're not disagreeing about anything, are we? Well, that's the way things go in moral disputes—at least, if Ruse is right. Jean Grey says, "Boo!" to mutant registration; Senator Kelly responds, "Hurrah!" They aren't disagreeing. For neither is making a factual claim; they're just venting their emotions. And yet this seems absurd. Anyone who watches the Grey-Kelly showdown can *see* genuine disagreement taking place. Sure, their emotions are engaged, but their *claims* aren't simply emotive eruptions. They're taking opposite positions on the question, "Is forced mutant registration *right*?" Senator Kelly says, "Yes"; Jean Grey disagrees.

Let's say that Senator Kelly decides to switch his position on mutant registration. He's now *against* it. Would you say that was an improvement or not? In the Ruse-Magneto view, it's neither better nor worse. It's just a change. In order to improve your views on any moral issue, you have to exchange the false beliefs you hold about something (e.g., "Slavery is good") for true ones (e.g., "Slavery is bad"). But if morality is all an illusion, then there is no right or wrong, good or bad. There's only cheers and boos. And this means that if Magneto were to switch his position on wiping out humanity, we couldn't say that it was a change *for the better* (only that it was a change). Nor would it be a moral failure if Charles Xavier decided to join forces with Magneto. It's no worse than deciding to hurl abuse at Phelps in the home stretch when you had started out applauding him.[19]

Some evolutionary ethicists have simply swallowed these difficulties wholesale without flinching.[20] What can we say to them? Well, let's temporarily concede that objective morality is an illusion, and that all we have are these "moral" instincts ingrained through natural selection. We obey our instincts because "there is more in it for us than if we do not."[21] Seriously? That sounds more like selfish (immoral) behavior to me. As Ruse admitted (thereby contradicting himself), "Morality means going out on a limb, because it is right to do so. Morality vanishes if you hope for payment."[22] Exactly.

Just think for a moment about Jean Grey's sacrifice for her comrades in *X-Men United*. Knowing that their ship isn't going to manage liftoff before the dam breaks and they are all crushed under its massive waters, Jean slips out the back. She then uses her considerable telepathic prowess to seal the hatch, block the water flow, and levitate the ship to safety. Unfortunately, she can't save herself and perishes in the process. Everyone is heartbroken. I'd say that's worthy of our praise and admiration. But all that the ethical illusionist can say here is that she followed her instincts. How praiseworthy is that? We do it all the time; it's actually pretty easy. If you're like me, when you wake up in the morning, you have a powerful urge to drink coffee. I almost always follow that urge—unless my coffeemaker is on the fritz and my local Starbucks has burned down! Do you admire me for that? I'll bet not. I'm simply acting on my desires. The same thing goes for Jean Grey. If dying for others is genetically hardwired into her, it's neither surprising nor praiseworthy if we find her doing just that.

Indeed, if you think about it long and hard enough, you might wonder (as I sometimes do) whether nature would even bother to select for this sort of behavior. As Darwin recognized long ago, "He who was ready to sacrifice his life . . . rather than betray his comrades, would often leave no offspring to inherit his noble nature."[23] So I'm rather inclined to think that natural selection, if it did anything, would eliminate such self-negating tendencies. But that's beside the point. Our question is, Why should we praise Jean Grey? As the ship clears the water, Logan cries out, "There had to be another way. Why did she leave the plane?" And Professor Xavier quietly replies, "Because she made a choice." It was a choice between two impulses; one propelling her to self-preservation, the other to save her friends. We praise her because she refused to follow the stronger impulse (which was no doubt self-preservation) and instead did what was right.[24] In this situation, I think we could make the case that Jean Grey actually had a moral obligation to give up her life. Only she had it within her power to save the team, and unless she were prepared to do that, they would all most certainly have died.[25] That's what morality's about. At its heart, it involves doing what is right, doing what we ought to do, even (and especially) when it runs at cross-purposes with our most selfish instincts.

What Einstein Can Learn from Xavier

If you're trying to figure out the moral life, Magneto's not your man. "If 'ought' cannot be derived from 'is,'" Dennett asks, "just what can 'ought' be derived from?"[26] Is there anything on which "to hang our deepest convictions" about right and wrong? In one of his lectures on ethics, Professor Xavier tells his class that since mutants have great power, they must ask themselves when the exercise of that power is permissible and when they have crossed the line "that turns us into tyrants over our fellow man." So there's one thing: you can cross the line in ethics; morality isn't an illusion fobbed off on us. A sharp student in the front row then sets a challenge: "But Einstein said that ethics are an exclusive human concern without any super-human authority behind it." Xavier's reply, delivered with a knowing smile, addresses only half the concern: "Einstein wasn't a mutant . . . so far as we know."

Students ask great questions. Sometimes they even stump their professors, who then try to answer different (much easier) questions instead. In this case, the professor dispels the myth that moral rules are merely evolutionary inventions applicable only to human beings. If Einstein were a mutant, Xavier is say-ing, he would have realized that morality is universal; it applies to all of us—mutants and humans alike. He would also have seen that right and wrong aren't subject to the changing tides of evolution, which might have gone in an entirely different direction, making hate our duty and Magneto our supreme moral example.[27] Good heavens! But what about that other concern? Is there a superhuman authority behind morality? Well, if there is, it cannot be anything in the natural world—not gobs of pleasure, evolutionary fitness, or even the character of a mutant as selfless and wise as Charles Xavier!

Anxious about the status of mathematical truths if grounded in either the physical world or human psychology, the German mathematician Gottlob Frege (1848–1925) placed them in what he called the "Third Realm": an absolute and unchanging realm of existence where nothing physical exists and natural selection has no foothold.[28] Would that mean that mathemat-ics was outside the reach of science? It would. And yet Frege wasn't exactly worried about positing a supranatural founda-tion for mathematics. After all, numbers aren't the sorts of things you can study under a microscope anyway. Of course, neither are moral oughts and duties; they completely defy scientific explanation. So perhaps the basis for morality is also beyond the natural. This view is open to the obvious objection that since duties and obligations can be owed only to persons, the ground for morality would have to be personal. No doubt some will see the attempt to invoke a supranatural person as the foundation for morality as obscure—maybe even wicked. (I can hear Darwin, Dennett, and Ruse howling!)

But one man's cost is another man's benefit. If you are already inclined to accept some form of supernatural theism, this suggestion may strike you as not only tolerable, but compelling. Of course, many questions remain. I only wish we could put Professor Xavier back together again for one more lecture![29]

NOTES

1. Daniel C. Dennett, *Darwin's Dangerous Idea: Evolution and the Meanings of Life* (London: Penguin Books, 1995), p. 21.

2. See, e.g., Richard Dawkins, *The God Delusion* (London: Bantam Press, 2006). See also Daniel C. Dennett, *Breaking the Spell: Religion as a Natural Phenomenon* (New York: Penguin Books, 2006).

3. Dennett, *Darwin's Dangerous Idea*, p. 21.

4. Michael Ruse, "Evolutionary Ethics: A Phoenix Arisen," *Zygon* 21 (1986): 99.

5. Charles Darwin, *The Descent of Man: And Selection in Relation to Sex* (London: Penguin Books, 2004), p. 130.

6. Dawkins, *The God Delusion*, p. 217.

7. Dennett, *Darwin's Dangerous Idea*, p. 507.

8. Compare Ruse: "our morality is a function of our actual human nature and . . . it cannot be divorced from the contingencies of our evolution" ("Evolutionary Ethics," p. 110).

9. Actually, *nearly* every member. Magneto, of course, is immune to telepathic attack because of that stylish helmet of his. Well, maybe not stylish, but certainly more pleasing than Xavier's Cerebro headset!

10. Edward O. Wilson, *Sociobiology: The New Synthesis* (Cambridge, Mass.: Harvard University Press, 1975), p. 127, emphasis mine.

11. James Rachels, *Created from Animals: The Moral Implications of Darwinism* (Oxford: Oxford University Press, 1991), p. 67.

12. See G. E. Moore, *Principia Ethica* (Cambridge: Cambridge University Press, 1948), Sec. 24.

13. Sam Harris, *The End of Faith: Religion, Terror and the Future of Reason* (New York: W. W. Norton, 2004), p. 146.

14. Compare Harris: "The practice of rape may have once conferred an adaptive advantage on our species—and rapists of all shapes and sizes can indeed be found in the natural world (dolphins, orangutans, chimpanzees, etc.) . . . From my genome's point of view, nothing could be more gratifying than the knowledge that I have fathered thousands of children for whom I now bear no financial responsibility" (*The End of Faith*, pp. 185–186).

15. Ibid., p. 185.

16. Ruse, "Evolutionary Ethics," p. 102, emphasis mine. By "objective," Ruse simply means "has a basis independent of what we think, feel, or believe."

17. Ibid., p. 102, emphasis mine.

18. The Oxford philosopher A. J. Ayer (1910–1989) made this point in his highly influential *Language, Truth, and Logic*, 2nd ed. (Mineola, NY: Dover Publications, 1952), chap. 6.

19. It's difficult to avoid making value judgments about what's better or worse. For example, Sam Harris laments the fact that "we must now confront whole societies whose moral and political development—in their treatment of women and children, in their prosecution of war, in their approach to criminal justice, and in their very intuitions about what constitutes cruelty—lags behind our own" (*The End of Faith*, p. 145). Harris quite clearly considers our society *better* than others—a value judgment that is ruled out in the Ruse-Magneto view.

20. Ayer is a perfect example here.

21. Ruse, "Evolutionary Ethics," p. 101.

22. Ibid., p. 105.

23. Darwin, *The Descent of Man*, p. 155.

24. Compare Darwin: "In a timid man . . . the instinct of self-preservation might be so strong that he would be unable to force himself to run any risk, perhaps not even for his own child" (*The Descent of Man*, p. 134).

25. You can read more about when self-sacrifice is and isn't our moral duty in Richard Davis, "Beyond the Call of Duty," in *24 and Philosophy: The World According to Jack*, edited by Jennifer Hart Weed, Richard Davis, and Ronald Weed (Malden, Mass.: Blackwell, 2007), pp. 31–42.

26. Dennett, *Darwin's Dangerous Idea*, p. 467.

27. Compare Ruse: "We might have developed so that we think we should hate our neighbors, when really we should love them. Worse than this even, perhaps we really should be hating our neighbors, even though we think we should love them!" ("Evolutionary Ethics," p. 108.)

28. See his essay "Thought," in *The Frege Reader*, edited by Michael Beaney (Malden, Mass.: Blackwell, 1997), pp. 325–345.

29. Special thanks to Caroline and Wesley Davis for their astute comments on an earlier draft.

PROFESSOR X
WANTS *YOU*

Christopher Robichaud

Be an X-Man?

"Help us! Fight with us!" Storm implores Wolverine midway through the first X-Men movie. "Fight with you?" Logan responds. "Join the team? Be an X-Man? Who the hell do you think you are? You're a mutant. The whole world out there is full of people who hate and fear you and you're wasting your time trying to protect them? I've got better things to do."

The choice Wolverine faces is not unique to him. Nor, perhaps, is his attitude. And that's one of the great things about the X-Men narrative. It focuses as much on groups as it does on individuals, giving us a world where superpowerful mutants are not a small-enough minority to avoid bumping into one another and the nonmutant public at large. As a result, mutants confront a complicated political landscape involving many factions that promote radically different agendas. Consider the two most popular mutant organizations: the X-Men, led by Professor Charles Xavier, and the Brotherhood of Mutants, led by Magneto. Under Professor X's guidance, the X-Men are devoted to working with nonmutants in finding mutually agreeable means for peaceful coexistence. Not so with the Brotherhood, which under Magneto's direction seeks to aggressively and often violently oppose the mutant prejudices it confronts. And these ideological differences often lead to bloody conflict between members of the X-Men and members of the Brotherhood.

Now suppose you find yourself in your teenage years waking up one day to discover that you shoot energy beams out of your eyes whenever you open them, or that everyone you touch loses his or her life energy. These really aren't the kinds of things you can keep under wraps. What should you do? Do you join the X-Men or the Brotherhood or perhaps neither?[1] Should your choice be guided only by considerations about what these groups will do for you specifically, or should it also be guided by considerations about what they stand for—the goals they're trying to accomplish and the consequences that pursuing those goals is likely to result in? And what about those goals in the first place? Is the Brotherhood's agenda morally defensible? The X-Men's? Which is better and how do you choose?

It's All about Me—or Is It?

Let's turn to the first set of issues. What factors should mutants take into consideration when deciding whether to go solo or to join the X-Men or the Brotherhood of Mutants? In answering this, let's focus on a specific case, Ororo Munroe (aka Storm). And let's consider her as she was some years ago in the X-Verse. At this point in time, she's doing pretty well for herself. She is, after all, being worshipped as a rain god in the Serengeti.[2] But then Professor X attempts to recruit her to the X-Men team. Ought she to join?

This might not seem to be a very deep or interesting question; we might be tempted to answer it by saying something like, "Well, she should join if she wants to join and she shouldn't join if she doesn't want to, and that's that." But this is too hasty a response. Our question is whether Storm *ought* to join the X-Men. And questions about what Storm—or any of us— ought to do are not, on the face of it, simply questions about what we *want* to do. Wolverine may want very much to extend his adamantium-laced claws straight through Cyclops's visor because of their jealous feud over the affections of Jean Grey. That doesn't mean he should! Then again, there's admittedly something to the idea that our desires matter, at least when it comes to determining what we ought to do. If, for example, Nightcrawler wants to teleport to the roof of the Xavier Institute to watch the sunset, it seems he should do so, all else remaining equal.

Philosophy can help us make progress on this issue by distinguishing two senses of "ought": the prudential sense and the moral sense. When we ask what we morally ought to do, on the one hand, we are asking what it is in our self-interest to do. We are asking about what will promote our own individual well-being; that is, what will bring about something that's good *for us*.[3] When we ask what we morally ought to do, on the other hand, we are asking a question with a larger scope; we're concerned with what will bring about the well-being of *others* in addition to our own well-being and, perhaps, with considerations involving respect for persons' rights and the promotion of social justice. Although this is a rough way of putting the distinction, it's enough to help us see that when we ask, "Ought Storm join the X-Men?" we could be asking either a prudential question or a moral one. Both are important. And our answers to them might be the same. Or they might not.[4]

How Badly Do You Want It, Bub?

It's tempting to think that when it comes to promoting our own well-being (i.e., prudential concerns), what fundamentally matters is what we want to do. In other words, the satisfaction of our desires or our preferences is what constitutes our well-being, and when we ask what we prudentially ought to do, the answer is that we ought to perform whatever action best realizes our desires. If that's right, then the impulsive response to the question of whether Storm ought to join the X-Men—she should if she wants to—is the correct one, at least when we restrict our attention to prudential considerations.

Many contemporary philosophers like this approach. One reason is that preferences are more or less easy to measure, allowing for substantive, specific answers to be given to the question of what a person should prudentially do in a particular situation. For example, suppose we're wondering what Wolverine prefers more: a date with Jean or an opportunity to avenge himself on the people who tried to turn him into the first Weapon X.[5] We could measure his preferences by seeing how much he'd hypothetically be willing to pay to satisfy each, that is, how much he'd be willing to spend to acquire a night on the town with Jean and how much he'd be willing to spend to acquire a night of vengeance against the members of Department K. The choice he's prepared to pay more for is the one he prefers more. Suppose it's the latter. If he then faces the decision of either going out with Jean or avenging himself, and he wonders what he ought to do, prudentially speaking, the answer is that he ought to pursue vengeance. That's what he prefers more, and optimizing the satisfaction of his preferences is, in this view, what constitutes his well-being—it's what's good for him.

Returning to Storm, we can answer the question of what she prudentially ought to do by determining what she prefers more: sticking around and being worshipped as a god, or, um, throwing herself in harm's way all the time by joining the X-Men and fighting, among other things, legions of Sentinels. Put this way, it's hard to imagine her wanting the latter more than the former. But another good feature of this approach to well-being is that it provides a clear goal for Professor X to have when recruiting the likes of Ororo. Simply put, he has to make her really, really want to join the X-Men. The same idea goes for Magneto when he's recruiting for the Brotherhood of Mutants. We therefore have in place the following picture about the relationship between mutants and the organizations that are interested in recruiting them. Groups need to work hard at being desirable for mutants to join, perhaps by making mutants want to achieve the same goals the group wants to achieve, or, if not actually instilling them with these desires, then at least emphasizing that mutants already do want what the groups want, if that's the case. Mutants, in turn, have a prudential obligation to join the specific group (if any) that optimizes the satisfaction of their preferences.

It should be obvious that this desire-based account of well-being is very much an "economic" one. The focus is on preference-satisfaction—getting what you want—and organizations are encouraged to create desires in persons when the desires aren't already there. For some, this guilt-by-association with a marketplace mentality might make them suspicious of this view as an adequate characterization of well-being. Before proceeding, then, it seems only fair to briefly examine the chief rival account of what well-being amounts to.

Once More, with Feeling

Long before the desire-based account of well-being was made popular, a different view, advanced by Jeremy Bentham (1748–1832), among others, had reached the status of orthodoxy.[6] At its heart is the idea that a person's well-being consists in her maximizing her pleasures and minimizing her pains.

Undoubtedly, there is a strong intuitive force to the idea that what is good for us consists in these sorts of experiences. Why is listening to Beethoven's Ninth good for Professor X?

It's good because of the pleasure it produces in him. Why are Mystique's shape-changing powers good for her? Because they allow her to avoid the pain that comes with being socially ostracized for her natural looks. How should Storm decide whether joining the X-Men is good for her? By weighing the pleasures and the pains that would likely result in doing so against the pleasures and the pains that would likely result from making other choices available to her. We can even accommodate the idea that satisfying preferences is good for us. That's true in this approach, but not because the story simply ends there, as it does with the desire-based account. Rather, satisfying desires is good in this view because of the pleasure associated with doing so, and having desires unsatisfied is bad because of the painful frustrations associated with doing so.

With all of the support for this account, it might seem curious that it hasn't remained the orthodoxy. As it turns out, though, it faces some surprising difficulties. We'll analyze just one, which is perhaps the most famous.[7] Suppose that Professor X is able to create something very much like the Danger Room. Its focus, however, is not on simulating combat for training purposes. Rather, it allows him to "plug" a child into the room and have her undergo, throughout the span of her life, exactly the same experiences that Rogue in fact undergoes, no more and no less. To appreciate this case, it's important to understand that the idea of Rogue and this child both sharing the very same experiences should be taken as meaning that they both share the same *mental* life, not that they both *do* the same thing. Obviously, they don't. This example is relying on the well-worn distinction between the way things are and the way we experience them as being; the distinction between, for instance, Beast discovering that his girlfriend is a spy and the rich array of experiences in his mind that accompany that discovery: visual, auditory, tactile, emotional, and so on.[8]

Suppose Professor X, who's been known to have a bit of a dark side from time to time, does plug this child into his experience room. Let's call the girl Eugor and let's further suppose that she never discovers what her situation is really like. So we have Rogue and Eugor, and they share the same mental life. Both have the experience of putting poor Cody Robbins into a coma by trying to steal a kiss from him, of being recruited to the Brotherhood of Mutants by Mystique, of later joining the X-Men, and so forth. Now, if well-being merely amounts to the set of pleasures and pains experienced, then it seems we're forced to conclude that the life Rogue lives and the life that Eugor lives are both on par as far as well-being is concerned; their lives both have the same prudential value. But that seems absolutely wrong! If we had a choice between which life we'd like to live, Rogue's (where the experiences undergone would point to things actually happening to *us*) or Eugor's (where the experiences undergone would be someone else's and would not at all be indicative of what our actual situation was like), it's pretty obvious we'd choose Rogue's life over Eugor's. Her life is better off in terms of well-being. If that's right, though, then well-being can't simply amount to the pleasures and the pains experienced, since Rogue and Eugor share all of those. Hence, there's something seriously amiss with the analysis of well-being in terms of pleasures and pains.

And the remedy, according to many contemporary philosophers, is to embrace the desire-satisfaction account of well-being that we began with. Rogue and Eugor both have the same desires, since they share the same mental life, but Rogue satisfies those desires, whereas Eugor, plausibly, does not. She thinks she does, of course. She thinks that she has done what she wanted to do and has, for instance, joined the X-Men, but in reality she hasn't. It just seems to her that she has, because she's being given someone else's experiences. It is the fact that Rogue satisfies her desires, while Eugor doesn't, that supports the intuitively correct verdict that her life is prudentially better than Eugor's.

Reporting for Duty

We'll stick to the idea, then, that when it comes to determining what a person ought prudentially to do, the best avenue to pursue is the one that focuses on determining what preferences would be satisfied, rather than on what pleasures and pains would result. Returning to the case of Storm, let's assume for the sake of argument that she would in fact optimize the realization of her desires if she joined the X-Men. That's what she prudentially should do, then. But is it what she morally ought to do; is it, at least, morally permissible for her to join the X-Men, if not obligatory?

Let's pause to ask why this question matters. Since we've already assumed that it's in Storm's prudential interest to join the team, why do we have to worry about whether it's morally permissible for her to do so? The answer is that we typically take moral concerns to trump prudential ones. In other words, if it turns out that Storm prudentially ought to join the X-Men but morally oughtn't, then it would be wrong for her to join the X-Men, all things considered. Acknowledging this is particularly important when we consider whether a mutant ought to join the Brotherhood. If it turns out that the Brotherhood engages in morally impermissible activities, then regardless of whether it's in Toad's or Pyro's or Sabretooth's personal best interest to join this group, it nevertheless would be wrong for them to do so, because they morally shouldn't, even granting that they prudentially should.

We're turning our attention, then, to the moral concerns associated with joining a group like the X-Men or the Brotherhood. And it seems reasonable to focus our attention on the goals and the activities of these groups, since doing so will help us determine whether they are acting morally appropriately and, hence, whether joining them would be morally permissible. We'll be using a broadly nonconsequentialist moral framework to evaluate these goals and activities, one that focuses not only on the overall well-being promoted by these groups, but also on whether the groups respect individuals' rights and whether they aim at contributing to social justice. And we'll acknowledge from the start that neither the X-Men nor the Brotherhood of Mutants *always* do the morally right thing or the morally wrong thing. Our interest is in the moral status of the *trends*, or the overall *agenda*, that these groups adopt.

It might still seem perplexing why there's anything here worth exploring. The X-Men are committed to *peaceful* cooperation between mutants and nonmutants, looking for mutually agreeable ways to exist side by side. The Brotherhood is at the minimum committed to aggressive resistance to anti-mutant policies and institutions, the latter of which they take to include most, if not all, governments. If these are the basic agendas of the two groups, is there really any question about which one has the moral high ground?

Absolutely. And that's because the universe of the X-Men is one of perpetual conflict, not simply between mutants, but between mutants and the nonmutant population at large. It is irresponsible to evaluate the agendas these different groups have adopted without acknowledging important details about the world in which these groups are situated. Specifically, with things such as mutant registration acts and, in the film *X-Men: The Last Stand*, a "cure" for mutanthood that ends up being weaponized, mutants are arguably the object of institutional prejudice, at best, and the targets of a potentially genocidal program, at worst. In light of these facts, it's an open question what a morally appropriate agenda is. The path of peace and persuasion is not obviously the morally right one to pursue, just as the path of violent resistance is not obviously the morally wrong one. The challenge is finding a plausible moral principle or set of principles that help determine when it's acceptable to move along the spectrum from peaceful persuasion to violent resistance.

You Say You Want a Revolution

Building on the work of contemporary political philosopher Ronald Dworkin (b. 1931) in his article "Civil Disobedience and Nuclear Protest," we can distinguish three different reasons mutants might disagree with the policies directed against them and then connect each type of disagreement with an intuitively plausible course of action.[9] The least severe kind of disagreement is policy-based. Beast, for instance, might think that the passage of the Mutant Registration Act is simply *bad* policy; it's going to increase tensions between the mutant and nonmutant communities. If that's the case, the morally appropriate course of action is persuasive engagement. Legitimate governments pass bad policies all the time; that doesn't warrant us in taking up arms against them or even forcing them to change their minds. Rather, the responsible course of action seems to be to take certain nonviolent steps, which may include protesting, to force the government to reconsider its position—to pick up the debate again, as it were.

The next kind of disagreement is justice-based. Jean Grey, for instance, might think that the Mutant Registration Act isn't merely bad policy, it's *unjust*. Since this is a more severe complaint against it, there is a more serious type of morally appropriate response available to change it. Persuasive strategies again are permitted, but so, too, are unpersuasive ones, where those are understood as being more aggressive, nonviolent ways of forcing the government to abandon its policy *even if it doesn't rethink its position*. The crucial idea is to force the policy change, circumventing the intervening step of requiring further deliberation. Jean Grey might therefore think it morally appropriate to send out a telepathic "ringing" in people's minds until the Mutant Registration Act is revoked.

The most severe kind of disagreement is integrity-based. Here the complaint against the policy is that it asks persons to do things that violate fundamental moral beliefs. Magneto, presumably, believes that being compelled to register as a mutant is just such a moral affront. This kind of disagreement morally permits most forms of resistance *short* of violent confrontation. For Magneto, then, destroying property or incapacitating government capabilities in the process of refusing to register is allowable.

Notice that none of these disagreements allow for violent resistance. But that is because they assume that the government responsible for the policy in question is still legitimate, even if the policy itself is unwise, unjust, or unethical. It seems reasonable, though, that if the government's policy moves beyond this last category and becomes not simply unethical but outright threatening to the lives of certain persons, then the government has lost its legitimacy and thereby has allowed for morally acceptable violent resistance to take place. The weaponization of the mutant cure is just such a problematic program. For Magneto and undoubtedly most of the Brotherhood, this government action is the equivalent of an enemy country putting tanks and army brigades on the borders of another. It's a clear and serious threat, and it morally permits a violent preemptive strike.

We might resist the seriousness of the supposed threat against mutants by arguing that the weapon in question will not kill them. Perhaps. But it will destroy what is distinctive about them. And that's quite significant. Moreover, it's not even clear that mutants wouldn't be killed, in a sense, by the cure. Some philosophers maintain that being human is essential to us; it's not possible for me to have been a dog or a toaster or the aurora borealis. Mutants, presumably, aren't born human. They're born mutants, who appear to be human but in fact aren't. If that's so, then just as I couldn't be a mutant, any more than I could be a dog, mutants *can't* be humans. So any drug that affects a mutant's biological kind thereby destroys that mutant. In its place is a human who shares a remarkable psychological history with a now-deceased mutant.

Thank You, Professor X, but I'll Make Up My Own Mind

Metaphysics aside, at least some case can be made for the moral appropriateness of the Brotherhood's agenda to a certain extent. This is not to suggest that the X-Men's agenda is incorrect; it's only to cast doubt on it being *obviously* right. Trying to peacefully persuade people who are directly or indirectly trying to destroy you is not necessarily a morally appropriate response. But if that's right, then we return to our original question: what ought Storm to do, morally speaking? And the answer, dissatisfying as it is, is that only she can determine that.

The X-Verse is compelling because of the many shades of moral gray it paints. Mutants are constantly faced with the two crucial questions we've posed here: What group, if any, is it in their best interest to join? And which group, if any, is doing what morally ought to be done? The answer to the first of these questions is manageable for a mutant to arrive at, since, as we've seen, it ultimately comes down to what preferences the mutant has. But the answer to the second of these questions is quite difficult. This is perhaps why the allegiance of so many mutants has switched from one organization to another throughout the history of *X-Men*. Ultimately, we may question their loyalty, but we understand their uncertainty.

NOTES

1. For simplicity's sake, I am *significantly* reducing the number of options available. We know that the organizations in the X-Verse are vast and varied, to say the least. Besides the many official X-Men teams and Brotherhood groups, there are, on the one hand (to name but a few), the New Mutants, X-Factor, X-Force, and Excalibur, while, on the other hand, there are (again, to name but a few) the Acolytes, the Marauders, the Alliance of Evil, and the Mutant Liberation Front.

2. *Uncanny X-Men* #102 (1976) and *Uncanny X-Men* #117 (1979).

3. An excellent survey of the literature on well-being, on which this article draws, can be found in Roger Crisp's entry "Well-being" for the *Stanford Encyclopedia of Philosophy*, http://plato.stanford.edu/entries/well-being/.

4. According to some *contractarian* moral views, the questions of what we prudentially and morally ought to do are permanently interwoven, because self-interest, in these accounts, is in some sense the ultimate ground of morality. We will be assuming that contractarian accounts of morality are false.

5. *Marvel Comics Presents* #72–84 (1991).

6. See Bentham's *An Introduction to the Principles of Morals and Legislation* (1789).

7. What follows is an adaptation of Robert Nozick's experience machine thought experiment, found in *Anarchy, State and Utopia* (New York: Basic Books, 1974), pp. 42–45.

8. *Amazing Adventures* #15 (1972).

9. In *A Matter of Principle* (Cambridge: Harvard University Press, 1985), pp. 104–116.

DIRTY HANDS AND DIRTY MINDS: THE ETHICS OF MIND READING AND MINDWRITING

Andrew Terjesen

The fear of mutants in the Marvel X-Verse often seems irrational, but there is an element of it that cannot be dismissed as easily as racism, sexism, or homophobia. Imagine living in a world where someone can read your thoughts without your knowing about it. Would you trust people to use this power ethically? Would you even know when they did? Imagine living in the Marvel X-Verse where Professor X, Jean Grey, or Emma Frost can alter your thoughts (what we'll call "mindwriting") so subtly that you wouldn't be able to tell whether an idea or an action is your own. Would you trust them to use their powers only when necessary?

If Professor X could tell who committed a crime by reading that person's thoughts, how many people would break the law? And if a group of telepaths could monitor our thoughts and detect when someone was planning to set off a bomb, how much safer would we be? Mindwriting would revolutionize therapy because telepaths could erase our traumatic memories and give us the ability to overcome various psychological obstacles. For all of the benefits, though, would we really want to turn over our law enforcement and clinical services to the X-Men?

This may seem like a very academic exercise—after all, no one can actually read minds (I hope)—but thinking about the ethics of telepathy can be very relevant to our everyday life. Ethics is the branch of philosophy that tries to discover principles that underlie moral behavior. Even though the specifics might be different, the general principles that help us distinguish good uses from bad uses of telepathy should also help us distinguish good and bad uses of optic blasts, adamantium claws, and personal property. In fact, thinking about unrealistic examples can be very helpful, because we don't get distracted by the similarities to our own personal situation that might lead us to approve of a principle just because it lets us do what we already want to do.

Should We Trust Telepaths?

In a very early issue of *Uncanny X-Men*, Professor X tried to get Johnny Storm (the Human Torch of the Fantastic Four) to help the X-Men fight the Juggernaut (*Uncanny X-Men* #13). But Johnny is unsure whether the Professor is really contacting him or whether it is a trap set by one of the Fantastic Four's enemies. His response makes a lot of sense. How does one distinguish the telepathic messages of Professor X from those of Jean Grey or the Shadow King? It's possible that they "sound" different, but how can we be sure of that? Plus, it's possible that telepaths could change their tone to "sound" like someone else. But let's extend this worry even further. Shouldn't Johnny Storm have been concerned that he was hallucinating, rather than receiving a deceptive message?

At this point, we seem to be exploring an epistemological (the name philosophers use for issues of truth and knowledge) and not an ethical question. But there's also an ethical issue behind this one: if we can't be sure about what we "see" with our minds, is it wrong to take actions based on what we think we see? That question is important even for mere mortals like us: when is it wrong to act if we lack certainty about the situation? When Cassandra Nova swapped bodies with Charles Xavier, the only evidence the X-Men had at first was telepathic, based on what Jean said she saw inside of the mind of a comatose Beak (*New X-Men* #119) and Jean's statement that Professor X's consciousness was lurking inside the body of Cassandra Nova (*New X-Men* #122). Admittedly, when Cassandra returned to Earth with the might of the Shi'ar Empire, she made no secret of the fact that she had switched bodies with Charles. But imagine if Cassandra had tried to maintain the ruse. Jean tells her fellow X-Men to attack and subdue someone who looks like Charles Xavier, based on her telepathic impressions of two comatose minds. Is that enough reason for the X-Men to fight with their mentor and the Shi'ar Imperial Guard?

The short answer is no. Jean seems to recognize this as Emma accompanies her inside the mind of Professor X, which is trapped in Cassandra's body (*New X-Men* #121). Of course, we should scrutinize telepathic evidence as much as possible before we take action, but we don't always have the luxury of asking for a second or third telepathic opinion. What do we do when one mind reader tells us that our beloved mentor is about to destroy the planet?

How Do I Tell Whether I'm a Mind Reader?

The larger question is: how does one determine the reliability of telepathy? During the Planet X Saga (in *X-Men* #149), the Cuckoos exonerate Beak for siding with Magneto because their telepathy confirms that he was under a subtle form of mind control. But how can they be sure that they were reading Beak's mind correctly? If they had been wrong, a traitor could have entered the X-Men's confidence and crimes would go unpunished.

Presumably, the Cuckoos would have justified their statement by comparing it to all of the other times they had probed someone's mind. But this only raises a deeper question: how can they be sure that they ever read someone's mind? From Professor X's and Jean Grey's origin stories, we can infer that most telepaths are initially overwhelmed by all of the thoughts they are picking up and they cannot tell who these thoughts are coming from. In that situation, how does one determine that one is experiencing telepathy as opposed to schizophrenia? It seems that telepaths have just as much a reason to be skeptical about their mind-reading abilities.

The difficulty here is a problem that stretches at least as far back as the philosopher René Descartes (1596–1650). In his *Meditations on First Philosophy*, Descartes wondered how he could be sure that other people had thoughts.[1] A well-constructed machine could talk and act like a person without ever having a single thought. This philosophical issue has become known as the Problem of Other Minds, and it has importance for the ethics of mind reading. If we cannot offer any reason for thinking that other people have thoughts, we have no reason to believe that we are reading their minds.

The most common answer to the Problem of Other Minds is offered by the philosopher Bertrand Russell (1872–1970), who argued that we are able to rely on an analogy between our own behavior and the behavior of others to conclude that they are also thinking beings.[2] The same logic could be applied to mind reading: if your mind reading tells you something that predicts how someone will behave and that person then does behave that way, you're probably reading the person's mind. For example, when Professor X was first discovering his mind-reading abilities, he used them to excel at sports

(*Uncanny X-Men* #12). His telepathy told him how the other athletes would react, and he used that information to outplay them—dodging attempts to tackle him on the football field, for example. No single instance would be enough evidence that Xavier had telepathy, but the repeated success in matching what he thought the other player was thinking and that person's actual behavior would be very good evidence.

It turns out that the X-Men could also use the method of analogy to determine the reliability of any telepath they work alongside. Cyclops has good reason to believe Jean when she says that Cassandra Nova has possessed Professor X's body because he has often observed her making statements about what someone thinks that are reflected in the person's behavior. Thus, the X-Men prepare for the return of Cassandra Nova and try to keep Cassandra Nova's body alive while it houses Professor X's consciousness.

How Much Ought the X-Men to Rely on Telepathy?

The X-Men often rely on their telepaths to serve as field communicators, issuing orders and relaying information to the whole team. But there are several reasons to think that a particular command might be unreliable. To start with, something might interfere with the transmission and it would be hard to make out, as often happens with a cell phone. Also, going back to Johnny Storm, there is the possibility that an evil telepath like Cassandra has taken over the telepathic line and is sending incorrect information. Or that the recipient is having a mental hallucination. Moreover, there is some risk in relying on the telepath to correctly read someone's thoughts and intentions. We can make mistakes with our vision and hearing, so why should telepathy be any different? Finally, the telepath must be trusted not to lie.

The appeal of telepathy has always been that it would give us guaranteed access to what people are thinking, but based on these considerations, telepathy is not much different from any method we use in the real world to try to predict how people will act.[3] The situations in which we are morally justified in acting on telepathy will be similar to the situations in which we are morally justified in acting on other fallible sources of information.

When trying to determine the ethics of a particular action, philosophers consider two main things: the results of acting that way and the things we owe (usually called "duties") to our fellow human beings. When Cassandra is in Charles's body, there will be very dire consequences if the X-Men do not treat her as a threat. On the other hand, we owe it to people to give them a chance to defend themselves against the accusation of being possessed; we should not attack them unless they provoke us. If we're going to figure out what the right thing to do is in this situation, we have to weigh the results against our perceived duties. The procedure is straightforward enough, but it is not simple. What weighs more: the deaths of several people or the right to trial by jury?

Some philosophers have favored the principle that the results should be weighed more than our duties. Those philosophers would argue that the danger posed by Cassandra requires one to treat Jean's telepathy as reliable. In general, they would have the attitude that the more dire the consequences, the more seriously we should take flimsy telepathic evidence. On the flip side, the less dire the issue, the more we can hesitate and try to verify the telepathic evidence through other means.

In *Utilitarianism*, John Stuart Mill (1806–1873) says that "actions are right in proportion as they tend to promote happiness, wrong as they tend to produce the reverse of happiness. By happiness is intended pleasure, and the absence of pain; by unhappiness, pain, and the privation of pleasure."[4] The action that results in the most overall happiness is better than any other action, according to utilitarians, and therefore is the right action to take. So, for example, even though it is a violation of our duty not to kill one another, if Wolverine's decapitation of Magneto-Xorn will save the planet, then it is the right thing to do. (And not only because Magneto-Xorn was a terrible retcon.)

Other philosophers are concerned that utilitarian thinking ends up licensing all sorts of things that we would normally call "wrong" (such as erasing your students' memories, as we'll discuss later) just because these produce the best consequences. As a result, they place greater weight on our duties. Duty-based moral theorists, called deontologists, would argue that it is never right for Wolverine to kill anyone, no matter how badly the person acts or how dangerous he or she is to society.[5]

Utilitarians often criticize deontologists for placing too high a value on moral purity. Although Mill never gives a conclusive argument for utilitarianism (he says it is impossible to do so), he points out a simple fact in favor of his theory. Everybody wants to be happy, and this suggests that there is something worthwhile about happiness. To state the idea more broadly: who doesn't want to have good results? If Wolverine's actions save six billion people, how could we call them wrong (especially if the only alternative is the deaths of six billion people)? Utilitarian thinking appeals to a simple moral principle that we all seem to recognize: actions that produce the greater good are better. So, if acting on Jean's telepathy is likely to produce greater good than ignoring her warning, the X-Men should act on it, even if it means running roughshod over the usual rules of civility and the duties of friendship.

Should One *Ever* Mindwrite?

Although utilitarians are willing to say that some things that we normally think of as bad (such as killing or lying) can actually be good, depending on their results, the application of the principle is more complex. Mind reading can involve some bad actions, like mental eavesdropping, but mindwriting opens up a whole different can of worms. An exchange between Polaris and Havok in *X-Men* #478 during the "Rise and Fall of the Shi'ar Empire" illustrates the utilitarian perspective on mindwriting.

> Polaris: Alex? Maybe I'm just noticing because he has to use Rachel to do it now. . . . But did the Professor always just push his will onto people like that?

> Alex: When he had to, I think. Yeah. Like, remember when Jean became the Phoenix? He made that whole airport full of people forget they'd seen any of us. . . . But don't forget the Shi'ar are the people who killed her the first time. And they'd do the same to Professor X if they got the chance. So I don't think him pushing a few minds to get us on our way is that bad, in the grand scheme of things.

> Polaris: No, probably not.

As Havok sees it, violating some "minor" duties to fellow sentient beings is permissible if it prevents even worse things from happening.

Over the history of the X-Men, telepaths have always been a bit cavalier in the use of the mindwriting abilities. Early in the X-Men run, Professor X was quick to take over people's minds in order to get their attention (*Uncanny X-Men* #16) or even to paralyze them (*Uncanny X-Men* #38). For the most part, these actions were done in the heat of the moment, when no other options were available, and the stakes were high. They also were temporary effects that did not seem to cause any lasting damage. Here, the utilitarian would argue that such actions produced the most good, as was the case when Professor X saved Nightcrawler from the people in an angry lynch mob by freezing them (*Giant-Size X-Men* #1).

Now let's consider mindwriting: erasing people's memories. In his early appearances, Professor X regularly erased the memories of the X-Men's friends and foes, such as the Vanisher (*Uncanny X-Men* #2), the Blob (*Uncanny X-Men* #3), Johnny Storm (*Uncanny X-Men* #13), and the Mimic (*Uncanny X-Men* #19). After faking his death, Professor X seemed to have abandoned that practice, perhaps recognizing that the immediate good of the action was not enough. When there are long-term consequences of an action, those must also be taken into account. If the overall result is negative, then the action is no longer morally permissible, no matter how good the short-term results might be. For instance, all of the people who had their memories erased regained them at some point and were pretty angry about what had happened, which caused them to have a grudge against the X-Men. We can also imagine that having your memory erased could create lasting psychological stress, as you cannot explain why you did some of the things that people said you did. It might also lead you to repeat the same mistakes or neglect certain responsibilities. Finally, knowing that there are people out there who can erase your memory might result in mutantphobia or a complete breakdown of social bonds, due to lack of trust in your memory and in other people.

Based on these consequences, utilitarians would advocate more restraint in mindwriting. But deontologists would find even a small number of mindwriting cases abhorrent. Mindwriting takes something personal from us and limits our freedom of choice in some circumstances.[6]

Is There Such a Thing as a Telepathic Affair?

During his marriage to Jean Grey, Cyclops sought out Emma Frost as a counselor to help him deal with his feelings after being possessed by Apocalypse (*New X-Men* #128). Of course, Emma was not the most professional counselor and used her powers to start a "telepathic affair" with Cyclops (*New X-Men* #131). As she described it, they were "only having a thought together" and it was in no way a violation of Cyclops's marriage vows (*New X-Men* #136). When Jean discovered Cyclops inside of Emma's thoughts, however, she was not willing to accept that what happened between Cyclops and Emma were only thoughts (*New X-Men* #139).[7]

From a utilitarian perspective, it does not seem that Emma and Cyclops did anything wrong. The consequences of their "telepathic affair" seem minimal—after all, just thinking about something is not the same as doing something or even intending to do something. The main consequence of the "affair" seems to be Jean's anger (and given that their relationship was already rocky, it did not seem to make things worse in that regard). Jean's response seems out of proportion with what was happening. Had Cyclops merely fantasized about having an affair with Emma, Jean would not have been justified in acting the way she did. As Emma describes it, "in a private thought, where we're safe to explore all those . . . difficult feelings without guilt" (*New X-Men* #138).

But to a deontologist, this example illustrates what is wrong with the utilitarian principle. Just because Cyclops and Emma's affair has no real consequences does not mean that it is okay. To begin with, since they were using telepathy, this was more than a simple fantasy. This was an example of Cyclops sharing a fantasy with Emma, and it was a secret that he was keeping from Jean. Although nothing "really" happened, Cyclops did violate a trust with Jean. Even if he thought there were things that Jean would not understand, he could have respected the trust between them by trying to go to therapy together with her. The deontologist would argue that the relationship between a married couple is an important foundation of what it means to be human, and no greater good could justify discarding that relationship.[8]

A deontologist would also disapprove of Jean's actions on learning of the affair. In her search for evidence of a physical affair (or plans to have one), Jean peers into many of Emma's most private memories and makes her relive them. Afterward, Emma is very upset because Jean, in her words, "saw right through me. She saw the truth and I had no defense . . . and she knows, too. Why did I allow myself to become so stupid and vulnerable . . . " (*New X-Men* #139).

Imagine if all of your thoughts were made public. Would you still be able to function in society? Wouldn't you have difficulty interacting with people who knew all of your fears, hopes, shames, and desires? More important, what would it mean to form a relationship with someone if there was nothing you could share with that person and nobody else? If you have no secrets, then there is no way to build intimacy with other human beings, and intimacy is an important part of the fabric of society. Utilitarians recognize this, to a certain extent, since they would say that most of the time we should not act as Jean did. Unless, of course, a million lives are at stake. To the deontologist, the utilitarian principle misses the point. If my privacy or my trust is always in danger of being violated (if the circumstances get dire enough), it seems that I cannot always rely on them or on other people. In which case, do I really have trust or privacy?

Getting Your Mind "Dirty"

The deontologist's point makes sense: there are just some things that one should not do. But once we accept the deontologist's argument, we open the door to situations where doing the right thing could have extremely bad consequences. So we must ask ourselves, are we willing to get our hands "dirty" to prevent a very bad thing from happening?

Let's assume for the moment that using one's mindwriting abilities to alter people's personalities is a violation of a basic right to independent thought that we all have. In several instances, telepaths in the X-Men disregard that basic right in order to stop a disaster. Jean uses mindwriting to corral humans in an orderly manner when the Shi'ar are attacking the school (*New X-Men* #124); Xavier uses mindwriting to defuse a terrorist situation (*New X-Men* #133); and Emma uses mindwriting to temporarily remove Jamie Madrox's objections to coming to the X-Mansion to discuss a plan to save the messiah baby (*Uncanny X-Men* #492). Xavier's actions seem most troubling as he hands the terrorists over to the police, saying, "I'm a telepath . . . and I can absolutely assure you that none of these men will ever again use violence in the service of abstract ideas." His statement that he had a talk with the lead terrorist and "explained some of the destructive inconsistencies and contradictions in his thinking" seems to be a euphemism for a complete rewrite of the former terrorist's personality. Changing someone's thinking permanently (as opposed to temporarily, in the cases of Jean and Emma) seems to be a gross violation of basic human rights.

Since the terrorist was a complete stranger, it seems a defensible action on Xavier's part, if the danger was great enough.[9] But it would be impossible to defend the same course of action against a loved one—for example, when the Professor tried to keep Amelia Voght from leaving him by making her see his point of view (*Uncanny X-Men* #309). Admittedly, he stopped himself before he went too far, but the damage was done. By exerting control over her mind, he forced her to respect his judgment, even though he would not respect hers. A more lasting action has come to light recently. Professor X admitted that he had erased Cyclops's memory of his brother Vulcan and altered his memories of the island Krakoa in order to hide how Xavier's poor judgment caused Vulcan's death (*X-Men: Deadly Genesis* #6). Cyclops was so stunned by the revelation that he cut all ties with the Professor and asked him to leave the X-Men.

Although Cyclops has begun to forgive the Professor, it is clear that his use of telepathy was viewed as a betrayal of basic trust. And while the Professor's intent was good (to spare Cyclops added emotional pain), his methods required him to get his hands (or at least his mind) dirty. The idea that the "ends justify the means" is often traced back to the political philosopher Niccolò Machiavelli (1469–1527), even though he never uttered that phrase. The closest he comes are passages such as the following:

> a prince, especially a new one, cannot observe all those things for which men are esteemed, being often forced, in order to maintain the state, to act contrary to fidelity, friendship, humanity, and religion. Therefore it is necessary for him to have a mind ready to turn itself accordingly as the winds and variations of fortune force it, yet, as I have said above, not to diverge from the good if he can avoid doing so, but, if compelled, then to know how to set about it.[10]

Machiavelli is not saying that one should violate the rules of morality whenever one has a good intention. Instead, he argues that one should do it only when it is absolutely necessary. Qualifiers such as "especially a new one" show that Machiavelli is thinking of his licensing of dirty hands (or minds) to be very limited in scope. Nevertheless, he seems to accept that we might need to act against fidelity and friendship, which seem to be basic moral principles we all abide by. Yet Machiavelli is not invoking the utilitarian principle and claiming that this is the right thing to do. He admits it is wrong, even though it is necessary.[11]

Trying to Clean a "Dirty" Mind

Professor X's greatest abuse of his powers comes when he completely mindwipes Magneto (*X-Men Vol. 2* #25). In part, this action is an emotional response to Magneto ripping the adamantium from Wolverine's body, but it is also something that Xavier had been considering as an option when Magneto began threatening the entire population of Earth. In mounting his assault on Magneto, Xavier states that "We do not have the luxury of time, or the occasion for nobility. . . . At this point, we are not fighting for the philosophy of a cause, a hope, or a dream—we are fighting for our very survival—and if we do not fight to win, this planet will be irrevocably lost to us." In his justification of his actions, Xavier's reasoning is very similar to Machiavelli's. The mindwipe of Magneto is a necessary action and it is also a wrong one, but it appears to be the only way to save the human population from extinction.

When confronted with "dirty minds" situations like these, philosophers invariably offer one of two responses: use some form of the utilitarian principle to argue that it is not a morally wrong action (so it's not really dirty) or admit that it is morally wrong, but that we must do it. Although the precise line may differ from person to person, it seems that no philosopher would deny that mindwiping (or even killing) Magneto is better than allowing the planet to be destroyed.[12]

Along these lines, Michael Walzer (b. 1935) is a modern political philosopher who argues that there are times when people must get their hands dirty. In a seminal article, he defended the practice, but he also recognized that we do not want to give free rein to "dirty hands" excuses.[13] As a result, he argued that you can be justified in getting your hands dirty, but you should feel guilt about it afterward; the guilt is evidence that you have acknowledged responsibility for committing a "moral crime." Xavier certainly fits the bill; he even seems to want to die in the act of stopping Magneto. Similarly, he seems remorseful about his actions toward Cyclops, which may be why Cyclops is willing to renew a relationship with him.

Some people (usually, staunch utilitarians) criticize Walzer for thinking that there is a real conflict between necessity and morality, but let's consider a different criticism: Walzer does not go far enough in recognizing the wrong of getting one's hands dirty, and he seems to offer no way to ever really get them clean. Once someone has done bad in order to bring about a good, it may be easier to rationalize similar actions in the future. Arguably, Xavier's violations of his friends' trust multiply and get worse over time, as he seems more and more willing to take such actions. Guilt does not seem sufficient to guarantee that Xavier would not find it easier to do the same thing to someone else. Moreover, it is often hard to predict unintended or long-term consequences of our actions. The good we try to do might end up making things much worse—as when Legion tried to assassinate Magneto and ended up creating the Age of Apocalypse.

Xavier's belief that his attack on Magneto is a suicide mission seems to excuse his behavior. The problem is that he survives and continues to make decisions that are morally questionable but that he claims are necessary.[14] If we are going to allay the concerns that make the deontologist disapprove of Xavier getting his mind dirty, then steps must be taken to ensure that he doesn't risk abusing his position. The best way to do that would be for him to voluntarily step down (and even forgo using his powers again) after getting his mind dirty. This might not be a permanent action, but even a period of not abusing his position and powers would send the right kind of signal about the importance of those basic duties that deontologists want to protect. Moreover, if Xavier knew that he would need to step down after getting his hands dirty, this would give him pause and maybe encourage him to seek a different solution. To step down from all he holds dear would be a tribute to those very important moral ideas like trust, friendship, and human dignity.[15]

In a (Real) World Like This

In his investigation of the murder of Emma Frost, Bishop comments that "In a world of mindreaders, shapechangers and disembodied consciousnesses . . . crime takes on a whole new meaning" (*New X-Men* #140). His observation turns out to be quite astute. One of the Cuckoos, Esme, uses her abilities to take possession of one of the X-Men to shoot Emma and creates a false alibi with her sisters and the Beast by altering their memories. In a world where something like that can happen, it is really important to reassure the average person by taking dramatic steps to wash one's dirty mind.[16] Otherwise, mutants such as Professor X, Emma Frost, and Jean Grey really are something to be feared, because they might sacrifice us at any moment to satisfy their notion of the greater good. Likewise, in the real world, the penalties for "dirty hands" must be severe so that the actions of dirty hands are rare.

NOTES

1. René Descartes, *Meditations on First Philosophy*, translated by Donald Cress (Indianapolis: Hackett, 1993). See Meditation II.

2. Bertrand Russell, "Analogy," in *Human Knowledge: Its Scope and Limits* (New York: Simon and Schuster, 1948).

3. Based on this fact, the parallel between relying on telepathically obtained information and relying on information obtained by torture is much stronger.

4. John Stuart Mill, *Utilitarianism* (Indianapolis: Hackett, 2002). The work is not very long and is a good introduction to the utilitarian way of thinking. The quote comes from the beginning of chapter 2.

5. The word *deontology* comes from the Greek word for "binding" and refers to the fact that deontologists think certain duties serve as constraints (or bounds) on the ways in which we can act. Unlike utilitarians, deontologists do not have a single principle they ascribe to. Various deontologists think we owe one another different things and for different reasons. One of the most famous deontologists is Immanuel Kant (1724–1804). Kant laid out his theory in his *Groundwork for the Metaphysics of Morals*, arguing that we have a duty to act on principles that can be universalized (applied to everyone) and to show a respect for human dignity. For a more thorough discussion of Kant, see Mark White's chapter in this volume. For simplicity's sake, we will treat deontology in a general way: as the belief that there is a limit on the actions we can take (no matter what the consequences are).

6. Interestingly, Professor Xavier of the Ultimate Universe refuses to erase the memory of May Parker when she learns Spider-Man's identity by accident (*Ultimate Spider-Man* #105). The reason he gives is very deontological: "It's not my place. People have to live *their* lives."

7. Jean seems concerned that the "telepathic affair" represented an intention to have an affair or that they had already done so, so it may not be the telepathic thoughts that upset her as much as what she thinks they represent. In fact, she rifles through Emma's memories looking for a one-night stand with Cyclops and is calmed down only when Cyclops invites her into his mind and she sees that he rebuffed Emma's physical advances when he had the opportunity. It would seem, then, that Jean would disagree with the idea that there is such a thing as "just thoughts." Yet to suggest that there is no such thing as a "fantasy" seems too strong.

8. If you're still not convinced that Cyclops has done anything wrong, ask yourself what you think of a spouse having "cybersex" without his or her partner's knowledge. Is that cheating? (And be sure to imagine yourself as the spouse who didn't know about it.)

9. Since we do seem to owe strangers less than we owe our family and friends.

10. Niccolò Machiavelli, *The Prince*, translated by W. K. Marriott (New York: Everyman's Library, 1992), chapter XVIII.

11. Elsewhere in the *Prince*, Machiavelli makes reference to using cruelty well. He seems to be recognizing the moral wrongness of the action by using the term *cruelty*. But one also needs to use it well if one's state is to survive.

12. In his article "Admirable Immorality, Dirty Hands, Ticking Bombs, and Torturing Innocents," *Southern Journal of Philosophy* 44, Howard Curzer tries to map out all of the possible positions when it comes to "dirty hands." Those who think that torture is wrong and we should never do it (even if the whole planet is at stake) he calls "Pauline Principle Purists," a reference to St. Paul. But Curzer does not think St. Paul ever ascribed to such an extreme view, nor can he identify anyone else who has argued for it.

13. Michael Walzer, "Political Action: The Problem of Dirty Hands," *Philosophy and Public Affairs* 2, no. 2 (Winter 1973): 160–180.

14. In *X-Men Vol. 2* #28, Jean and Cyclops confront him about his recent decisions (including the Magneto mindwipe) but do not suggest that he step down. In fact, they seem to go out of their way to make it clear that they still trust him and will abide by his decisions.

15. A great example of this is in the film *The Dark Knight* (2008). Batman creates a city-wide sonar monitoring system based on cell phones in order to find the Joker before he kills ferry loads of people. Although the results will be very good if Batman succeeds, it still tramples people's privacy. In recognition of how dirty this gets his hands, he gives this immense power to Lucius Fox (who is not comfortable with it at all and thinks it is wrong but sees the necessity of the situation). In addition, when the danger has passed, Batman "steps down" by designing the system to self-destruct right after Lucius is finished, even though it could help avert other disasters in the future.

16. Although this sounds like strictly utilitarian reasoning, reassurance might also be something that we owe (regardless of the consequences) to those who lack telepathy. Similarly, we might owe it to people not to cause them to live in fear of what we might do.

THE MUTANT CURE
OR SOCIAL CHANGE:
DEBATING DISABILITY

Ramona Ilea

Rogue (excited): Is it true? They can cure us?

Storm: No. They can't cure us. You wanna know
why? Because there's nothing to cure. Nothing's
wrong with you. Or any of us, for that matter.

The cure for the mutant gene developed by Worthington
Labs in *X-Men: The Last Stand* presents a difficult choice for
mutants, and their reaction is, not surprisingly, mixed. Some
line up to receive it. Others protest against it. Many are angry
that people see them as defective, as needing help.

Just as mutants worry that thanks to fear and stereotypes,
the new "cure" will be used to eliminate them, some disability activists worry that stereotypes about disabled people will
lead to their elimination. For example, fear and stereotypes
overwhelmingly compel women to have abortions if the babies
they carry have Down syndrome. Of course, the comparison

between mutants and disabled people might seem strange. After all, mutants are superheroes, whereas disabled people are impaired. But we should question these assumptions. Is disability always a terrible impairment, something to be fixed? And are mutants always superheroes whose powers are desirable traits? How should we conceive of bodily difference? *The Last Stand* illustrates the diversity of reactions to so-called cures, and it challenges viewers to understand both the side of those who long for a cure and the side of disability activists who argue forcefully against a cure.

The Medical Model and the Social Model

When Warren Worthington II publicly announces that his lab has found a cure for the mutant gene, he argues that the mutants' "affliction is nothing more than a disease, a corruption of healthy cellular activity," a medical problem that the cure will fix. Listening to him, Storm angrily asks, "Since when have we become a disease?"

Worthington adheres to a physical model of disability, while Storm subscribes to a social model. In the social model, the problem is not physical. Rather, society creates disability by labeling, maintaining, and closing off options for certain people. Following this approach, the society in which the disabled/mutants live is to blame for the difficulties they encounter. (More will be said later about the social model of disability.) In the medical model, disability (or being a mutant) is seen as an undesirable and painful condition that needs to be fixed.[1] Medicine and science can provide cures and thus enable disabled people and mutants to enjoy all of the freedoms that "normal" people have.

Unlike the social model, which highlights the need for social change—legal protection, increased access, more social support, less prejudice—the medical model assumes that what is needed is more money and support for research into cures for disability. The medical model has been and still is the main way that doctors and scientists view disability. So it is no coincidence that the primary voice for the medical model in the movie is the head of Worthington Labs, a scientist. Consider Worthington's speech:

> These so-called mutants are people just like us. Their affliction is nothing more than a disease, a corruption of healthy cellular activity. But I stand here today to tell you that there's hope. This site, once the world's most famous prison, will now be the source of freedom for all mutants who choose it. Ladies and gentlemen . . . I proudly present the answer to mutation. Finally, we have a cure.

Worthington is not unique in his belief that the cure will offer freedom to mutants who choose it. Believing fervently in a medical model of disability, scientists have tried for a long time to find a cure for deaf people, and they have succeeded with cochlear implants, which are fairly effective if implanted in deaf children at an early age. The "cure" enables the deaf to hear and finally be "normal." Who wouldn't want this? Many deaf people, as it turns out. The reaction from some deaf people has been about as positive as the mutants' reaction to the cure for the mutant gene.

Many disability activists argue that when scientists look for diagnoses and "cures" for disabilities, they send the message that people with disabilities are less worthwhile or, in fact, "defective." Instead, disability activists suggest that disabled people should take pride in their bodies, just as some mutants have argued that pride is the appropriate attitude toward their unusual bodies.

Of course, disabled people form a diverse community, and not all of them have the same reaction. Some deaf and hard-of-hearing people, for example, have not been so quick to dismiss cochlear implants, and even some of those who have initially dismissed them have recently warmed up to them.

Jean, Rogue, and the Medical Model

It is tempting to think that all mutant powers are desirable traits that are radically dissimilar to any actual disability. But some mutant powers are, in certain ways, disabling. Wolverine's power to heal allowed the painful and intrusive implantation of adamantium claws and the coating of his bones, but since Wolverine's hands don't have openings for his claws, he experiences intense pain when they cut through this flesh. Similarly, Cyclops must wear glasses to control the beams of energy coming out of his eyes; he can't even remove them to make eye contact with his girlfriend. Furthermore, many mutants, such as Beast and Nightcrawler, look rather strange; their appearance prevents them from fitting into society.

But the strongest examples are Jean Grey/Phoenix and Rogue. Jean Grey is a class 5 mutant with extraordinarily powerful telepathic and telekinetic powers. Though her powers may seem enviable, *The Last Stand* suggests that she is in some ways disabled by her powers, which she cannot control. Even Xavier, who is so accepting of mutants that he has dedicated his life to leading a school for them, tries to control her "problem." Is he buying into the medical model, as Magneto seems to suggest when he tells Xavier that he is similar to Jean's parents in thinking of her as ill? Is Jean really sick, or is Xavier's "treatment" causing her to be sick? The answer is not clear. What is clear is that Jean has strong recurring headaches, and once the negative side of her personality takes over, she does terrible things that she does not actually want to do, such as killing Scott, her lover, and Xavier, her mentor.

Not surprisingly, Rogue is one of the few X-Men who wants to be cured. She has one of the few disabilities that no amount of societal support can help: she cannot touch anyone without injuring that person. In the first ten minutes of the first X-Men film, we see Rogue seriously injure her boyfriend when she kisses him; later, we find out that he actually went into a coma. When Rogue first hears about the cure, she rushes into Xavier's room. "Is it true? They can cure us?" she asks, her eyes sparking with excitement. She tells Logan, "I want to be able to touch people. A hug. A handshake. A kiss." (One of the main people she wants to hug and kiss is, of course, her boyfriend, Bobby Drake.) Rogue's eagerness to be cured reflects the fact that she views her power as a disability. She cannot touch anyone without absorbing the person's life force, a trait that is useful in combat but not in interacting with loved ones.

The Social Model

Unlike Rogue, many mutants reject the cure and the attitude of those who think that they need to be cured. Disability activists have also been angry that others persist in seeing them as defective. Encouraged by the women's movement and the civil rights movement, the disability rights movement gained momentum during the 1970s. Over time, disability activists and theorists began to challenge the medical model of disability and propose a new social model of disability. Adherents to this model argue that "people with impairments were disabled by a social system which erected barriers to their participation."[2] The social model politicizes disability, stating that the problem lies not in the body but in the social restrictions, "ranging from individual prejudice to institutional discrimination, from inaccessible buildings to unusable transport systems, from segregated education to excluding work arrangements."[3]

Just consider that all of us with poor eyesight would be labeled disabled in a society where eyeglasses and contact lenses were not available. We would not be able to see well, our opportunities for jobs would be limited, and our interactions with other people would be impaired. Similarly, in a society where people have to travel long distances to get firewood, water, and food, athletically challenged people like me (and most Americans) would have difficulty getting materials that are essential to survival, and we would be considered disabled. In the United States and many other countries, though, we rely on tap water, electricity and gas, cars and public transportation, and we do not need to have much physical strength or endurance. So we are not disabled.

Similarly, at schools for the deaf or communities designed for deaf people, being deaf is not a disability.[4] Deaf and hard-of-hearing people can communicate just as well with sign language as others do with the spoken word, and they have rich and happy communities. They are able to thrive and flourish, just as mutants do at Xavier's School for the Gifted. In fact, many Deaf people do not consider themselves disabled.[5] Rather, they see themselves as a cultural group that uses a different language than the majority. Deaf culture is rich with distinct experiences and a complex language. Many deaf parents of deaf children have actually resisted cochlear implants for their children. Such parents want their children to share in the rich deaf culture, and they want to contradict the message that deaf people are defective. Deaf people are disabled in the hearing world only if accommodations are not made for them and if they are discriminated against (just as hearing people would be in a place that used only sign language and where people had negative prejudices against the hearing).

Thus, according to the social model, it is not the physical impairment that causes disability. Rather, "it is society which disables physically impaired people. Disability is something imposed on top of our impairments by the way we are unnecessarily isolated and excluded from full participation in society."[6] If the problems that some deaf and hard-of-hearing people encounter are due to social and institutional causes, we need to change the society, not the people, just as we need to deal with racism and homophobia, not make all blacks white and all gays straight.[7]

Dilemmas

Very early in the film, we are introduced to Warren Worthington's son, Angel, a boy with wings. While this might seem like an enviable mythical power, the boy clearly does not see it this way; the portrayal of him trying to cut off the growth on his back is one of the more gruesome and touching parts of the film. Later, we see Angel as a young man. Underneath his clothes are his large wings, making him look like a hunchback. We can imagine that as he grew up, he was probably picked on by his human peers and he was likely unable to undress in gym class. So Worthington was probably motivated by his son's suffering to work on a cure for the mutant gene. The father seems to subscribe to a medical model: he sees his son's unusual body as a disability, and he sets out to fix it by developing a cure. Although Worthington is, of course, very different from Xavier, there are similarities between the two: Xavier also thought of Jean—who is almost like an adopted daughter to him—as being sick and consequently attempted to use his power to control her.

After the mutant cure is developed, Angel is supposed to be the first to undergo the treatment. At the last minute, however, he changes his mind. Just as Angel frees himself from the medical chair, his father tries one last time to remind him that he wants the cure.

Father: It's a better life. It's what we all want.

Son: No. It's what you want.

Being a caring, loving parent who wants his child to have the best life possible fits the very idea of a virtuous parent. Many parents who want their deaf children to get cochlear implants simply want the best for their children. If indeed Worthington developed the cure to help Angel, he might also be a virtuous parent. But the dialogue indicates Worthington is less interested in the cure because he wants the best for Angel and more because he wants to eliminate the feeling that he is an inadequate parent (for having an "abnormal" child). Or perhaps, like some hearing parents who have deaf children, he simply has overly negative ideas about what being different is like; he cannot imagine living in his son's body and he thinks his son does not want to live in that body either— he thinks that his son wants to be "normal" because that is the only life the father knows.

Implications of the cure for mutant parents are not explored in the movie, except for Angel and his father. We do know how some of the other parents feel, though. Mystique tells the prosecutor at one point, "My family tried to kill me, you pathetic meatsack." Bobby's parents are not so extreme but seem terrified and shocked to find out that he is a mutant. Jean's father refers to her "illness." If these parents knew about the cure, they would likely have made their children undergo treatment. But what would the world of the X-Men be without Bobby, Jean, Mystique, and Angel? And without all of the other mutants whose parents would have chosen to "cure" them of their abnormalities early on?

Although it is tempting to assume that being a mutant is better than being disabled, it's not clear whether this is always the case. How is brutal Sabretooth (or even Bobby or Pyro) better than a child with Down syndrome? Some parents of children with Down syndrome describe them as "stars in an increasingly materialistic world," "without exception magic children" and capable of "unconditional love"; it seems likely that some parents would rather have a child with Down syndrome than a child like Sabretooth, Pyro, or Rogue.[8] In fact, it's possible to think of children with Down syndrome as having special powers: one parent of a child with Down syndrome even said, "[We] often wish that all our children had this extraordinary syndrome, which deletes anger and malice, replacing them with humor, thoughtfulness and devotion to friends and family."[9]

In the ethics of medicine and health-care, the principles of beneficence and nonmaleficence have extraordinary importance. Simply put, the principle of beneficence says that we should do good whenever possible, while the principle of nonmaleficence says that we should do no harm. But applying these principles can be tricky. Is the child being harmed by not getting a cochlear implant? Or is she harmed by getting it? Would Rogue be harmed if she was no longer a mutant? Would Bobby be harmed if he could not create ice? The answers to these questions are not clear. Parents are supposed to look out for the best interests of their children, and most of them do. The reason why they disagree so much is that it is not obvious what the best thing to do is. X-Men fans are attached to all of the quirky attributes of the X-Men, but if we had a child like Beast or Nightcrawler, would we seek treatment for him? What if the child was like Rogue?

The issue is even more complicated when we start considering not only the well-being of the child but also the well-being of society. The principle of utility says that we should act so as to promote the greatest overall good or happiness, taking into account both short- and long-term consequences. Is the cure maximizing the greatest overall good? If Sabretooth's mutant gene is causing him to be brutal and sadistic, would his parents be justified in "curing" him? Assuming that we knew Jean would end up killing her boyfriend and Xavier, as well as a lot of other mutants and human beings, would we be obligated to seek treatment for her?

How we treat those with so-called disabilities shows what kind of values we have. What sort of virtues and principles do we value? How do we conceive of equality, justice, fairness, personhood, good parenting, autonomy, individualism, abnormality, dependence, happiness, freedom, community, duties of the state toward its citizens, or the likelihood of social change?

Curing Oneself of Persecution

When the cure is first introduced, Storm asks, her voice filled with dismay and anger, "Who would want this cure? I mean, what kind of coward would take it just to fit in?" Hank/Beast gives the answer that many parents of children with disabilities would give: "Is it cowardice to save oneself from persecution?" Later, Hank, who is covered in blue fur, points out to the beautiful Storm, "Not all of us can fit in so easily."

Like many disabled people, the mutants are not well understood or well liked by their fellow human beings. In the first X-Men movie, Dr. Grey explains to Congress that the mutants have been met with fear, hostility, and even violence. Much like Rogue and those who line up to receive the treatment, some disabled people draw attention to the pain, the isolation, and the social difficulties they encounter. And unlike Rogue, who can live in Xavier's school, many of them do not live in supportive communities, in places where they can thrive and flourish, surrounded by others like them.

Society is not structured to protect disabled people or enable them to participate in society. Rather, societal structures perpetuate or exacerbate their disempowerment. Our buses, cars, buildings, and household appliances have not been made for people with mobility or vision problems. People with disabilities of all kinds are still often denied the social support that they need, such as appropriate accommodations in the workplace, schools, and public spaces. Furthermore, disability is often accompanied by poverty, especially in the United States, where forty-eight million people are without health insurance. So for many parents, cochlear implants represent the opportunity to save themselves and their children from the persecution that accompanies being different.

The Cure as a Weapon

One way to fight against the discrimination is to work on legislative campaigns that change the social barriers encountered by those with disabilities. *The Last Stand*, however, does not have a sympathetic portrayal of this approach. At a large meeting held by a group of mutants after they hear about the cure, one mutant who seems to be the organizer of the event explains,

"This is about getting organized, voicing our complaints to the right people. We need to put together a committee and talk to the government." Would this approach work? The film suggests it wouldn't. The mutant seems naïve in his belief that the government will change. The dialogue that follows is instructive:

> Arclight (interrupting him): They wanna exterminate us.
>
> Organizer: This cure is voluntary. Nobody is talking about extermination.
>
> Magneto: No one ever talks about it. They just do it. And you'll go on with your lives ignoring the signs all around you. And then one day . . . they come for you. Then you realize, while you're talking about organizing and committees, the extermination has already begun. Make no mistake, my brothers. They will draw first blood. They will force their cure upon us.

In a movie made in the United States, a country whose history includes colonialism and racism, is it a coincidence that Magneto's army—suspicious of the government's intention—is predominantly Hispanic, Asian, and black? And that Xavier's group—much less suspicious of the government, much more willing to work within the system—is mostly white? (Except for Storm, but she is also the one who is most outraged about the cure.) It is surely not a coincidence that Magneto himself is a Holocaust survivor (and he reminds us of this by showing his tattoo soon after he expresses his thoughts about an extermination), and he seems determined to never let anyone persecute him or his kind ever again. It is well known that during the Holocaust, the Nazis euthanized and sterilized those they deemed to be "defective." It is less well known that in the United States, the eugenics movement was also widespread in the early twentieth century. For example, in 1931, almost thirty states had sterilization laws aimed at the feebleminded, and twenty thousand people were forcibly sterilized at that time.[10]

Mindful of this history, some people argue that fetal screening for disabilities and the selective abortion that often follows has the effect of decimating people with disabilities. Many parents, for example, are horrified to find out that their children have Down syndrome; indeed, about 90 percent of women choose to terminate their pregnancies after prenatal diagnoses show that they are carrying children with Down syndrome.[11] Similarly, because implanting deaf children with cochlear implants allows them to perceive sound and learn spoken language, cochlear implants have the effect of eliminating new generations of deaf people. Thus, while some, like Worthington, see technological advances as "cures" and "sources of freedom," others are suspicious, seeing weapons and genocide.

Indeed, although the mutant cure was initially available as an option for those who wanted it, it quickly became a weapon in the hands of the government. First, they use it against Mystique; then, at the end of the movie, against all mutants. But the government is not the only one using it; some mutants also use it against other mutants. Wolverine and Beast stab Magneto with it in attempt to take away his mutant powers.

Stereotypes and prejudices against disabled people abound. People imagine that a disability is a defect, something to be fixed, and they assume that disabled people will be delighted to hear about scientific discoveries that are aimed to cure them. Some of them are. But other disabled people might relate more with Storm, who, on hearing about the cure, argues with pathos that there is nothing to be cured. With extraordinary power, *The Last Stand* calls into question the intuition that the first stance is the only justified one: that mutants, or the "disabled" require a cure to lead meaningful lives. As Storm insists, there's nothing to "cure."

NOTES

1. When I refer to "disability issues," I refer to a wide range of disabilities, of many different kinds: visible or invisible; mental, physical, or emotional/social; inherited or acquired; common or uncommon; minor or severe; and so on.

2. William Hughes and Kevin Patterson, "The Social Model of Disability and the Disappearing Body: Towards a Sociology of Impairment," *Disability and Society* 12, no. 3 (1997): 328.

3. Michael Oliver, *Understanding Disability: From Theory to Practice* (Basingstoke, UK: Macmillan, 1996), p. 33.

4. See, for example, Neil Levy's "Reconsidering Cochlear Implants: The Lessons of Martha's Vineyard," *Bioethics* 16, no. 2 (2002): 134–153.

5. Deaf people capitalize the word *Deaf* to refer to their culture, in a similar way to our capitalization of the words *American* or *French*, while *deaf* with a small "d" refers simply to being deaf.

6. Oliver, *Understanding Disability: From Theory to Practice*, p. 22.

7. For more information on the social model of disability, see Susan Wendell's influential book *The Rejected Body: Feminist Philosophical Reflections on Disability* (New York: Routledge, 1996).

8. Quoted in Peter Singer's "Shopping at the Genetic Supermarket," in *Asian Bioethics in the 21st Century*, edited by S. Y. Song, Y. M. Koo, and D. R. J. Macer (Tsukuba, Japan: Tsukuba University Press, 2003), pp. 143–156.

9. Quoted in Ann Bradley's "Why Shouldn't Women Abort Disabled Fetuses?" *Living Marxism* 82 (September 1995); See www.informinc.co.uk/LM/LM82/LM82_Taboos.html.

10. Ruth Hubbard and Mary Sue Henifin, "Genetic Screening of Prospective Parents and of Workers: Some Scientific and Social Issues," in *Biomedical Ethics Reviews*, edited by James Humber and Robert Almeder (Clifton, NJ: Humana Press, 1984), p. 77.

11. Cited in Rayna Rapp's *Testing Women, Testing the Fetus: The Social Impact of Amniocentesis in America* (London: Routledge, 1999), p. 223.

MUTANTS AND THE
METAPHYSICS OF RACE

Jeremy Pierce

> Mutation—it is the key to our evolution. It has
> enabled us to evolve from a single-celled organism
> to the dominant species on the planet. This process
> is slow, normally taking thousands and thousands
> of years, but every few hundred millennia evolution
> leaps forward.

Professor Charles Xavier makes the statement above about the
evolution of Homo sapiens in the opening monologue of
the first film, *X-Men*. But what about Homo superior? As any
X-pert can tell you, Magneto coins the phrase in the original
1963 comic *X-Men* #1, claiming, "The human race no longer deserves dominion over the planet earth! The day of the
mutants is upon us! The first phase of my plan shall be to show
my power . . . to make Homo sapiens bow to Homo superior!"
 The way many of the X-Men characters talk makes it sound
like mutants are a new species, a new "race" separate from the
human race. Yet this is not the way we use the word *race* most

of the time, when we refer to different groups of people within humanity. Rather, mutants sound like the kind of races we see in *The Lord of the Rings*, where humans, dwarves, elves, and hobbits are all different races.

There's a big problem with thinking of mutants as a race in the sense of a new species, though. There's little in common among mutants besides what's already common to all of humanity. If they're a species, the only thing that marks them as a species is that each has a different mutation. Even the X-Gene, which we'll consider in detail shortly, occurred within the general human population and not only in mutants (until very recently in the comic books, at least, when the Scarlet Witch removed the X-Gene from almost everyone). To coalesce into a species, mutants would need much more in common than one gene or a cluster of genes. A group with an extremely diverse set of mutations isn't coherent enough to be a species. At best, it's the first step toward a new species.

So even though Magneto assigns the name *Homo superior* to mutants, it seems premature to think of mutants as a species. If mutants have not yet formed a race in the sense of a separate species, are they then a race in the same sense as races within humanity (the races that we distinguish based on characteristics like skin color, hair type, and so on)?

Race and the X-Gene

If we want to find out whether Nightcrawler, Mystique, Havok, and Rogue, as mutants, are members of a race, then the first task is to look at some views of what races are.

One view is that races are biological categories based purely in genetic difference and/or ancestry relations. This was probably the dominant understanding of race for most of the time from the African slave trade until the middle of the twentieth century, when many scientists' understanding of DNA led them to reject the idea of race altogether. If races are something like a subspecies of humanity, then we would expect the genetic similarity within each race and the genetic differences between races to be similar to the genetic similarity within, and the differences between, subspecies groups of nonhuman animals (for example, dog breeds).

This turns out to be false, though. Only .2 percent of human genetic material will differ between any two randomly selected people. Only 6 percent of that .2 percent is due to differences between racial groups, which amounts to .012 percent of all human variation. This means that almost all of human genetic variation appears within each racial group. Only a tiny amount of the ways that human beings differ can have anything to do with racial differences.[1]

Compare this with subspecies groups in other animals. The genetic similarity between human racial groups is much closer than the genetic similarity between any nonhuman subspecies groups. Scientists can measure how close two populations are genetically.[2] Gray wolf subspecies are measured at .7. Lizard subspecies a mile apart in the Ozarks are .4. Human populations average at around .15 but can range between .08 and .25.[3] Human populations aren't as genetically distinct as subspecies of other species are, and most scientists don't treat human races as subspecies the way we consider German shepherds to be a subspecies of dog and Rhode Island reds to be a subspecies of chicken.

Now apply this reasoning to mutants. Mutations in the Marvel X-Verse occur in all of the major racial and ethnic groups. For many years, the X-Men comic books didn't give much explanation for why some people are mutants. They simply treated mutants as having some special powers that they were born with (and that often became activated at puberty). The powers were the result of mutations in DNA. By the time of *X-Factor* #1 in the eighties, they began calling it a special X-Factor, which is still pretty unclear but does suggest a common cause to all mutations among mutants. More recently, the comic books and the movie series have both provided a much more specific explanation. *X-Men: The Last Stand* explains mutant powers as coming from one single gene, called the mutant X-Gene. Every mutant has it, and it somehow causes his or her powers, although we're not given any more explanation than that in the movie. Warren Worthington II, the father of the Angel, develops a method of suppressing the gene and neutralizing the special abilities it leads to.

Recent comic books supply a little more information, which is relevant to whether mutants are a race. Several facts are important. First, the X-Gene does not appear only in mutants. Many mutants received the X-Gene from their nonmutant parents. The X-Gene, which occurs on the twenty-third chromosome, is not activated in every person who has it. A group of ancient aliens, called the Celestials, seeded the gene into the population, and it was passed on until the current generation. Normal humans have had the X-Gene for quite a while without being mutants.

The situation is also more complicated than simply one gene explaining all of the varied mutations, which would be scientifically implausible. In *House of M* #2, the Beast explains mutant abilities as coming from a cluster of genes, rather than just one, and perhaps that cluster of genes is what the term *X-Gene* actually refers to. The Beast describes the X-Gene in *Astonishing X-Men* #25 as releasing "exotic proteins" that cause other cells to produce mutations. So the mutations themselves are not directly due to the X-Gene, and that's why the X-Gene can be the same gene or cluster of genes while producing such radically different mutations in all of the different mutants. Something else determines exactly what mutations occur. The X-Gene, if activated, only explains why the mutations occur at all. If not activated, the gene simply sits there not doing anything, except getting passed on to the next generation.

Mutants and Biological Race

So, what do mutants have in common genetically that distinguishes them from the rest of humanity? Not the X-Gene, apparently, since that's been present in humanity since the Celestials planted it in our ancestors. Even so, one gene or a cluster of genes is much less significant than the number of genes that affect the traits we usually associate with a race. And as we've seen, it's hard to see race as a biological category because the variation among members of a race is not much less than the variation among all humans. Just think about the variety of racial backgrounds and national origins among mutants. Storm is from Kenya; Forge is Native American; Sunfire is from Japan; Rictor is Latino; Colossus and his siblings are from Siberia; Gateway is an aboriginal Australian; Wolverine is from northern Alberta in Canada; Cannonball and his siblings are from Kentucky; Banshee is Irish; Jubilee is Chinese American; Wolfsbane is Scottish; Apocalypse is from ancient Egypt; and Arclight is Dominican.

Mutants come from virtually every racial background, and thus the group of all mutants is quite diverse genetically. Now add all of the genetic modifications that cause their powers, and you find far more diversity than occurs in any one race. Mutants are even farther from being a biological subspecies than races are.

In addition, mutants aren't self-contained or reproductively isolated, even if they might end up like that in the future (for example, in *Days of Future Past*, which we'll consider shortly). If races are biological, then they must constitute some kind of genetic population. In the first generation of large numbers of mutants, you simply don't have a population, even if you might later end up with one. Also consider that mutants do not reproduce only with one another, but with humans, too; this makes it nearly impossible to see mutants as a biological race.

One view, now very much out of favor but once highly influential, took races to have what might be called biological essences. The members of any race have a biological essence that they share with all other members of their race. These essences were supposed to have explained why certain visible features were common to each race but different from those of most other races. Contemporary science has especially refuted the idea that these essences give rise to differences in intelligence, moral character, and so on.

Not many scientists accept this view about race today, but if you found a population with a biological essence, you might see it as a reason for thinking of that population as a subspecies race. The X-Gene does at first seem like a good candidate for such a racial essence, except that many humans also have it. Apart from that, it's hard to see what might be a racial essence for mutants. Since mutants don't come from any common stock, the only thing they have in common is that they each have a power.

There is the X-Gene itself, but, as we've seen, that wouldn't distinguish mutants from humans. The best we could say is that *activated* X-Genes could be a very minimal biological essence. But a racial essence in the classical sense was supposed to explain *all* of the distinctive characteristics of a race, and the X-Gene alone doesn't do that. So, for all of these reasons, mutants are not a biological race. But since races probably aren't biological anyway, maybe that's not a serious problem. If races by definition are biological, and if there are no biological races, then there are no races.

Mutants and Social Races

Many contemporary philosophers take a different approach to race, however. They reject race as a biological category but insist on race as a social reality. If this view is right, then perhaps mutants are a social race, even if they're not a biological race.

A lot of what we mean by race isn't biological at all. People base racial categories on things that result from biological facts, such as physical appearance. But if we were to use similar methods of categorizing mutants, we would end up placing the Beast into the same race as Nightcrawler, because he is *blue and furry* (sometimes, anyway) and not because of any similarity in their powers. And once we as a society begin to categorize people along such lines, we tend to include cultural differences that aren't determined by DNA and ancestry alone. For example, without any biological basis, some races have been thought of as having moral, intellectual, or physical capabilities and deficiencies. Stereotypes thus emerge. Having blue fur, pointy ears, and a tail doesn't make Nightcrawler satanic, and the mutation that led to his fur, ears, and tail has nothing to do with his religious views. In fact, he is a pious Roman Catholic who almost became a priest. Having dark-colored skin, fur, horns, or wings doesn't make someone religious or nonreligious, smart or stupid, moral or immoral, cowardly or courageous. Racial prejudices have conceived the people we call black as intellectually inferior. Similarly, prejudice against mutants suggests that they are to be feared because of how they look or what they can do, without any genuine basis in reality.

So, what sense can we make of the social reality of race? We all accept the reality of categories that don't have their basis in biology or DNA. For instance, when we talk about politics, we refer to certain people as liberals or progressives and others as conservatives, libertarians, Democratic socialists, and so on. When we come up with such categories, we are picking out genuine features of the people we're classifying that don't depend on genetics. Granted, there are complicating factors: we sometimes oversimplify, some people defy categorization, there are borderline cases, and there are categories that might be useful in explaining voting behavior or political philosophy that we haven't thought to put a name to. Nevertheless, things that people do and things we think about people's political beliefs allow us to categorize them usefully.

So, too, with races. We can often identify someone's race by looking at him or her, at least with most racial classifications in the United States. (This was not always so. For example, Irish people were sometimes classified as black in the nineteenth century.) The features we use to identify someone's race may well have been determined by his DNA—for example, skin color. But we need to realize that historical and social factors partly determine which biological traits we've picked out as ways of determining who is in what group. The populations that developed into the groups we call races were different according to skin color, hair type, and bone structure and as a result suffered much wrongful treatment. Imagine if their differences had instead been in height, right- or left-handedness, and whether their earlobes were attached. We would still have something like races.

Along these lines, you could imagine a society that turns mutants into a social race. We see the beginnings of isolation in several X-Men stories. For example, in *Days of Future Past*, we're given a possible future in which mutants are hunted down and put into concentration camps, where their powers are inhibited. We're not told much about the details, but we could certainly expect such a world to lead to mutants becoming a separate group, whose mutations might pass on to the next generation if they're allowed to breed and whose social separation allows them to be treated as their own group with a biological element common to all of them (having an activated X-Gene that causes mutation).

Another example involves the island nation of Genosha, which secretly rounded up mutants to be reconditioned and genetically manipulated in order to serve Genosha as slaves, with their names and identities removed and their resistance to enslavement replaced with a desire only to serve. Mutants weren't allowed to breed on their own in the story, as writer Chris Claremont told it in the comic books. Instead, their genetic information was combined with the genetic information of

others to produce ideal mutant slaves in the next generation. Whether this would satisfy the ancestry requirement
some people want to include probably depends on what people
might mean by ancestry, but the case could easily be modified
to produce a situation more like *Days of Future Past*.

One reason to consider the Genoshan nation is that
Claremont worked into the story several features that connect it
nicely with historical and current features of race. In Genosha,
mutants have a derogatory name—*Genejoke* (*X-Men* #235).
Genoshans refer to someone testing gene-positive and thus
qualifying for slavery as mutants (*X-Men* #236), which parallels
the negative treatment of people who are HIV-positive.
Although that's not a racial issue, it does involve similar kinds
of negative treatment, and if enforced segregation of any races
were to occur nowadays in a technologically developed society,
it almost certainly would involve gene testing.

Claremont puts an unintentionally ironic race comparison
into the words of an official Genoshan informatape promoting Genosha in *X-Men* #237, which says, "Ours is a free land,
where people are judged by deeds and character, not the color
of their skin." The irony of a nation that enslaves mutants
pointing out that it doesn't discriminate on the basis of skin
color is very effective in communicating that what's going on in
Genosha is similar to what's far too often happened along racial
lines. Indeed, mutants, like some racial minorities, are not even
thought of as people. As the Carol Danvers personality, who
controls Rogue during part of the Genoshan storyline, says,
"Effectively, they become extensions of their jobs—perceived
not as people any longer but organic machines" (*X-Men* #238).

Of course, mutants have been called Muties for a long
time in the comic books, and the fear of mutants by some in
the general populace was Magneto's original motivation for
wanting mutants to rule humans. But the Genoshan case is
particularly vivid in the comparison it invites with the treatment of slaves in the United States.

The Difference between
Mutants and Race

So, are mutants a race? One difficulty is that Bishop is black, but he's also a mutant. Cable is white, and he's a mutant, too. Every mutant has a racial background. Being able to talk about diversity of race is one thing, but being able to talk about diversity of race among mutants means if mutants are a race, then it's not the sort that prevents you from being a member of more than one race. It's not as if Cable is mixed race, with one parent who is a mutant and another who is human. Both of his parents are fully mutants and fully white. Of course, it's possible that someone could be both black and white. So being both black and a mutant doesn't mean absolutely that mutants aren't a race.

In addition, races are usually thought of as being identifiable by visible characteristics. You might call powers visible, since once you know about the power, you might guess that the person is a mutant (although in the Marvel Universe we should remember that people can have powers without getting them because of a mutation, such as Spider-Man or the Hulk, who are both superpowered because of radiation). Then again, some powers could be so insignificant that we might miss them, and even the person who has them might never discover them. This feels like it's pushing the helpful analogy between mutants and race.

Mutants as Racelike

On the other hand, we often speak loosely and use certain classificatory terms in an extended or even metaphorical sense. For example, people sometimes refer to coworkers as family. They aren't related, and in the primary meaning of the term *family*, they simply aren't one. But it has become acceptable to use the term to describe people who are like a family in their closeness. Public debate over same-sex marriage has sometimes centered on whether a couple of the same sex should call their relationship a marriage, when marriage has traditionally been a relationship between a man and a woman. Yet we frequently speak of bonds as marriages, even if they have nothing to do with a man and a woman. William Blake (1757–1827) wrote a book called *The Marriage of Heaven and Hell*, and he didn't think of heaven or hell as a man or a woman.

So, are comic book characters just speaking loosely when they use racial language with reference to mutants? One indication that they might be is that they move back and forth between referring to mutants as a species (using the label *Homo superior*) and calling mutants a part of humanity. Magneto does this in several of his appearances, even within the same comic book issue, and he does it in the films as well. So there might be some truth to what they're saying, if we don't take it as literally as the writers may have intended it. X-Men stories draw a helpful analogy with the racial problems in our society, even if mutants aren't really a race.[4]

NOTES

1. K. Anthony Appiah's "Race, Culture, Identity: Misunderstood Connections" in K. Anthony Appiah and Amy Gutmann's *Color Conscious: The Political Morality of Race* (Princeton, NJ: Princeton University Press, 1996), pp. 30–105.

2. This measure is called *heterozygosity*.

3. See, for example, Tina Hesman, "No Trace of Race: Genome Sequencing Project Proves Nothing Biological Separates Peoples," *St. Louis Post-Dispatch*, June 4, 2003.

4. I'd like to thank Winky Chin, Jonathan Ichikawa, Avery Tooley, and the editors of this volume for help at various stages of development of this chapter.

WAR, TECHNOLOGY, DEATH, AND MUTANTKIND

MUTANT
PHENOMENOLOGY

J. Jeremy Wisnewski

Good. The title didn't scare you away. You made it into the chapter and into an exploration of what it's like to be a mutant—into "mutant being-there," as I'll call it. As you'll see, I'm skeptical that we can know what it's like to be a mutant. In this respect—please try not to get mad—my title is really false advertising. But don't go anywhere. I do think we can learn a lot about *ourselves* if we try to figure out how mutant consciousness might be different from our own. Trust me when I say that phenomenology is worth all the effort.

Phenomenology is a philosophical movement that has its roots in late-nineteenth- and early-twentieth-century thought, in thinkers such as Edmund Husserl (1859–1938) and Martin Heidegger (1889–1976). It is a systematic investigation into *phenomena*—that is, into the way things present themselves to us in experience. Both Husserl and Heidegger thought that things present themselves as they really are in our experiences, but that we often distort the truth that experience presents.

We impose particular theories onto phenomena and insist that they conform to our preconceived notions about how the world is. To do phenomenology is to try to set aside our preconceptions and to uncover the actual *being* of things as they reveal themselves to us. In a way, it is to see past our preconceptions into the heart of things—past, for example, Hank McCoy's beastly blue exterior and into what is really presented to us there: a being not like us, to be sure, but also strangely familiar.

But I'm getting ahead of myself here (something Madrox is particularly good at).[1] Phenomenology is also interested in uncovering the structures in which experience occurs. As thinkers such as Heidegger and Maurice Merleau-Ponty (1908–1961) have argued, by clarifying the way that all experience presupposes embodiment in the world, we can clear away some significant sources of philosophical error. If, in investigating the structure of experience, we come to see that all experience presupposes our being embodied, it won't make sense to ask the question (as René Descartes [1596–1650] once did): how do I know I have a body? Likewise, if our being is, as Heidegger said, a Being-in-the-world—that is, if having experiences involves already presupposing a context of meaning within which we act—there's really no place to ask questions (again, as Descartes once did) about whether there is an external world. In doing phenomenology, we can thus learn about the world as it is, and we can do some philosophical house-cleaning to boot, highlighting what kind of philosophical questions rest on silly misunderstandings of the world around us.

Sounds fancy, I know. And it is. What adds to the already rather high level of fanciness here is that the X-Verse presents a *Marvel*ous site for phenomenology by playing with things that we all take for granted in encountering the world: touch, death, companionship, and the possession of immense power (to name only a few examples). By allowing us to see what life might be like without our substantial limitations, we also see what our own phenomenology involves.

Mutant and Human Being-There

Merleau-Ponty claimed that our bodies are our point of view on the world.[2] This means that my body is not something that I *have* but something that I *am*. My body should not be confused with "one of the objects of the world."[3] Indeed, it *isn't* an object at all. It is *me*. The way our bodies occupy the world is, in turn, the grounding of all of our awareness. As Merleau-Ponty strikingly noted, "Consciousness is in the first place not a matter of 'I think that' but of 'I can.'"[4] My body is "the nexus of living meanings": it is that through which I have a world at all. The implication of this is clear: if our bodies were different, so, too, would our understanding of the world—our very consciousness—be different. The world we occupy—the things we take to be significant, the way we understand and interact with these things, and much more besides—would be unlike anything we currently know.

Mutants exist in a way that we do not. They occupy the world in a way that we can only imagine. Our being-there (that is, our "concernful" existence in the world) is characterized essentially by some rather stunning things. We are mortal. We have bodies that are, in many ways, the very prisons that house us: the limits of our bodies help determine how we encounter things and how we judge the meanings of things. Our significant limitations mark the contours of our understanding of the world, as well as of one another. If we were otherwise, our interactions would differ dramatically.

The X-Verse allows us to see this in vivid detail.

On Occupying Space, Phenomenology-Style

For most of us, the space we occupy is never much of an occasion for reflection. But space (not "outer space," of course, but three-dimensional space) actually infiltrates everything about our perceptual experience.

In one sense, of course, this is totally obvious: if there were no space, then we couldn't actually have experiences of things in the world or of things that were not us. After all, for me to experience something, I must be able to distinguish that thing from *myself*. If I can't, then I won't be able to experience that thing. For example, how many Wisnewskis are there below? (I would have preferred to use an actual mutant, but copyright has powers that exceed even those of the Dark Phoenix!)

Now, assuming you can count, you'll say there are five. Imagine that I insist there are actually six thousand photos of Wisnewski here, but that these six thousand photos occupy exactly the same positions and hence cannot be distinguished. Obviously, this doesn't make much sense. The only way to know that there are more than five photos would be to actually be able to distinguish at least one more.

But there are bigger photos to fry here, to mix metaphors shamelessly. As you read this, space informs what you're doing in a much more personal and pervasive way. You know where your fingers are in relation to your legs. You understand this book as blocking your view of the world beyond the book (at least partially). You know that, as you turn your head, there will be a world waiting to fill your experiential field or that, if you were to move your hand *behind* this book, there would be space in which you could *move* your hand. As you look at the Wisnewski pictures, you know each one is a picture of a person moving in space, with a world on all sides of him. You know it as much as you know that there is a world behind you now, even if you do not bother to look at it.

Our consciousness is spatial in this deeper existential sense. Our understanding of things, and of ourselves, is an understanding of ourselves as *haunting* space.[5] We don't just occupy space, like the book you hold in your hands. We permeate it, and through it, we understand our world: we are capable of walking around in it, finding food, making friends, and reading X-Men comics. To exist in space as we do is central to what we are and how we understand the world.

And one of the fundamental features of our existence in the world—our existence as embodied beings in the world—is our limitation. We cannot do everything. Our bodies deny us at every turn. I cannot fly, I cannot go without food or sleep or connection with others. The limitations we face in the world are the result of how we *are* in the world, of the kinds of bodily existence we have. The way I understand things, such as bullets, sharks, and angry killer bees, reflects my bodily reality: these things can kill me. The way I understand the X-Men themselves is informed by my bodily permeation in the world: these mutants show me what I cannot do and thus reveal to me what *my* bodily "being-in-the-world" is like.[6]

Whatever else is true of mutants, phenomenology teaches us this: their understanding of things is fundamentally different from our own. They *live in their world* in a way that we simply cannot. To be a mutant—to have a body without the limitations that we have (or with different limitations)—is to be connected to the world in a radically different way. If consciousness is a matter of "I can," as Merleau-Ponty said, then mutant consciousness lives in a world well beyond the human.

On Occupying Mutant Space

Imagine that I have locked myself out of a building and need to get in desperately. My entire understanding of the situation reflects what I am able to do and what I am not able to do. Certain possibilities never occur to me (for example, to walk *through* the closed door, as Kitty Pryde might). Indeed, for a mutant who can walk through walls, the very meaning of "walls"—the very significance these things have to her in everyday life—must be totally alien to us. We understand walls as things that keep us out and in, things that mark boundaries, literally and symbolically. To be a being unaffected by walls is to be more than merely a being with a power—it is to be a being who lives in a different world altogether, one where there simply *are not walls* (at least, in the ways that we understand them).

Almost everything in our lives is a reflection of our abilities and limitations. If I find myself stuck under a heavy object or in a prison or on a high precipice, my finitude (my limitedness) is painfully apparent to me. This kind of finitude *makes me what I am*. I am constituted by what I can and cannot do. To be human is to be weak, subject to gravity, and restrainable with relative ease. Mutants such as Juggernaut, Angel, Strong Guy, Colossus, Madrox, and Nightcrawler, to name a small subset of the vast array of mutancy, inhabit worlds where such finitude is absent, and it is the absence of this finitude that allows us to see how much our bodies dictate about what we understand.[7]

The space I exist in is one that must be moved through gradually. Nightcrawler's ability to teleport makes the way he haunts space completely unlike mine—so much so that Nightcrawler's "space" just isn't the sort of space I can ever *really* understand. So, too, with Angel and Juggernaut: to be able to fly at will or to gain such momentum that nothing can stop me is to possess a mastery of finitude that would change the entire experience of my world. Madrox, too, presents a possibility that gnaws at the imagination: to be able to occupy multiple spaces at once, and to confront oneself as something that is *external to oneself.* These possibilities present the phenomenologist with data to be explored, ways of being in the world that are so fundamentally different from what we are able to do that they force us to look more closely at what our own being-in-the-world presupposes.

Rogue's inability to touch others without hurting them allows us to examine something else we routinely ignore, perhaps only because it is as basic to our experience of the world as things can get. Indeed, the importance of touch is something that we do not often reflect upon, but its absence is enough for Rogue to choose to give up her mutantcy in *X-Men: The Last Stand*. Seeing Rogue's torment calls attention to our own primordial need for contact with other living beings.

Consider this: young human children can actually die from lack of physical contact with other persons.[8] Though we might not understand (at the conscious level) how central touch is to our everyday lives, there can be no doubt that it is absolutely essential to our understanding of ourselves and our connection to other persons. We are indeed social animals, as Aristotle (384–322 BCE) recognized—so much so, that our very lives depend on being in physical contact with those around us. We express ourselves, as well as our relations to others, through the medium of touch and hence through our bodily being-in-the-world. To live Rogue's life is to live a life that is in many ways *not human*.

Death and Apocalypse, Mutant-Style

For philosophers such as Heidegger, our mortality is perhaps the most important feature of our finitude. Death is the only thing, Heidegger contended, we must truly do alone. The fact that we will not live forever allows us to distinguish ourselves from everyone else. Although I might like to lose myself in the views and actions of the masses, my own impending death will not allow me to. At the end of the day, I, too, must die, and this is something that no one can do for me. The fact of mortality is a central fact of human life and, in a certain respect, gives meaning to absolutely everything else.

Here things get very interesting in the X-Verse. In our world, death is not something that *gets undone*. Death *is* the end, not simply a pause in the action. This is part of the way we generally understand death, even granting the popularity of that one zombie story where the guy gets up after three days and leaves his tomb.[9] But death is rather different with the X-Men. Consider our mutant friend Apocalypse.

Apocalypse is five thousand years old—he is the first mutant, having his origins in ancient Egypt, under the name En Sabah Nur.[10] As a shape-shifter, he can change any part of his body into a weapon. This means, essentially, that he *is* his body armor, his shield (when he wants it), and any other weapon he happens to have. He is a living weapon, and one that seems nearly impossible to kill. Notice that I say "nearly." In one story arc, he lives until the thirty-ninth century (that's a total of seven thousand years, folks!), when he apparently dies at the hands of Cyclops, Phoenix, and teenage Cable.

Is Apocalypse mortal? Well, certainly not in the way that I am (or you are, reader). Our meager eighty years is barely comparable to the seven thousand years of this mutant. To see so many generations come and go is virtually unthinkable to us. To have the memories of ancient civilizations piled endlessly on one another would be a form of consciousness unlike anything we can realistically imagine. The sense of history that *is* Apocalypse would render his world vastly unlike our own.

But things are actually more complicated than this. We know that in the X-Verse, death can be (and often is) a temporary state. There have been plenty of storylines where we were sure Apocalypse (or Jean Grey or Cyclops or Wolverine) was dead. We also know (from alternate timelines) that visions of the future, such as the one where Apocalypse dies, cannot be relied on. As Charles Xavier reminds us, we've "seen too many conflicting futures to accept only one as inevitable."[11] Indeed, as we see in M-Day, Apocalypse attempts to flee into death, only to be immediately resurrected by the Celestials from which he derives technology. As they say, *"We cannot let you die. Not yet. It is time, Apocalypse . . . it is time."*[12]

In a world where death is so . . . well . . . temporary, can there be anything like human understanding? Once again, the mutants present us with a powerful example of how different things might be, and it is this very example that allows us to reflect with nuance on what our own world is actually like. Death pervades all that we do, and its denial is crucial to our proper functioning. As philosopher and psychologist Ernest Becker (1924–1974) said, "Everything that man does in his symbolic world is an attempt to deny and overcome his grotesque fate."[13] Furthermore, "all culture, all man's creative life-ways, are in some basic part of them a fabricated protest against natural reality, a denial of the truth of the human condition, and an attempt to forget the pathetic creature that man is."[14]

The need to hide from our own inevitable fate by constructing elaborate systems of meaning is simply not present in Apocalypse and other death-defying mutants. Apocalypse is interested in engineering wars among mutants, mutants and humans, humans and humans, and others. The fear of mortality does not inform his actions in the way that my own fear of mortality informs mine. Perhaps I read X-Men to imagine a deathless world. Perhaps I attend church to build up hope of a life after this one. Perhaps I write this chapter in the silly belief that I will live on through my writing.

Now I ask you: would Apocalypse ever write a chapter for a book on X-Men? Is Apocalypse like us: scurrying around, denying that we are decaying hunks of flesh that are rushing headlong into the abyss? Of course not. Apocalypse doesn't need to deny death. He just needs to kick ass.

What It's Like to Be a Mutant

I want to understand what it's like to be Wolverine, Apocalypse, Magneto, and the rest of mutantdom. But given how weak and frail I am as Homo sapiens, it's doubtful that I ever will. The way I haunt the world, thrown into a finite body that is hurtling toward death, makes this just about impossible. Even if I imagine being a mutant, I am merely imagining *myself* being that mutant, rather than imagining a *true* mutant.

The contemporary philosopher Thomas Nagel famously raised exactly this problem with the far less interesting example of bats:

> But bat sonar, though clearly a form of perception, is not similar in its operation to any sense that we possess, and there is no reason to suppose that it is subjectively like anything we can experience or imagine. . . . In so far as I can imagine this (which is not very far), it tells me only what it would be like for *me* to behave as a bat behaves. But that is not the question. I want to know what it is like for a *bat* to be a bat.[15]

And I want to know what it is like to be a mutant, but my own embodiment seems to preclude this possibility. Nevertheless, even if I cannot know what it is like to be Kitty Pryde running through walls or Nightcrawler teleporting or Apocalypse being oblivious to mortality, I am still offered an occasion to reflect on my own being-in-the-world through these mutants and to see exactly what my limits are and why these are so important to my understanding of myself and the world around me.

In the end, perhaps I can only imagine what *my* mutantcy would be like—how my being-in-the-world, and hence my understanding of both myself *and* the world, would be altered by the activation of my X-Gene. This makes things better than trying to imagine bats, and, I daresay, much more interesting.[16]

Although I can't envision what my understanding would be like, I'm fairly sure I'd look like the image on the next page.

Even in phenomenology, one can dream. . . .

NOTES

1. For more on Madrox, please see Jason Southworth's "Amnesia, Personal Identity, and the Many Lives of Wolverine," chapter 2 of this book.

2. Maurice Merleau-Ponty, *The Phenomenology of Perception*, translated by Colin Smith (London: Routledge Press, 2002), p. 81.

3. Ibid.

4. Ibid., p. 159.

5. The term *haunting* comes from Merleau-Ponty.

6. I know, that's a mouthful. The term is Heidegger's. It means to exist in a context of meaning—to exist among things and projects that provide life with a sense.

7. Wolverine provides one of the clearest cases of getting beyond finitude, although his escape is nowhere near as complete as we might expect. Wolverine's capacity to regenerate defies our understanding. In this way, he does indeed occupy a world that is not our own. The fact that he is capable of being hurt, even killed (if only briefly), though, shows that he is subject to finitude. He is not a god, but he is much closer to Mt. Olympus than any of us.

8. This finding is all over the place. Some cite Spitz's 1940 study of contact and disease as the earliest source. If you want to read more in depth about this interesting biological fact, just pick your favorite search engine and get to it!

9. Yes, that's right. I'm calling Jesus a zombie.

10. *X-Factor Vol. 1* (1986).

11. Quoted in Michael Mallory, *X-Men: The Characters and Their Universe* (New York: Hugh Lauter Levin Associates, 2006), p. 255.

12. *X-Men Vol. 2* #186.

13. Ernest Becker, *The Denial of Death* (New York: Free Press, 1973), p. 27.

14. Ibid., pp. 32–33.

15. Thomas Nagel, "What Is It Like to Be a Bat?" in *The Nature of Mind* (New York and Oxford: Oxford University Press, 1991), pp. 422–428.

16. If we could imagine what it is like to be a frog, we might be getting closer to imagining what it's like to be Wolverine. To wit: "Some African frogs carry concealed weapons: when threatened, these species puncture their own skin with sharp bones in their toes, using the bones as claws capable of wounding predators. At least 11 species kick at predators with sharp, protruding bones as a defense mechanism." For more, see "When Threatened, A Few African Frogs Can Morph Toes into Claws," *ScienceDaily* (June 25, 2008), www.sciencedaily.com/releases/2008/06/080623125003.htm, accessed June 30, 2008.

WAR AND PEACE, POWER AND FAITH

Katherine E. Kirby

> When an individual acquires great power, the use or misuse of that power is everything. Will it be used for the greater good, or will it be used for personal, or for destructive, ends?[1]

Charles Xavier delivers this line to his students at the beginning of *X-Men: The Last Stand (X-3)*, highlighting the theme of T. H. White's *The Once and Future King* (the book Magneto reads in his plastic prison, and the book Xavier begins to discuss with students at the end of *X-2: X-Men United*). In this chapter we'll take the French philosopher Emmanuel Levinas (1906–1995) as our guide in examining the use and abuse of power and the nature of war and peace as depicted in the X-Men trilogy.

Real Peace

Sometimes we find a rational resolution to our wars and conflicts, and we make agreements of nonaggression—a halt to active violence or a cease-fire. We deem this suspension of active, physical violence or domination to be a "time of peace." The Brotherhood sometimes works with the X-Men, after all. For Levinas, however, such a social climate was not the truest, most fundamental kind of peace. In his famous essay "Peace and Proximity," Levinas articulated the difference between a false peace and a true peace, saying, "It is necessary to ask oneself if peace, instead of being the result of an absorption or disappearance of alterity, would not . . . be the *fraternal* mode of a proximity to the other (*autrui*), which . . . would signify precisely the *surplus* of sociality over every solitude—the *surplus* of sociality and of love."[2]

By "alterity," Levinas means the uniqueness of the individual, the absolute difference that makes the other person unique and irreplaceable. False peace involves two parties who are still opposed to each other, but who temporarily coexist without negative interaction. Levinas's goal, on the other hand, was a "project of peace different from the political peace spoken of above. . . . [I]n ethical peace, the relation is with the inassimilable other, the irreducible other, the other, unique."[3] Furthermore, this is "peace as love" for the other individual.[4] Peace is not about finding similarities or common interests. It is about embracing difference. Genuine peace is not simply the temporary halting of physical aggression or domination. Rather, true peace lies in a genuine ethical *love* for the other, which we can describe as faith in the goodness and preciousness of the other.

We can recognize these distinctions quite clearly in the X-Men trilogy. For Levinas, it all boiled down to *power*. War is the exertion of one's power over others, through oppression, manipulation, and violence. Peace is the restraint of one's power for the sake of cultivating the abilities and freedom of the other. Such peace and restraint require an incredible and seemingly irrational leap of faith—a belief in the other's goodness and her ability to choose and act responsibly.

Fear, Oppression, and Violence

As Magneto wisely recognizes in the beginning of the first X-Men movie, "Mankind has always feared what it doesn't understand."[5] This truism finds confirmation throughout human history. In recent history, we see the slaughter of American Indians, the enslavement of Africans and others, the systematic isolation and labeling of individuals on the basis of race or religion, and, of course, the genocide we've witnessed in nations and regions across the globe. Why do we fear difference? Why do we fear what we don't understand?

X-Men begins with a flashback to a Nazi concentration camp, one of the clearest possible examples of oppression and violence based on the distinction between "us" and "them." The film then jumps to a time in the not-so-distant future, and we see a room full of important individuals. Jean Grey is there, speaking as a scientist; Senator Kelly is there; and presumably the room is filled with politicians and other influential leaders of society. The discussion centers around the controversial registration or licensing of mutants for the purpose of protecting society. It is pointed out that the powers that mutants have are *dangerous* and could be used against the greater good of society for personal gain or the domination of humans. The senator goes so far as to refer to mutant children as "weapons in our schools." Clearly, there is a presumption on the part of society that those who are "different" are dangerous, because they threaten the current way of life. They have power beyond our own. We can have control over that which we can understand, identify, categorize, and label. That which we cannot understand, we cannot control. In this example, fear of the unknown is transformed into oppression.

Sharing Magneto's recognition that humankind fears what it cannot understand, Professor Charles Xavier opens *X-2: X-Men United*, saying, "Sharing the world has never been humanity's defining attribute."[6] In this second film, humanity's fear of the unknown takes a more radical form than oppression or registration. In Colonel William Stryker, we see fear transformed into outright violence against "the other." Using his son Jason, he concocts a formula that allows him to forcefully take over the will of another person, literally paralyzing his victim and stealing his way into the victim's mind. This same man who manipulated Wolverine's healing power to create an indestructible "beast," as he calls him, invades Magneto's mind and then endeavors to manipulate Xavier's telepathic power in order to murder all mutants. Fear of the unknown *other* compels him to eradicate all of those who are different, to completely do away with that which threatens humanity's superiority. He feels free to recklessly *use* those who are different from him for his own selfish purposes.

Finally, in *X-Men: The Last Stand*, fear of the other results in what is often considered the rational, "peaceful" solution to conflict based on difference: eradicate difference through assimilation. Those who are different can now be "cured," so that they are just like everyone else. Government scientists at Worthington Labs have developed a "mutant antibody" that can suppress the mutant gene, permanently. Of course, the first intention in dispersing the "cure" is that participation is voluntary. It is not long, however, before the "cure" is weaponized and used against mutants who refuse to be cured voluntarily.

Here we have a situation similar to many historical attempts to "unify" communities or nations through assimilation. Colonial powers, for example, typically conceive of themselves as bringing "civilization" to "barbarian" tribes—American Indians, Africans, Aborigines, and so forth—by forcing them, sometimes violently, to abandon their ancestral languages, cultural practices, and religious beliefs. *X-3* gives us an illustration of the consequences of such violent, forced assimilation by way of a "cure" for dangerous, "barbaric" difference.

The Mutant Other

A simplistic view sees Xavier as the leader of the "good guys" and Magneto as the leader of the "bad guys," or at least one group of "bad guys." Magneto is, after all, a villain, right? On closer investigation, however, we find that Magneto and Xavier share a couple of very important commonalities. These two old friends both recognize the evil in the world: the self-seeking, fearful oppression of, and violence against, mutants. Their actions and attitudes are responses to that recognition. They also both recognize the goodness within each unique individual that must be protected, especially the goodness within each other.

In *X-Men*, we discover that Magneto helped Xavier create Cerebro, the machine that was designed to allow Xavier to locate mutants and humans around the world. Clearly, they both seek to ensure that mutants are cared for and protected. For example, Xavier's School for Gifted Youngsters, as well, is a place where mutants can find acceptance, care, and guidance in cultivating and understanding their powers—powers that are acknowledged as remarkable and incredibly valuable. Xavier wants the mutants to know that their differences from other humans are not faults but gifts.

It is clear from the very beginning that Magneto is convinced of the preciousness and uniqueness of mutants, as shown in his complete dedication to their survival and flourishing. But *X-2* more clearly shows Magneto's appreciation of the unique powers mutants possess. When Wolverine says about Mystique, "She's good," Magneto replies, "You have no idea." He has a definite respect for her abilities, and he recognizes the great gifts of Xavier's team of mutants as well. When Pyro laments that he can only *control* fire, not create it, Magneto replies, "You are a god among insects. Never let anyone tell you different." Though we can recognize the blatant attitude of superiority in this comment, there is no doubt that Magneto believes each mutant to be unique, precious, and irreplaceable.

Finally, in *X-3*, we once again see Magneto's utter respect for Xavier and his gifts, both his mutant gifts and his uniqueness and preciousness as a human being. When Pyro flippantly suggests that he would have killed Xavier himself, Magneto stops him in his tracks, reprimanding him, saying, "Charles Xavier did more for mutants than you'll ever know. My single greatest regret is that he had to die for our dream to live." Despite their radically different solutions to the conflict between humans and mutants, Magneto never forgets Xavier's profound goodness.

X-3 also reveals that Jean is a "class 5" mutant, the only one yet to be discovered. Her power is so great that it was able to wrap her in a "cocoon of telekinetic energy," protecting her from death at the end of *X-2*. When Magneto and Xavier first encountered her, twenty years ago at her parents' home, Xavier told Magneto, "This one's special." Jean is unique even among mutants. She is capable of almost anything, and we learn that her power is so great that it eclipses her human side if unleashed. (Later, we'll consider whether this excuses Xavier's limitation of her power.)

Perhaps one of the most relevant lines in the trilogy is spoken by Mystique, who has the power to hide her true self and take on the identity of any other individual, human or mutant. Kurt Wagner—a character who clearly cannot hide within society—asks her, in *X-2*, why she doesn't stay in disguise all the time. She bluntly replies, "Because we shouldn't have to." A person should not have to hide her differences to assimilate into society. Her differences are what make her unique. As Levinas insisted, the uniqueness of the other is to be embraced.

War

At the end of *X-Men*, Magneto says to Xavier, "The war is still coming, Charles, and I intend to fight it *by any means necessary*." He responds to the war being waged against him by exerting his own power; he becomes the evil against which he is fighting, adopting an attitude of superiority and domination. In fact, Magneto agrees to "play by their rules," as he says in *X-2*. He, Stryker, and others engage in the violent use of their power to take what they want. This, as Levinas would say, is the arbitrary violence of the *I*, "for itself."

In his essay "Uniqueness," Levinas explained the self and its freedom and power, saying, "The human individual lives in the will to live, that is to say in freedom, in *his* freedom which affirms itself as an egotism of the *I*. . . . But the human individual is also negativity in his freedom, in excluding the freedom of others which limits his own . . . an eventual war of each against all."[7] The individual—the *I*, for Levinas—enacts his or her freedom for the purposes of survival, pleasure, happiness, and so on. Using one's power and freedom to secure such benefits for the self, however, entails limiting the freedom and benefits of the other, especially when one's interests conflict with the other's interests.

Many characters in the X-Verse have powers that enable them to take what they need or desire from others or to force others to conform to their will. Mystique, for example, imitates others in order to manipulate, gain trust, or deceive her way into positions of access to what she desires. Storm holds the extraordinary power to control the weather, literally harnessing the forces of nature to create tornadolike wind and lightning. And Charles Xavier has the incomparable power of communicating directly with other minds. Indeed, he acknowledges that if he were to concentrate too hard, he would kill the person whose mind he enters. Mere concentration of his power can kill!

Perhaps the strongest power imagery we find in the trilogy, however, is used to announce the extraordinary might and supremacy of Magneto. He is able to manipulate metals of all kinds: creating pathways before him that allow him to walk across gaping voids; paralyzing and stretching Wolverine's adamantium frame; holding guns to the heads of dozens of police officers at once; halting the X-Men jet in midair; extracting the iron out of a security guard's blood to create a tool to demolish his plastic prison; and even moving the entire Golden Gate Bridge! Magneto's incredible power makes him capable of truly astounding feats. He could potentially harness his power for the benefit of others, without ethical compromise. But instead, he uses his power to enact retribution on those who threaten him. He chooses to engage in acts of war in response to the war being waged against mutants.

In *X-Men*, Magneto uses his power violently to transform the senator into a mutant, calling on the theory of evolution but deciding that "God works too slowly." Having succeeded, Magneto sets his sights on a similar transformation of all humankind. And to enact his plan, he steals Rogue and sacrifices her. Knowing that his mutant-making machine would drain him to the point of death, he chooses to transfer his power to Rogue, which actually means *stealing her power* in order to save himself from death. Magneto conceives of his act as one of strength, rather than of cowardice, as we might surmise from his earlier comment to Xavier: "Still unwilling to make sacrifices—that's what makes you weak." Magneto believes that strength comes not through self-sacrifice for others, but rather through the willingness to *sacrifice others*—to make ethical compromises—to reach his own selfish goals.

In *X-2*, we actually see the softer side of Magneto, as he teams up with the X-Men to fight the evil Stryker's plan to annihilate all mutants. We can recognize his vulnerability as one of Stryker's victims, and we even see remorse when he reveals to Xavier and the others that it was he who told Stryker about the true purpose of Xavier's school. As soon as he gets the chance, however, Magneto strikes back violently. He is not content with stopping Stryker; rather, he turns the war on the war-maker, thus becoming the war-maker. As soon as he makes his way into the inner chamber of Stryker's homemade Cerebro, he simply reverses the target of violence from mutant to human.

He chooses to engage in war, rather than to stop the warring. He uses his power not to protect those who are other than him, but rather to destroy those who are other, just as he sought to do in *X-Men*. Stryker and he become brothers in war.

In *X-3*, we once again see Magneto's mentality of war between "us" and "them." During his speech in the woods, he insists, "Make no mistake, my brothers. They will draw first blood. They will force their cure upon us. The only question is: will you join my brotherhood and fight? Or wait for the inevitable genocide? Who will you stand with—humans or us?" Sadly, Magneto fails to recognize that his own fight is a kind of genocide, an intentional destruction of human beings simply because they are not mutants. In fact, he once again adopts the tactics of his enemy, saying, "*We* are the cure," and encouraging his followers to strike back against both humans and traitor-mutants "with vengeance and fury." Magneto becomes a terrorist leader, as we might recognize from his televised message to humans following Pyro's flaming attack on the medical lab. He even abandons his most beloved follower, Mystique, when she is "cured," saying, "I'm sorry, dear. You're not one of us anymore."

Surely, a discussion of power and war would be incomplete without acknowledging Jean's turn to the dark side: her transformation into the dark, almost sinister Phoenix. Her power overtakes her, and she seems to revel in it. When Wolverine suggests that Xavier can "fix it" by re-creating the psychic barriers that once contained her power, Jean hisses, "I don't *want* to fix it," with a terrifying intensity that hints at the true darkness possible in her power. And, of course, we see this prophetic moment fulfilled when she lifts Xavier out of his wheelchair and viciously murders her former teacher and mentor. Even Magneto looks petrified on witnessing her display of unrestrained power, a feeling to which he returns at the end of the film. When he has been "cured," he watches Jean as she obliterates everyone and everything in sight, asking, "What have I done?"

Peace

In Xavier, we see a kind of peace that is not simply a temporary halt of physical aggression. Rather, peace occurs when the two warring parties disengage from *any exertion* of their individual power. Such peace requires trust in the Other to make responsible choices in using his or her power, as Xavier teaches. Levinas told us that peace exists only when we recognize the Other's uniqueness, and, as I would put it, we *believe in the goodness of the Other*. In one of his books, *Totality and Infinity*, Levinas explained that the encounter with the unique and precious Other calls into question the arbitrary use of my own powers and freedom. He said, "Conscience welcomes the Other. It is the revelation of a resistance to my powers that does not counter them as a greater force, but calls in question the naive right of my powers, my glorious spontaneity as a living being. Morality begins when freedom, instead of being justified by itself, feels itself to be arbitrary and violent."[8] Morality begins, according to Levinas, when I realize that the uncritical use of my power can cause harm to others. I become moral, or ethical, when I choose to be very careful with my power so as not to harm or limit the freedom of others. In fact, being ethical means *suspending* my own powers, desires, and endeavors for the good of the other person. And it also means engaging in "discourse" with the other person so that she can reveal her goodness to me.

Xavier is able to *hear* people and *discourse* with them, and he is very aware of his power's potential to harm. He chooses to *listen to others* and to use his powers to protect mutants, and he tries to teach his students to understand their powers and learn to control them, responsibly. The professor believes in his students' ability to use their powers responsibly, and he believes in their capacity for goodness, as he does even with Magneto and the humans who might threaten what he has created.

In the very beginning of *X-Men*, when Magneto asks him what he's looking to find inside his mind, Xavier replies, "I'm looking for hope." He wants, more than anything, to enable those around him to have faith and trust that people can choose what is right: that peace is possible. In the scene where Magneto is about to murder dozens of police officers, Xavier takes over the mind of one of Magneto's minions and tells him to let them go. In that moment, we see that Xavier could kill Magneto if he wanted to, as he has him by the throat. Rather than killing him, he gives him the choice to stand down. By the end of the film, when Magneto insists that he will fight the war, "by any means necessary," Xavier calmly and almost lovingly replies, "And I will always be there, old friend." Xavier clearly has faith even in Magneto and even in the very moments during which Magneto is enacting war. Whereas Magneto believes only in the goodness of his own kind—Mystique and other mutants—Xavier believes in the goodness of all individuals.

A particularly clear example of Xavier's wise guidance can be found in his relationship with Wolverine, a fairly complex character. When we first meet Wolverine in *X-Men*, he is quite the loner. He doesn't want anything to do with Rogue or the school . . . at least, not until he encounters Xavier. Wolverine accepts Xavier's offer to help him piece together his past, and he does not resist Xavier's request to give him a chance to help him. In *X-2*, when Xavier shows Wolverine how Cerebro works, he says, "Through Cerebro, I'm connected to [all mutants], and they to me. You see, Logan, we're not as alone as you think." He wants Wolverine to believe that there are people he can trust and depend on.

In all three films, of course, Wolverine kills *a lot* of people. But we also see him adopt Xavier's attitude of faith in others and commitment to protecting them, although he certainly takes on this attitude only selectively. When Rogue runs away from the school in *X-Men*, Wolverine tracks her down and convinces her to follow her own instincts. He admits that Xavier seems to be someone who genuinely wants to help them, and he tells her to "give these geeks one more shot." In other words, he encourages her to have faith in them, even though reason has previously taught her to be suspicious. Wolverine's own growing faith in the goodness of others—the very lesson that Xavier teaches—is further evidenced by his sacrifice for Rogue at the end of *X-Men*. He volunteers to be the one to approach Magneto's machine, so that if he fails, Cyclops will still have the chance to save the day. Wolverine then *gives his very life force* to Rogue to save her, literally shedding his blood for her. He sacrifices his own good because he has such strong faith in Rogue's goodness and preciousness.

In *X-2*, Kurt Wagner attests to the power of faith more explicitly than any other character, wisely telling us, "Most people will never know anything beyond what they see with their own two eyes." Surely, the faith that Xavier teaches is precisely a belief in the goodness in others, which we often cannot see by their actions alone. At the end of the film, Xavier's X-Men appear in the president's office, and Xavier extends to him an offer of peace, saying, "Mr. President, this is not a threat. It is an opportunity. There are forces in this world, both mutant and human alike, who believe a war is coming . . . and there have been casualties, losses on both sides. Mr. President, what you are about to tell the world is true. This is a moment . . . to repeat the mistakes of the past, or to work together for a better future. We're here to stay, Mr. President. The next move is yours." Herein lies the Levinasian point: peace is found through discourse, commitment to cooperation, and faith in the other's ability to enact goodness.

In *X-3*, the peace Xavier teaches becomes far more difficult. His message remains the same, as poignantly articulated by Storm at Xavier's funeral. We might think of nonviolent leaders in our own world, such as Martin Luther King Jr. and Gandhi, when we hear her words: "We live in an age of darkness—a world full of fear, hate, and intolerance. But in every age, there are those who fight against it. Charles Xavier was born into a world divided—a world he tried to heal. . . . It seems the destiny of great men to see their goals unfulfilled. Charles was more than a leader—more than a teacher. He was a friend. When we were afraid, he gave us strength. And when we were alone, he gave us a family." Xavier's commitment to peace and his faith in the goodness of others never wavered, even up to the end of his life. He once said to Jean, "You have more power than you can imagine, Jean. The question is: will you control that power? Or let it control you?"

Though it seems that Xavier's intention was always to teach Jean to control her own powers, his creation of the aforementioned "psychic barriers," which were designed to "cage the beast" within her, is certainly problematic. He created within her a dual consciousness, keeping the full power of the Phoenix hidden from her conscious mind. Is this a violation of her uniqueness, similar to the oppressive or violent use of power that we have identified in Magneto and others? On the one hand, perhaps Xavier was merely *protecting* her from powers that *no individual*—and especially a young child—could control alone. Perhaps he was helping her by containing such overwhelming power until she was wise enough and strong enough to control the Phoenix on her own. On the other hand, his act of control over her seems to indicate a lack of faith in her ability to restrain herself. Xavier himself acknowledges this, saying that he "chose the lesser of two evils." Such a choice is still a choice in favor of evil, after all! It is an *ethical compromise* that violates his genuinely peaceful intention to trust others' abilities to do the right thing.

During the initial flashback to Jean's childhood home, Magneto asks, "Couldn't you just make [her parents] say yes?" Xavier answers, "Yes, I could, but it's not my way." And Magneto replies, "Ah, power corrupts and all that." Xavier's desire for peace requires relinquishing control and having faith in the other to make free, *yet responsible*, choices. On return to Jean's home, when the Phoenix has taken over and she is torturing Xavier, he asks her to trust him—to "let him in" to her mind—and he tells her that he wants to help her, not control her. He begs her to restrain her power, saying, "Don't let it control you." Here, we see him pleading with her, encouraging her to refrain from enacting her power over him for her own purposes. He is asking her to choose responsibly: to choose peace, rather than war. Even to the very end of his own life, Xavier holds onto the difficult, radical faith that is the belief in the goodness of the other, even the other who chooses war. Peace can never be attained through war, as the two endeavors arise out of diametrically opposed dispositions or orientations. War is enacted out of suspicion, distrust of the other, and devotion to the survival and benefit of the self. Peace is enacted out of love, faith in the goodness of the other, and commitment of the self to the survival and flourishing of others.

NOTES

1. See Brett Ratner's *X-Men: The Last Stand* (Twentieth Century Fox, 2006), DVD.

2. Emmanuel Levinas, "Peace and Proximity," in *Basic Philosophical Writings*, edited by Adriaan T, Peperzak, Simon Critchley, and Robert Bernasconi (Bloomington: Indiana University Press, 1996), p. 165.

3. Ibid., p. 166.

4. Ibid., p. 166.

5. See Bryan Singer's *X-Men* (Twentieth Century Fox, 2000), DVD.

6. See Bryan Singer's *X-2: X-Men United* (Twentieth Century Fox, 2003), DVD.

7. Emmanuel Levinas, "Uniqueness," in *Entre Nous: Thinking-of-the-Other*, translated by Michael B. Smith and Barbara Harshav (New York: Columbia University Press, 1998), pp. 189–190.

8. Emmanuel Levinas, *Totality and Infinity: An Essay on Exteriority*, translated by Alphonso Lingis (Pittsburgh: Duquesne University Press, 1969), p. 84.

HIGH-TECH MYTHOLOGY IN X-MEN

George Teschner

Creating and believing in mythical heroes and heroic deeds are ways that human consciousness conceptualizes major forces and conflicts. The ancient Greeks satisfied the need to understand the how, the why, the origin of things, and the destiny of human beings beyond social and biological life through an elaborate polytheism that invested divinities with powers and personalities beyond the human. Mythology is a figurative and metaphorical way the human intellect grasps its world and answers and resolves some of the most fundamental questions. Unlike ancient Greece, today's society faces one of its most pressing issues in the relationship between humanity and technology. Contemporary technology has created the machine, which has dwarfed the natural abilities of the human body. The native capacities of the human mind are slow and meager compared to the speed and processing power of the computer. The major events of the nineteenth and twentieth centuries have been shaped by the use and development of the machine in manufacturing, war, transportation, and scientific research.

The machine produces a sense of both awe and dread. The imagery of the X-Men narratives and characters, therefore, provides a way to represent the relationship between man and machine in mythical imagery.

Within the X-Men narratives, questions arise concerning the relationship between the machine and the natural and biological capabilities of human beings, such as the extent to which technological powers can be controlled or whether technology serves good or evil ends, what role the political system has in controlling technological power, and what the differences are between humans and machines when the machine takes over more and more physical and intellectual human functions. Graphic representations in both comic book and film imagery, compared to conceptual modes of understanding, touch a deeper and more subconscious level at which these concerns are felt. On the surface, the X-Men imagery appeals to our sense of entertainment and adventure. When the images are interpreted symbolically, however, something deeper than the storyline and the characters is taking place. The X-Men imagery reaches the roots of the human psyche and addresses some of the deepest anxieties regarding the relationship between human existence and its increasingly technological environment.

Dream Works

The X-Men stories can be interpreted as myths and dreams. In what Sigmund Freud (1856–1939) called the "dream work," we find unconscious wishes that the conscious mind cannot face directly. The wishes, if acknowledged, would destroy the ego and the world that the ego inhabits. Among the most primordial wishes is the desire to heal the break between nature and culture. Nature is spontaneous, unplanned, organic, and contextual, holistic rather than atomistic. Culture is planned, deliberated, linear, and analytic. Culture is embodied in utilitarian technological consciousness, which thinks exclusively in terms of means and ends and is directed away from the present toward the future.

Dreaming allows for the symbolic satisfaction of unconscious desires. The symbolism creates images that escape the censorship of the conscious ego by using distortion and disguise. The psychic value of images that would excite desire is displaced onto images that are of less psychic intensity. Male characters such as Magneto, Xavier, and Wolverine and female characters like Storm, Mystique, Jean Grey, and Rogue are images that displace deeper and more primordial wishes in the collective cultural psyche. To interpret them requires separating elements that are part of the narrative representational structure from elements that are rooted in deeper latent unconscious meanings.

The work of dreams is to displace the lust for power, which, if left uncensored, would violate social norms and destroy the ego's image of itself, and to transfer desire into images that are larger than life, of human beings who use their power to achieve beneficial social ends. The heroes of X-Men, like the heroes of ancient mythology, have extraordinary powers and find themselves in conflicts with human and nonhuman beings who are equal in strength. Narrative drama demands that their victory or defeat remains uncertain. Also like classical mythology, X-Men relax the criteria for what reason may accept as real. As science fiction, the X-Men series only marginally attempts to incorporate orthodox scientific theory into its storyline. Concepts of mutation, such as telepathic and telekinetic powers and the instantaneous repair of human tissue, make no claim to scientific credibility. Storm's ability to alter the weather, Magneto's magnetic power that is capable of lifting and moving objects of great weight, and Cyclops's eye blasts that produce thousands of pounds of force all violate the most elementary principles of energy conservation. But the scientific implausibility does not detract from the value of the X-Men narrative.

The suspension of the reality principle as a literary device correlates with the silencing of censorship in dreams. The world of the X-Men is both dream and myth and must be decoded accordingly. In the dream, the image of the superhero represents our own wish for power. The specific kind of power that the X-Men represent is technological power that they have embodied physically and psychically.

Human and Machine

In technological society, the prospect of unlimited power expresses itself in the image of the machine, rather than in the form of supernatural beings who have the power to alter natural events and who can be influenced by prayer and sacrifice. Secularism, the loss of the belief in the supernatural, and scientific-technological culture go hand in hand. For example, the movie *Forbidden Planet* describes a civilization called the Krell that designed a machine so vast and so powerful that a wish could be made real by a mere act of thought. Once the machine was activated, it took only one night for the entire civilization to destroy itself. The movie script explains the mystery of its annihilation in one phrase: "monsters from the id." With their technological reasoning, the Krell engineers were oblivious to the danger of the unconscious. The utilitarian wishes that the machine was intended to satisfy were merely the surface manifestation of deeper desires that had the capacity to destroy the social order. Clearly, the Frankenstein thesis, that technology will destroy its creator, runs through many science fiction movies.[1]

Wolverine in particular represents the union of the human and the machine in the X-Verse. His entire body has been fused with the mechanical, giving him enormous strength. Only because his mutant body can instantaneously heal was such a procedure possible. His body, even on a molecular level, is laced with a nearly indestructible metal, adamantium. When

Rogue asks him in the first X-Men movie whether it is painful when his mechanical claws push through the flesh of his hands, he replies that it is painful every time. This pain symbolizes the alienation people have experienced as a result of their subordination to machines ever since the Industrial Revolution.

Consider also that Wolverine's memory has been erased from the time before the adamantium. A large part of his quest is to find his identity and recover his memory, that is, his own personal history before his body was fused with the metal associated with machines. Wolverine's brooding anger represents human culture seeking to find its own metaphysical identity in the face of a society that is becoming increasingly more technological and industrialized. Wolverine represents our inability to meaningfully recall humanity's preindustrial identity before our lives were governed by the rhythm of the machine.

Mutation

The X-Verse is unique in representing superpowers as a result of a natural biological process, mutation. Other popular superheroes develop superpowers after accidents or from the use of certain special technologies. For example, the Fantastic Four were exposed to cosmic rays and Spiderman was bitten by a radioactive spider. The mutation that gives the X-Men their powers is not, however, strictly speaking, the result of an evolutionary mechanism. Rather, it is the actualization of a potential that had been hidden within the human genome. In the X-Men, the body and the mind have undergone metamorphoses; perhaps it would be more symbolic to call mutants *metamorphs*. The metamorphosis is from preindustrial culture to technological society. The superpowers are often more mechanical than biological. For example, the electromagnetic power of Magneto is not an enhancement of a normal biological function; it is an addition from a different order than the biological—namely, the mechanical.

The same is true of Cyclops's ability to produce energy bolts from apertures of the body where the eyes are usually located. What replaced his eyes are interdimensional openings that connect different universes. The physics is quite complex. What emerges from the apertures are gravitational particles, which, when focused, transfer great kinetic force. Besides having mass, the particles are lightlike and can be focused. The diameter and focus of the beam can be changed by the ruby crystal lenses of his glasses and by his mind's psionic (pronounced "sigh-onic") field. Cyclops's powers derive from a universe that is in a dimension different from the world that normal humans inhabit. The interdimensional ability arises from, and depends on, the psionic mind's openness to other dimensional realities, to other worlds and worldviews. That the opening to the other dimensions is located where the eyes are normally found is significant, because the eyes are common symbols of knowledge, intelligence, and insight—in Cyclops's case, the insight has given him other-dimensional powers. Cyclops derives his abilities by possessing powers that result from his being in touch with a world that functions according to laws that are different from, and beyond, our own. These laws can be understood as the laws of mathematical physics, but, more symbolically, they are the laws and customs of society.

In one of the many narratives that mention mutation, Charles Xavier claims that the mutations come from what scientists call "junk DNA."[2] The junk DNA, as Xavier describes it, is a latent potential in the human genetic makeup that is the source of the extraordinary powers possessed by mutants. Jean Grey, in her address before the U.S. Senate, speaks of a mutator gene, the X-Factor, which lies dormant as long as the environment remains stable. Here again, the distinction between latent and manifest appears. Powers result from a part of the human genetic makeup that has been dismissed by orthodox genetics and systematically censored and ignored by mainstream culture. The stable environment to which Jean

Grey refers is the environment of familiar human artifacts, but for some unknown reason, she claims, the mutator gene has activated in response to a change in the environment. That unknown reason is, of course, advances in technology that blur the distinction between man and machine.

The Psionic Mind

Many of the powers that the X-Men possess result from the "psionic mind's" telepathic or telekinetic abilities. Magneto has the power of manipulating magnetism; Storm possesses power over water, aquakinesis, and air, aerokinesis, and therefore can affect the weather. Cyclops is able to control interdimensional gravitational energy. Jean Grey possesses chronokinesis and is able to interact causally with future events. All have a degree of telepathic power. Telepathy symbolizes the upper limit of tele-communication technology, while telekinesis symbolizes the union of knowledge and action in technological know-how.

The psionic mind is parapsychological, both telepathic and telekinetic. Mind and matter directly interact. According to the Western tradition, which is rooted in Cartesian dualism, the mind and the body are two separate substances, and it is not possible for one to directly affect the other except through neurological and muscular processes. (And even then, the connection between mind and body remains problematic.) The ordinary human mind is able to affect the physical world through the mediation of the body. Its control of the body, however, is limited, and most bodily processes are autonomic. By contrast, for the psionic mind what is autonomic is voluntary—again, an upper limit of technological control. The psionic mind is able to influence objects directly and thus does not have a need for instruments. The psionic mind does not have mass but can exert force and cause motion. Unlike matter, the psionic mind remains motionless in imparting motion. It is both physical and spiritual. The psionic mind is the ordinary mind when the separation from conscious to unconscious mind, the thou-shalts and the thou-shalt-nots of society, is removed. Psionic minds possess powers that the conscious mind can only entertain in dreams, for to face them without the disguise of symbolism would profoundly undercut conventional culture and self-identity.

Psionic Blocks

Jean Grey was born with telepathic abilities that manifested at an early age; she is the most powerful form of mutation, an omega-level mutant, and has unlimited potential. Jean's telepathic abilities are so strong that Professor Xavier had to use psionic blocks to prevent her subliminal powers from injuring her conscious mind. If Jean Grey's psyche were fully liberated, she would become the host of the godlike Phoenix Force, giving her limitless psionic powers to manipulate matter and energy and, in particular, the power of pyrokenesis, the primal cosmic fire that symbolizes death and rebirth, making her indestructible. It is significant that the capacity for psychic transfiguration resides within the female characters of the X-Men narrative, symbolizing the infinite depth of the feminine psyche, in contrast to the shallow rationality of the rigidly focused masculine mind. This fluid transformative feminine nature is present in other female characters, such as Mystique, who is a shape-shifter, and Rogue, who is capable of absorbing the powers of other mutants.

Professor Xavier represents the repressive side of human nature. He upholds the morality of cooperation and self-sacrifice. He blocks Jean's self-destructive power, but he fails to recognize that the self Jean would destroy is the ego, a fabrication of normal human society. Professor Xavier is a paraplegic and therefore paralyzed in a world where, paradoxically, other mutants are capable of nonambulatory movement. Xavier's nemesis, Magneto, moves through space by virtue of psychokinetic-magnetic power. His ability to fly, a symbol of liberation, in contrast to Xavier's paralysis, is the result of his having seen through the façade of orthodox society and the duplicity of political institutions. The horror of the Nazi concentration camp has taught him that the ruling laws are ultimately not laws of a civil society. Magneto recognizes the pattern: discrimination, segregation, and extermination. Professor Xavier has created a school for socializing young mutants who otherwise would not know how to control their extraordinary powers. But here again, we see that Xavier is a symbol of repression and control, insofar as he seeks to limit mutant powers by having them submit to the rules ordinary humans live by.

Magneto represents a morality of might, and he sees no reason to treat normal humans as equals. Xavier is his antithesis and imagines that a being with power can be taught to treat as equals others who are his inferiors in power. That is the purpose of Xavier's School for Gifted Youngsters. The term *gifted* is a euphemism for a power that, if fully acknowledged or unleashed, could overturn conventional morality and replace it with a morality in which might makes right. One may wonder why it is not a school for adult mutants as well. The "youngsters" whom the name of the school refers to are children who have entered puberty, a time when physical and psychological forces become manifest and threaten the social order.

Xavier's Telepathic Probe

Magneto's view of human society was formed from the experience of losing his family in a Nazi concentration camp. He understands how power can overturn civil society and deny citizenship and rights to a class of people that it no longer regards in the same category as itself. In front of the train station, when the Brotherhood is about to abduct Rogue, it is necessary for Magneto to shield himself from the telepathic probes of Xavier with a specially designed helmet that silences the voice of traditional morality. Xavier counters Magneto's defenses by superimposing his own telepathic will on the animal-like and naive psyche of Sabretooth, who then symbolically grabs Magneto's throat, preventing him from communicating other than through the telepathic link with Xavier. In the standoff, where policemen, as enforcers of law and order, are held hostage, Magneto says to Xavier, "Still unwilling to make sacrifices. That is what makes you weak."[3] The sacrifice is of the ego and the social norms that constitute it. Xavier's telepathic power is more than an ability to read minds. It is an ability to take over minds, to possess them, so that the mind that is possessed experiences Xavier's will as its own. The identity that is rooted in nature, which is one with nature, is replaced by the ego that is constituted by culture.

Magneto's Mutant *Machina*

Magneto designed a machine that is capable of inducing mutant powers in ordinary human beings, transforming human consciousness and making it aware of its latent destructive and simultaneously creative potential. In order for the machine to function, Magneto must be hooked up like a battery, as the energy source of the machine. The device drains Magneto of his energy before he can transfer his own power to Rogue and use her to power the machine. Rogue's mutation is unique. She is in effect a universal mutant, capable of taking on the mutant power of any other mutant by simply coming into physical contact with that person. She symbolizes the power of the unconscious mind and the genius of the dream work to transfer its wishes to different objects and various dream images. Physical contact with Rogue, however, proves deadly for ordinary humans, which is a problem for her, because she longs for intimate contact. Deadly also to the conscious ego would be the removal of the repressive barrier separating the conscious from the unconscious. Rogue's protector is Wolverine, living at the interface of human and machine, a place of transformation and transference in advanced technological culture. Rogue becomes the necessary means by which mutant powers can be transferred to ordinary humans.

Magneto speaks about humans "becoming like us," or becoming mutants. Humans fear mutants because of their extraordinary powers. To make them "like us" is to remove the fear by transforming the human into a mutant. Magneto intends to accomplish his plan at Liberty Island, while a few miles away world leaders are assembled on Ellis Island. Liberty Island is the location of the Statue of Liberty, a symbol of freedom and transition from the old to the new. It is appropriate that Magneto has chosen this place as the place to transform the human into the mutant. Magneto often refers to his battle as a war with humanity, but Magneto's *machina* is more a device of diplomacy and communication than a weapon of war. The purpose of his mutant machine is to induce mutation in humans, to make them understand the point of view of mutants who hitherto have been regarded as objects of fear. Magneto must be imprisoned in a nonmetallic, plastic cell. Any nonmetallic substance would work, so why clear plastic? Transparency represents an instant of insight into the unconscious, a moment of catharsis, a relaxation of the tension between social prohibitions and unconscious desires that is normally disguised in symbol. The dream work is one of disguise and disclosure, of concealment and revealment. On a manifest level, Xavier represents what is good, and Magneto, what is evil. On the latent level, however, Xavier symbolizes the forces of repression and Magneto the acceptance of a redefinition of humanity in the light of technology and the machine and in the power that would result from such a union.

The X-Men Metanarrative

The characters and the narrative structure of X-Men are rich in symbolism and have the power to generate new mythical imagery. The mythology speaks to concerns about the relation between humanity and the expanding technological power it possesses, about the distinction between man and machine, and about changes in gender roles that rapidly occur in changing technological environments. The mythology is also about how governments and political institutions *must* respond to technological change. Technology has created a new world of desire, but these desires are difficult to face directly and acknowledge on a conscious level because of their intensity in defining who we are and in determining the social, physical, and metaphysical world we encompass. The X-Men series is an ongoing metanarrative, perhaps the most potent in contemporary culture, permitting a way for us to contemplate the possibilities outside of the worn, archaic mythical structures that are offered in traditional religions and institutions whose origins stem from a nontechnological environment.

NOTES

1. In *Blade Runner*, artificial human beings called "replicants," which have artificial memories and limited life spans, rebel against the laws of human society and destroy their makers. A combat replicant called Roy, the leader of the group of rebels, kills the geneticist who designed him. Thus, *Blade Runner* calls into question the distinction between what is real and what is artifact. Rachael, a replicant who at first thinks that she is human, discovers that her memories of her mother are implants. She has the ability to play the piano, has memories of taking lessons, but is not sure whether her memories are hers or belong to someone else. She is a product of the Tyrell Corporation, which specializes in genetically designed organisms. The movie leaves uncertain whether Deckard, who works for LAPD and who hunts down replicants, is himself a replicant. Replicants feel pain; they long for normal lives; they have friendships, feel love, and fear death. The distinction between the human and the nonhuman is unclear.

The character Data of *Star Trek* also exists on the borderline between the human and the technological. Data is entirely an artifact of a cyberneticist of the twenty-fourth century who invented Data's positronic brain. In the episode *The Measure of a Man*, however, when Star Fleet Command gives permission to dissemble Data, evaluate his (its) software, and dump his (its) core memory into a computer, a legal battle ensues in which Captain Picard argues that Data is not "property" and that it is no easier trying to prove that humans are sentient than it is proving that Data is sentient. Again, the boundary between the human and the machine becomes ambiguous. The legal justification for not treating Data as property in the end was the admission by the court that it was ignorant of a real distinction between the human and a machine that simulates the human.

Similarly, in *I, Robot*, the boundary separating the human from the nonhuman becomes unclear in the image of the corporate computer VIKI (Virtual Interactive Kinetic

Intelligence), who decides on her own to destroy those who made her, because, as she (it) claims, humans are a self-destructive species who "toxify the earth." The robot, who names himself Sonny and who has a unique positronic brain that allows him to dream, feel emotion, and fear death, thwarts VIKI's attempt to enslave mankind. In one scene, the camera pans in on the hands of Sonny and detective Spooner in a handshake that symbolizes the acknowledgment of Sonny's personhood and humanity. Both the *Star Trek* episode and the movie *I, Robot* seek to elicit in the viewer a compassion for the machine and argue that to treat a machine, which simulates the human, as anything less than a person is prejudice and discrimination. In *I, Robot*, Dr. Lanning, the scientist who designed Sonny, suggests that the distinction between the human and the machine begins to blur as its behavioral repertoire increases. Lanning speaks of "random bits of code that have assembled together to form unexpected protocols . . . that engender questions of free will, creativity."

2. See editor Mike Marts's book *X-Men: The Movie Beginnings* (New York: Marvel Comics, 2000), p. 3.

3. Ibid., chap. 14.

CONTRIBUTORS

And Now, We'd Like to Introduce the X-Perts: Ladies and Gentlemen, the Amazing, Astonishing, Uncanny, Ultimate Authors from Xavier's School for Gifted Philosophers!

Andrew Burnett teaches philosophy at Augustana College and medical ethics at Sanford School of Medicine, University of South Dakota. His research interests include the problem of natural evil, psychiatric ethics, and issues of (real-world) genetic discrimination. Current projects include an interdisciplinary seminar on "mad science" and transforming the family basement into a fully equipped Danger Room.

Joseph J. Darowski is a Ph.D. candidate in the American Studies Program at Michigan State University. His research focuses on American popular culture, American literature, and Latino culture. As soon as his mutant superpowers emerge, he will use the persona of a mild-mannered academic as a ruse while pursuing a career within the superhero field, preferably as an X-Man.

Richard Davis is an associate professor of philosophy at Tyndale University College in Toronto, Canada. He coedited the volume *24 and Philosophy* with Jennifer Hart Weed and Ronald Weed (John Wiley & Sons, 2007). As an active member of the

Brotherhood of Evil Mutants, Davis uses his mutant superpowers to influence the masses to reason in an evil attempt to flood American pop culture with intelligent thought.

George A. Dunn regularly coteaches a course called "Philosophy through Pop Culture" at the Indiana University–Purdue University at Indianapolis. His publications include articles on philosophy in *Battlestar Galactica* and *Buffy the Vampire Slayer*. He has been a visiting lecturer at Purdue University, the University of Indianapolis, and the Ningbo Institute of Technology in the People's Republic of China. Unlike his hero Layla Miller, he doesn't know a damn thing.

Patrick D. Hopkins teaches philosophy and science and technology studies at Millsaps College in Mississippi. He is the author of numerous articles on bioethics, technology studies, gender studies, and religious studies. He is the editor of *Sex/Machine: Readings in Culture, Gender, and Technology* (Indiana University Press, 1999). Through his numerous mutant superpowers as a college professor, Hopkins uses nothing but *Star Trek* episodes as texts and uses the term "Buffyverse" un-ironically. Yes, he is that kind of mutant.

Rebecca Housel teaches writing and popular culture at a secret mutant university in western New York. She is an active member of *Excalibur* on an alternate Earth and started a separate branch for Aussie X-Men while attending the University of New South Wales in Sydney after thwarting a plot by Mojo to kill her. Luckily, Housel only lost the use of one leg during the unfortunate Mojo encounter. Her mutant superpowers have been used for articles on poker, *Monty Python*, and, of course, superheroes, as well as a novel series for middle-grade to adult literacy. Housel's dream is to write for Marvel comics. She eagerly awaits Joe Quesada's call. Any day now . . .

Ramona Ilea is an assistant professor of philosophy at Pacific University and lives in Portland, Oregon. Her work focuses on normative and applied ethics, especially animal and environmental ethics. Although born in Transylvania, Ramona doesn't have any vampiric superpowers; in fact, as a vegan-philosopher, she has ethical objections to drinking any kind of blood.

Jesse Kavadlo is an associate professor of English and humanities at Maryville University of St. Louis, where he teaches courses in writing, literature, and interdisciplinary topics such as superheroes, rock and roll, conspiracies, and monsters. He is the author of the book *Don DeLillo: Balance at the Edge of Belief* (Peter Lang, 2004), as well as journal articles and book chapters on contemporary American fiction, popular culture, and writing pedagogy. When no one is looking, Jesse puts three pencils between his closed fingers and imagines adamantium claws.

Katherine E. Kirby is an assistant professor of philosophy and global studies at Saint Michael's College in Vermont. She specializes in the work of Emmanuel Levinas, continental philosophy, and ethics and has created courses examining genocide, marginalization, propaganda and the media, and heroic action or character. She has written and presented essays on ethical and moral philosophy, heroism, the Holocaust, ethical pedagogy, and ethical faith. Katherine is looking forward to having Hugh Jackman over for dinner to discuss the complex nature of his character in regard to her essay.

Cynthia McWilliams is an assistant professor of philosophy at the University of Texas-Pan American, where she serves as the codirector of the Pan American Collaboration for Ethics in the Professions (PACE). She has published in biomedical ethics, animal ethics, and intelligence ethics. Sadly, Cynthia has never recovered from having the worst mutant power ever: glow-in-the-dark freckles.

Jeremy Pierce is a Ph.D. student in philosophy at Syracuse University and an adjunct instructor at Le Moyne College. His Ph.D. dissertation examines issues in the philosophy of race and metaphysics with research interests in the philosophy of religion. Jeremy's X-Gene produced a higher-than-normal level of ambidexterity with a lower-than-normal level of dexterity itself. The result is bad but passable handwriting with both hands and the ability to play equally badly on either side of the soccer field.

Christopher Robichaud is an instructor of public policy at the Harvard Kennedy School of Government. He trained as a boy at Professor X's prestigious school, and although it's unclear whether his ability to question everything is really a mutant power, he certainly finds himself more at home in mutant company. Wolverine won't suffer his nonsense, but Beast and he get along just fine.

Jason Southworth is an ABD graduate student at the University of Oklahoma and an instructor of philosophy at Fort Hays State University in Kansas. He has published articles on *Batman*, *Heroes*, and Stephen Colbert. In the late 1980s and early 1990s, Jason enjoyed reading all of the X-books, even those drawn and plotted by Rob Liefeld. Please don't hold that against him, though, as he was too young to know any better; he is still working toward absolution of this horrible mistake in judgment.

Andrew Terjesen is currently a visiting assistant professor of philosophy at Rhodes College in Memphis, Tennessee. In the past, he has taught at Washington and Lee University, Austin College, and Duke University. He is mainly interested in ethics, moral psychology, early modern philosophy, and the philosophy of economics. He has had essays published in this series on the connections between philosophy and *Family Guy*, *The Office*, and *Battlestar Galactica* and is also working on essays involving *Heroes* and *Watchmen*. If Terjesen had telepathy as a superpower, he'd find out what Brett Ratner was thinking when making *The Last Stand* (and whether Ratner feels any shame).

George Teschner is a professor of philosophy at Christopher Newport University, where he teaches a variety of courses in comparative philosophy, continental philosophy, and philosophy in popular culture. He has published articles in the areas of Asian philosophy, phenomenology, continental philosophy, and the philosophy of technology. Teschner grew up with the stigma of having super-philosophical powers, so he relates strongly to the plight of X-Men and mutants everywhere.

Mark D. White is an associate professor in the Department of Political Science, Economics, and Philosophy at the College of Staten Island/CUNY, where he teaches courses that combine economics, philosophy, and law. He has edited *Watchmen and Philosophy* (John Wiley & Sons, 2009), *Batman and Philosophy* (with Robert Arp, John Wiley & Sons, 2008), *Theoretical Foundations of Law and Economics* (Cambridge University Press, 2009), and *Economics and the Mind*, with Barbara Montero (Routledge, 2007). Since puberty, he has had the mutant power to repel intelligent, beautiful women, and he sadly has no control over it.

J. Jeremy Wisnewski was an assistant professor of philosophy at the Xavier School for Gifted Youngsters. He published several articles on mutant affairs, including "Your Inner Mutant," "Magneto as Infantile Narcissist," and "Can't Anyone Die around Here?" These titles, unfortunately, were insufficient for him to be granted tenure at the prestigious academy. After working for a time in various convenience stores and fast-food establishments, Wisnewski edited *Family Guy and Philosophy* (Blackwell Publishing, 2007) and *The Office and Philosophy* (Blackwell Publishing, 2008). He hopes eventually to land a job in retail.

INDEX